Cy
of
Life

About the Author

Rod Suskin (South Africa) is the best-known astrologer in his country. A professional consultant for fifteen years, he has a radio program and often appears on national television to talk about astrology. He writes a monthly astrology column in Cape Town's largest daily newspaper and regularly contributes to journals and magazines, including the official magazine of the South African Parliament, who commissioned him to write an article commenting on the astrological chart of the newly democratic country.

To Write to the Author

If you wish to contact the author or would like more information about this book, please write to the author in care of Llewellyn Worldwide and we will forward your request. Both the author and publisher appreciate hearing from you and learning of your enjoyment of this book and how it has helped you. Llewellyn Worldwide cannot guarantee that every letter written to the author can be answered, but all will be forwarded. Please write to:

Rod Suskin
℅ Llewellyn Worldwide
P.O. Box 64383, Dept. 0-7387-0659-0
St. Paul, MN 55164-0383, U.S.A.
Please enclose a self-addressed stamped envelope for reply,
or $1.00 to cover costs. If outside U.S.A., enclose
international postal reply coupon.

Many of Llewellyn's authors have websites with additional
information and resources. For more information,
please visit our website at
www.llewellyn.com

CYCLES
of
LIFE

UNDERSTANDING THE PRINCIPLES
OF PREDICTIVE ASTROLOGY

ROD SUSKIN

Llewellyn Publications
St. Paul, Minnesota

First Edition
First Printing, 2005

Background texture © 2004 by PhotoDisc
Cover design by Ellen Dahl
Graph courtesy of Rod Suskin
Interior illustrations by Llewellyn Art Department

Llewellyn is a registered trademark of Llewellyn Worldwide, Ltd.

Library of Congress Cataloging-in-Publication Data
Suskin, Rod, 1963–
    Cycles of life : understanding the principles of predictive astrology / Rod Suskin.—
1st ed.
      p. cm.
    Includes bibliographical references and index.
    ISBN 0-7387-0659-0
     1. Predictive astrology. I. Title.
  BF1720.5.R89 2005
  133.5—dc22   2004057711

Llewellyn Publications
A Division of Llewellyn Worldwide, Ltd.
P.O. Box 64383, Dept. 0-7387-0659-0
St. Paul, MN 55164-0383, U.S.A.
www.llewellyn.com

Printed in the United States of America

For Chris Ntombemhlophe, who was so patient.

And God said, Let there be lights in the firmament of the heaven to divide the day from the night; and let them be for signs, and for seasons, and for days, and years.

—*Genesis 1:14*

Also by Rod Suskin

Soul Talks
(DoubleStorey, 2004)

Acknowledgements

Many people helped test the simplified astrological predictive system in this book and helped make the text much easier to read. Thanks to Lauren Sweet, Christine Nachmann, Martin Hahn, Brian Barker and especially Simon Chislett, as well as everyone at Llewellyn who helped shape and grow the book.

Many of my clients shared the experience of their own cycles and allowed me to use them as illustrations, and my students have done as much to shape my astrology as I have theirs.

Finally, special thanks to Noel Tyl, whose ceaseless encouragement and inspiration opened my path and finally brought me to put my ideas onto paper.

Contents

FOREWORD

The title of this book is magnificent! And, for several reasons:

First, it promises us much. And I tell you, the book comes through with that promise: we learn what time it is in our life development on a continuing basis, into the future—easily, clearly, sometimes dramatically—through, would you believe, *ten* special hands on our life clock!

Second, it makes us think about time in terms more than of hours, days, weeks, etc. The book alerts us to *cycles*, to the interplay of time considerations that reveals the purpose within our life, the strategy to develop that purpose, and the identity confirmation we get from learning what we're about!

And third, "Cycles of Life" speaks of joy, of happiness to come from being in synch with our developmental phases from birth to death.

Rod Suskin is known and celebrated—radio, magazines, lectures—throughout South Africa for sensitive thought, clear vision, and practical spirituality. All these strengths are here in *Cycles of Life,* explaining the face-to-face interplay between the undeniable natural rhythms that guide our development and our life experience of them. Instead of just asking "what time is it?" in terms of "when do I leave for work," we should be asking "what time is it?" in terms of our development at this or that stage of our life plan. Am I building up for a big change in my life? How have I been fooling myself for the past three years? Are my difficulties teaching me a lesson? When will rewards come to lift me up and over? Suskin answers scores of questions like these!

Our developmental plan *is* time, it *is* age. The natural rhythms make sense; they have even entered our language: the "seven-year itch," "here today, gone tomorrow," "It just wasn't my time," "My time has come!"

Rod Suskin brings these concepts down to earth, into our workaday life; into our arsenal of strategies, which we use to make things happen. In a flash—with a bit of study here—we can see our cycles, know our cycles vividly. We will know *why* "life begins at forty!" We'll predict and understand and alleviate the "midlife crisis"; we'll even know *when* the raise should come on the job!

And even more: we learn how to influence, to *change* each day. Knowing the cycles allows us to condition our behavior through the first planning thoughts of every morning, let alone family or career projections for the year ahead!—That's a major statement: you can change confusion into knowing anticipation. Instead of being alerted to the clear-cut happenings of *past* cycles—"Oh, *that's* when I made the biggest change in my life," or "That was a terrible time, when nothing went right."—we can be alerted to the changes to come in the future and make the *very best* of them! We know what we're about and *when* we are *who* we are!

Suskin shares one particularly beautiful and powerful teaching image (among many!) that bears a pre-echo here: in talking about the times when we must meet obstacles to become wiser and stronger, he shows a river meeting a mountain. "The river does not suffer; it simply adjusts and turns, and reaches its destination by solving the problem of the mountain." Eventually, of course, both the river *and* the mountain are changing in this process, over time. That's the cycle of things, and knowing the timing of our *individual* cycles—ten of them, mind you!—we learn *when* the mountains appear, and we learn the path of our river.

Now, this book is beautiful—don't even think twice about that! It is also *practical*. Don't let the numbers frighten you: they are simply references to the real stuff, and you will quickly learn how it all works.

Finally, you may be thinking, how can I speak so enthusiastically and authoritatively about this book? Let me explain: I am an astrologer with a substantial reputation throughout much of the world and I have written twenty-nine books of my own. I know time and cycles very, very well. But no one anywhere has brought the times of our individual heavens down to earth as practically and aptly as Rod Suskin has. This is a book for *everyone*, not special students of cosmic matters. This is an original work with ageless principles.

Rod Suskin's book represents the time of *everyone's* life, and it's about time we rejoice in the knowledge that gives us such opportunity to live better lives.

Noel Tyl
Phoenix, AZ, USA

PREFACE

Some years ago friends from New York were briefly passing through my hometown Cape Town, and sorely needed a guide to what they could expect in their busy lives over the coming year. Since we had so little time I provided them with a "Graphical Ephemeris," a diagram that converted planetary positions to points on a 90-degree scale and indicated when these positions would overlap with the positions of the planets at the time of their births.

On my friends' Graphical Ephemeris printout I simply circled critical crossing points and provided them with simple keywords for each of the planets. Back in the Big Apple, my friends stuck this on their refrigerator, and proceeded to watch in astonishment as each critical event took place on all the circled dates on their graphs.

From this principle I devised a simplified set of tables for the present book that allows the beginning astrologer to apply the same method to be able to look at an entire lifetime on a single chart. You don't need any sophisticated software and you will be able learn a hands-on method for cosmobiology without worrying about technicalities.

INTRODUCTION

The system of representing planetary cycles on a 90-degree scale was devised in the last century by astrologer Reinhold Ebertin.[1] It is simply a new way of representing the same information that astrologers have always used. But it is a powerful tool and one that is even accessible to nonastrologers.

This fresh approach to an old concept allows beginner astrologers to extend their understanding into the principles behind predictive astrology as well as quickly acquiring a hands-on approach to working with these principles without special software or finicky mathematics. With a little patience, even those with no astrological knowledge at all will be able to make use of this technique and have the best possible time of the journey that is your life.

Why this was so amazing is because on paper in black and white such cycles look like almost any other scientific diagrams, except that these diagrams seemed to predict the future! I realized that this provided great evidence to the layperson that astrology had something serious to offer, and how someone with the most basic grasp of cyclical concepts could effectively use it to understand change—and so this book was born.

I have devised a simplified set of tables that allow you to apply astrological principles to your whole life on a single chart and learn to make accurate predictions of those changes—and hopefully good use of them, too. This book will teach you that method. No matter your age or stage of growth, you will be able to look back and forward over your life to understand changes of the past and predict those still to come.

What This Book Will Do

This book will show you how to master change. You will learn:

- that the changes life offers are much more predictable than we think.

- that a simple understanding of cycles will help you understand past events and learning experiences.

- how to predict major changes still to come in your life.

- why success in business and in romance depend on proper timing more than anything else—and knowing when those proper times occur.

---

1. Ebertin called himself a "cosmobiologist" and his method of representing planetary cycles, Cosmobiology, was a modernization of an idea by an earlier astrologer. The chart he drew to represent planetary cycles in "yearly rhythms," and which is often used by astrologers today, is called a "Graphical Ephemeris."

PART ONE

THE PLANETARY CYCLES

1

THE CYCLES OF LIFE

Was life simpler before? We live in a world of so much freedom and choice compared with our ancestors, especially in choosing our beliefs about life, but along with this freedom comes a great deal of uncertainty. While the freedom to pursue and believe our own spiritual truths offers us a great opportunity to find fulfillment, the lack of sureness allows change to surprise us, makes us feel that unlike previous generations we have little certainty of what to expect from life.

Perhaps our ancestors never really had a much simpler time than us; perhaps they knew something about the rhythms of nature and of life itself that made things seem more certain to them.

Predictability does not consign us to the limitations of fate but rather offers us an opportunity to take charge and steer our choices and actions in a direction that will help us fulfill our goals more easily. Ultimately, you will understand the present moment in a way that makes it easier to "live in the now."

Using a simple set of numbers firmly based in the well-established techniques of astrology, you will be able to predict when changes will happen in your life, what they will entail, and what are the best strategies to deal with them. Although some knowledge of astrology will be helpful, you will be able to grasp the method with only the most basic understanding of astrological principles. Should you study astrology further you will be more easily able to grasp the complexities of predictive techniques when you finally get to that exciting stage.

Cycles Equate to Changes

Astrologers observe ten major cycles in our lives, how they work and when they change. Each cycle is associated with different events, issues and experiences. These associations are not merely superstitious beliefs; they are observations that have accumulated over thousands of years. The cycles also interconnect and "cross over" to describe more detailed changes.

These are the same cycles astrologers use to make their detailed predictions using the ten planets. They are called transits, and they describe the movements of the planets through time compared with where they were at the subject's birth, shown in the natal chart.[1]

As our earth sciences show, some of the most powerful cycles we know are those of the Earth itself. With your birth time and place, an astrologer can locate the start of your cycles and pinpoint fine details about your cycles using your natal chart. It's likely that once you have a grasp of this system, you will eagerly and easily learn more advanced principles of prediction.

Creating Your Life Worksheet

Each of the cycles is associated with one of the planets, and a set of tables is used to quickly find your own starting points for each of the planets. The tables represent the planets' positions in a way that allows you to identify four-stage cycle used in this book.

The cycles have a simple four-stage rhythm. You will create your own "chart" of numbers to indicate when cycles change and when they interact with each other. A special worksheet is provided to make the task simpler. Once you have created your worksheet, the rest of the book will show you how to read it and become the master of your own destiny.

A Guide Through the Stages of Life

In each chapter we'll examine some of the cycles that unfold as we grow. We'll see how the length of a cycle explains many age-related experiences. We'll also look at what happens when you divide a cycle into its four main stages—the real heart of our method. You'll learn strategies to work with the cycles and how to cope with the changes, when to expect them, and when to make some changes yourself. More than anything, this method can become a strategy for your success in all areas of life, not simply a "weather report." Later you'll use the cycles in combination and in analyzing your relationships.

To illustrate the effects of the cycles, we will look at the chart of singer-actress Madonna, on page 12. Since she is an iconic figure for her generation, her well-publicized life events epitomize much of the best and worst of life's changes.

You're not required to *believe* anything here; you can match everything to your own *past* experience and test the system for yourself before you make any big life plans based on it!

Astrology Is about Cycles

Astrology is really the study of our relationship with time and with the cycles of nature. It works because we are cyclical creatures bound in the web of time, like all other living things. Astrology is not merely a way to describe our personalities and not a magical belief system. It is the study of cycles and the art of understanding just how we fit into them.

The Cosmic Clock

In the same way that we correlate the movement of the hour hand and the minute hand of the clock with the passing of time, so too we correlate the passage of the Sun and Moon through the sky with the passing of time. With only two hands on a clock we have accurate information about time, although we know we can add a third hand and be more precise. We can do the same with the sky clock of Sun and Moon.

Astrology Is a Way of Describing Time

Astrology is like a vast cosmic clock. By adding the other planets, it gives us more hands for our clock. By correlating ten cycles with human events, we form a detailed picture of natural cycles in our activities. Astrologers correlate periods of time with the movement of the planets around the zodiac.

Astrologers have learned to read a ten-handed clock (ten cycles of ten planets) that has been correlated for 6,000 years with human experience. The planetary cycles are not the *cause* of events any more than the hands of a clock cause time to pass. They simply describe the event, as one o'clock *describes* lunchtime rather than *causes* it to be lunchtime.

Table of Planets and Corresponding Life Cycles

Planet	Time cycle it measures
Sun	The daily and yearly pulse of our lives, the feeling of being each age, the feel of each day, short-term goals
Moon	Monthly emotional cycles—only a general guide to these is given in this book
Mercury	Patterns of communication and mental cycle
Venus	Patterns of values and relationship cycle
Mars	Short- and medium-term goals and drives, and relationship cycles (especially sexual)
Jupiter	Reward cycles of 3 and 12 years*
Saturn	Challenge, growth, maturity and karmic cycles of 7 and 29 years*
Uranus	Change cycles of sudden, dramatic or exciting nature; 21, 42 and 84 year cycle of self-discovery*
Neptune	Change cycles of subtle, slow or confusing nature, spiritual growth cycle of 42 and 84 years*
Pluto	Change cycles of transformational and traumatic nature as well as endings—karmic cycles of 36–65 years**

*varies slightly in length from person to person
**varies dramatically from one generation to another

Characteristics that Cycles Share

All these cycles follow a similar pattern. Each planet has its own period, or the amount of time it takes for the cycle to move through the stages. Each reflects clear and radical change every one-quarter of a cycle.

How Cycles Indicate Change

The twelve-stage (month) cycle of the year changes season every three months, producing the four major stages of the year. This cycle corresponds to the apparent movement of the Sun through four stages: from the equator to the tropic, from the tropic to the equator, from the equator to the opposite tropic, and back again to the equator. The Sun takes exactly three months to complete each of these stages, and the weather changes significantly each time. If we represent the cycle graphically, it is easy to see why (see figure 1 below).

In figure 1, which represents the flow of time as a line travelling in the direction indicated by arrowheads, each of the four change-points is represented by a black dot. As you can see, each time such a point is reached, the cycle changes "direction." These are critical points, where change happens—and so we have our seasons. In fact, this is the natural shape of a cycle, or a "sine curve." All cycles essentially have these same four change-points.[2]

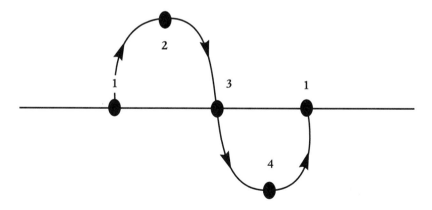

Figure 1

Twelve Steps Through a Cycle

The evolution of the calendar into a twelve-month period reflects the observation that each of the four seasons—or stages—goes through a beginning, middle, and end. A season flows from early season to high season to late season. The three stages can be useful in helping us ensure that fulfilling our goals also provides rewards.

Astrologers measure the twelve steps through each cycle by observing the Sun's apparent movement through the twelve signs of the zodiac. Like the dial of a clock, the zodiac is a manmade template to measure a pre-existing natural cycle. Understanding the meaning of each of the twelve stages is the source of much of astrology's power.

Personal Cycles

This principle of four basic stages, or four critical points in the cycle, applies to every single cycle that we can measure, whatever its length. This simple principle is the heart of this book. Each of us is individually attuned to these natural rhythms.

There is nothing at all occult about this discovery: it is a natural rhythm, as natural as all your other physical bodily processes. Once you learn how to work with your own cycles, you will experience the power of this knowledge.

Even though we have distanced ourselves from nature so much that we barely recognize the seasons, we retain some of this knowledge. The familiar seven-year cycle is mentioned everywhere, from the Bible to the "seven-year itch." Most of us have experienced things in our lives that seem to change about every seven years. You'll discover that the seven-year cycle is a quarter of Saturn's cycle, one of the cycles we will consider.

Overlapping Cycles

The cycles are not acting independently. They all happen at the same time and work together. If your drive cycle is at a high when your opportunity cycle is at a low, you can expect the drive to be somewhat frustrated. The simplified numerical tables used later in this book will allow us to examine the points where two cycles overlap in this way and provide more accurate predictions of change.

Human cycles and planetary cycles follow a pattern found in all of nature. On the one hand, every cycle goes about its own rhythm as if the others are not there. At times, though, the cycles may overlap, adding their frequencies or subtracting them and creating a strong interference effect.

The real adventure is seeing the effect of overlapping cycles in your own life. By the end of the book you will be set on the road of combining cycles to make accurate predictions. Putting two of the cycles together will suddenly focus your ability to understand and anticipate changes. Soon you will easily add more overlapping cycles. Learning this technique will help you anticipate changes, understand them, and discover when you should exploit changes and when you should lie low.

By definition, you are working with your own personal cycles, which began when you were born. A book that was not written personally for you must therefore have some limitations. If you have your natal chart, an understanding of how each planet works for you will greatly improve your ability to know what type of events happen for each of the ten cycles. In turn, watching the cycles change and seeing what happens will help you learn more about your natal planets too.

Practice and Make It Your Own

The most important principle in astrology is that it is not mere belief: it proves itself. Experiment with this method, use it to look back at times in your life to see if it truly bears out events, and use it as the months and years unfold. You'll begin to feel more in touch with your own life and more in control. Sure, it can't help you avoid every difficulty, but it will equip you to understand these fluctuations, help you grow from them, and help you be prepared for the future.

---

1. Astrological terms such as this are defined in the Glossary, page 235.

2. Observing these neat cycles from a tilted, orbiting Earth makes each quarter uneven, and so we need tables to measure them rather than simple division by four.

Name: Madonna   Birthdate: 8/16/1958

Birth position	Sun-All	Sun-Jup.	Venus	Mars	Jup.	Sat.	Uran.	Nept.	Pluto
	53	23	30	45	86	79	43	32	62

Date	Sun-All	Sun-Jup.	Venus	Mars	Jup.	Sat.	Uran.	Nept.	Pluto
1987						(S)			
1988									
1989				P			P		
1990							P		
1991			S					S	
1992				S			S		
1993	SP				(J)				
1994									S
1995			U			S			
1996			U						(P)
1997			N						
1998			SN				(U)	(N) S	
1999			S	SU			(U) S	(N) S	
2000				S					
2001	SU								S
2002						S			
2003						P	N		U
2004				N			N		U
2005			S	N				S	
2006	S			S		S			
2007	S					U			S
2008	N					U			S
2009						S			

Dates every year the Sun changes cycle

Feb. 12	May 14	Aug. 16	Nov. 16

Person	Venus	Mars
Me	30	45
Sean	68	69
Guy	9	53

2

FINDING YOUR OWN CYCLES

For the information in this book to be meaningful and useful right from the beginning, it's best to use your own cycles as your reference point. You'll be able to start predicting changes right away.

In this chapter

- Using the tables
- Finding your basic numbers
- Filling out the worksheet
- Overlapping cycles

Cycles Start from Birth

The cycles start ticking at the moment we are born, so you need to know the starting positions of each of the cycles on the day of your birth. I have provided very simple representations of these cycles in tables that you'll quickly find easy to use. You don't need any math ability. You are simply going to look up numbers and write them down.

In the tables each cycle is represented by one of the planets, and each of the planets has a list of numbers covering a span of time. These numbers represent the positions of the planets in their cycle over this period of time. You will be creating a list of numbers that represents your birth chart.

Looking Up Your Own Numbers

On page 20 is a form you can photocopy that makes it easier to find and keep track of your own personal cycle numbers. Once you have completed it you will have everything you need to learn about your life changes through astrology. We are able to explore nine of the planetary cycles using this book, so we'll find our nine basic numbers before we start.

Why Table Numbers Go in Both Directions

If you look through the lists of numbers, you'll see two apparently strange characteristics of these cycles: 1) they speed up and slow down, or 2) they travel backward as well as forward. This is the apparent backward (retrograde) motion of the planets, caused by observing them from the faster-moving Earth.

Astrology studies these cycles with regard to their relevance on the Earth, so it is necessary for astrologers to consider the Earth-centered perspective as the most important one. We must take retrograde into account to time the arrival of a planet at a point in the cycle even though it's not a true movement of the planet.

You'll also notice that this causes numbers to often repeat three times in a short span of time. That accounts for the familiar phenomenon of things happening in threes.

Filling In the Numbers

Right now you won't know what these numbers mean, but soon you'll discover their power. We are going to use Madonna as an example. Follow along, using your own birthdate and filling in the blank form.

Step 1: Find your nine basic numbers

- Turn to Table 1 on page 149. Here you can fill in the first two numbers.

- Find your date of birth (day and month) in this table in the Date column.

- Copy the number you find at this date from the Sun-All column and the number from the Sun-Jup column into the boxes on the form with the same designations.

- Madonna was born on August 16. On that date you find 53 in the Sun-All column and 23 in the Sun-Jup column. These are the numbers you'd write into the first two boxes if you had that birthday.

- Now turn to Table 2 on page 155.

- Find the date closest to your birthdate in the Date column. Copy the numbers from all five columns into the boxes with the same planets' names.

Madonna was born on August 16, 1958. The closest date we find is 8/14/1958. At this date we find the numbers 86, 79, 43, 32, 62. These are copied into the columns. Madonna's sheet now looks like this:

Name: Madonna   Birthdate: 8/16/1958

Birth position	Sun-All	Sun-Jup.	Venus	Mars	Jup.	Sat.	Uran.	Nept.	Pluto
	53	23			86	79	43	32	62

Finally, turn to Table 3 on page 189. Once again, find the date closest to your birthdate and copy down the Venus and Mars numbers for that date.

If your date falls between two dates, notice how the Venus number increases or decreases by about one per day, and Mars about one per two days. You can adjust your number to be more accurate by adding to or subtracting from the number closest to your date. If you're not comfortable doing this, just stick to the numbers closest to your birthdate.

In Madonna's case, the closest date is 8/18/58. The numbers on that day are 32 and 46. If you look at the previous date in the table, 8/11, it is a week earlier. The Venus number on that date is 24, a difference of 8. Over seven days, that's about one per day. So, on the 16th, the Venus number was closer to 30, two less than the number on the 18th. Two days earlier, Mars would probably be one number less, so that makes it 45. Inserting these numbers into the table we now have this:

Birth position	Sun-All	Sun-Jup	Venus	Mars	Jup.	Sat.	Uran.	Nept.	Pluto
	53	23	30	45	86	79	43	32	62

Sometimes you'll notice that the numbers change much more slowly. In those cases you don't need to do much adjusting at all.

That's it! You have found your nine major cycle numbers.

Step 2: Adding changes of the Sun
Using Table 1:

- Find the number in the Sun-All column for your birthday.
- Find the three other dates in the year when this same number recurs in the Sun-All column.
- Fill in the three dates in the small table marked "Dates every year the sun cycle changes." You'll see the first block in this section is your birthdate.

Step 3: Adding your years
The next step is to list the years for dating events. The first column in the table is listed "Date." This is where you list the years of your life. Start from as early as you are interested in the events in your life, even in the year after your birth. List the sequential years as far as you are interested in.

In the example, Madonna was born in 1958. We have listed the years from 1987 to 2009 in the first column of her table.

Step 4: Adding special cycle numbers
At the bottom of the first page of the worksheet, you see a box called Relationships. Copy your Venus and Mars numbers to this box, and look up the Venus and Mars numbers for your romantic and business partners in Table 3 and fill them in below yours.

Step 5: Adding change points of the four major growth and change cycles

Now you'll find the quarter-mark changes of the major change cycles. We'll use initials to represent the cycles: J = Jupiter, S = Saturn, U = Uranus, N = Neptune, P = Pluto.

Using Table 2:

- Look at your Saturn cycle number.

- In the Saturn column in Table 2, scan ahead from your birthdate, or from today if you are interested only in looking ahead. When the same number comes up again, or a number very close to it, put an S in the block under "Saturn" for that year. If you like, put a small digit with it to represent the month.

- Remember that things happen in threes, so that same number may occur twice more within a year from the date you have found. Note these in the same way. You'll probably find that, in many cases, the repeating cycle causes the Saturn cycle to appear two years in succession as it spreads itself over a few months each time. Again, look at the filled-in example on the next page.

- Jump ahead seven years and repeat the process.

- Proceed the same way for every seventh year after that.

- Circle the S's on the **fourth** appearance of Saturn, around the age of 29. Do the same for the one around the age of 58.

- Repeat the process with Uranus, looking for repeats of the Uranus number in the Uranus column every 19–22 years (age around 21, 40, and 62), and filling in a "U" in the Uranus column at these dates. Circle the **second** and **fourth** "U."

- Do the same with Neptune, repeating every 40–44 years. Circle the **first** "N" and the **second,** if there is one.

- Finally, find the single repeat of the Pluto number in the Pluto column and fill in a "P" which you circle. It may be worth checking to see if you have a possible second one—Britain's Queen Mother had it at her death at age 101.

- Now do Jupiter. We've saved this step because Jupiter uses a differ-ent cycle system, a three-part cycle instead of a four-part one. Jupiter numbers will repeat about every 4 years, and you need to circle **every third "J"** in the Jupiter column, around ages 12, 24, 36, 48, 60, and so on.

- The Mars cycle changes every five-to-nine months, so we will only look at it for the current few years in year life. Look for repeats of your Mars number over the last year or two and the next year or two.

That was quite a task—you may want to stretch or take a walk before you do the final stage.

If you're eager to get going, you have filled in enough information on your worksheet to use most of this book. You will need to come back here to finish the last few steps when you get to chapter 10.

Step 6: Adding your overlapping cycles
Now spend a last half hour listing all your overlapping cycles on the worksheet so you can see how cycles operate together. Pour a cup of tea, sit in a well-lit place, and prepare to consult the tables one last time.

- Check your Sun-All number on your worksheet.

- Starting with the year of your birth, scan through the Saturn list in Table 2 to see in which years Saturn crosses the Sun number or reaches in two digits of it. In the Sun column for that year, write an S, just as you did with the Saturn column. This is a year that the Saturn cycle overlaps the Sun cycle.

- Go forward seven years and repeat the exercise. Keep on going until you reach the end of your worksheet.

- Now do the same for each of the other planet numbers, checking to see when Saturn reaches the positions of Venus, Mars, and the rest all the way to Pluto, and filling in the S at the appropriate years in each planet's column. This is the part that will take half an hour! For each of the planets, you will find Saturn reaching or crossing that number approximately every seven or eight years.

- Now repeat the exercise for Uranus, Neptune, and Pluto, checking to see when they reach the positions of all the planets before them. This task will be much quicker, because they appear only twice for each of the other planet's columns.

Turn to the completed table for Madonna on page 12. You can see it's not that much work, and that there are immediately some years visible where many things are happening, and some when there is little.

Optional step: Using color

If you haven't had enough of messing about with your worksheet yet, and you have a bunch of colored pencils or highlighters, you can color each planet's letter a different color. It will make it much easier to predict changes later on. If you only have a few colors, concentrate on Saturn, Uranus, Neptune, and Pluto.

Seeing the Whole Picture at a Glance

I mentioned in the Introduction that what brought me to write this book was demonstrating to some friends how overlapping cycles worked on a graph. If you are a visual person and are wont to see a holistic, graphical view, consult the Appendix to see how to create the graph. For now, though, we have some predictions to make.

Let's Go

Now you can finally put down your pens and get ready to take control from today.

Name: _____   Birthdate: _____

Birth position	Sun-All	Sun-Jup.	Venus	Mars	Jup.	Sat.	Uran.	Nept.	Pluto

Date									

Dates every year the Sun changes cycle

Person	Venus	Mars
Me		

PART TWO

PLANNING FOR SUCCESS WITH EVERYDAY CYCLES

3

BUILDING BLOCKS:
THE SUN'S CYCLE

The main benefit of understanding cycles is more than just predicting and understanding change. Similarly, the Sun and Moon are more than just a way to measure time. Once we understand the natural cycles they measure, we can gain significantly more mastery over our daily lives and what is often the drudgery of the daily grind.

In this chapter

- You will learn to master the two most basic units of time: the day and the year, measured by the Sun's cycle.

- You will learn how to attune yourself to the natural rhythm of the day and make it more rewarding and enjoyable.

- You will rediscover the importance of leisure time.

- You will learn the two special cycles that the year holds so that you can succeed at short-term goals and make birthdays something to look forward to. A practical example will show you how to use these principles to re-establish natural good health.

Using Your Worksheet

All you need to measure your solar cycles is the block of four dates filled in on the worksheet in the section "Dates every year the sun changes." Have those dates handy now.

The Day Is the Most Basic Time Unit

Our way of measuring time is based on the apparent movement of the Sun, which allows us to measure the passage of the day and of the year. These two periods are the basis of our calendar. Added to that, we incorporate the twenty-nine-day cycle of the Moon. These two lights in the sky, Sun and Moon in their endless cycles, respectively illuminate and reflect our consciousness of self in our world. These are the lights of self, and they have the dual status of timekeeper and personal mirror.

At any given moment the fundamental concern with "what do I do with my life" is about *today*. After the artificial measurement of the hours and minutes, the natural day is our most basic unit of time. The day is our real meaning of now, the present. It is the only time we can really apprehend, because the future is always unknown and the past is recalled, somewhat inaccurately, only as memory.

Many people, in their pursuit of philosophical and spiritual understanding, have encountered the concept in both physics and metaphysics that time is part of the actual, ever-present fabric of space—it is not really moving or passing. This means it is always the present. Although impossible for us to grasp in the intellectual sense, the idea of the eternal present is fundamental to both metaphysics and our modern, post-Einstein way of understanding the nature of time and space.

When you consider this, the importance of today takes on much greater significance: mastering the daily cycle can truly mean mastering your entire life. As buildings are made from single bricks, living things from single cells, and great journeys from single steps, so the day is the very heartbeat of our personal journey through life.

Natural Attunement to the Daily Cycle

Like other creatures on Earth, we and our body processes are timed according to an approximate twenty-four-hour cycle. This is known as the "circadian rhythm," or more commonly as the "biological clock" and it helps maintain the most fundamental life processes. For most animals, including humans, this rhythm helps us sleep and eat at the right times, and it controls processes down to the level of individual cells. Although the body's own chemical processes are responsible for running these clocks, it is the daily exposure to light that helps adjust the inner clocks to the true daily rhythm.

Of course, the apparent motion of the Sun through a cycle is actually the motion of the Earth observed by watching the Sun. This means that we are really measuring Earth cycles. When we talk of the Sun as representing the everyday self, we are really describing ourselves as being Earth-based and subject to Earth cycles.

When our clocks lose synchronization with the natural light cycle, the body operates much less efficiently. It is precisely this phenomenon that is responsible for jet lag, and probably much of the common problems of tiredness before bedtime.

Most people are out of synchronization every day, even without the luxury of air travel. This desynchronization has come about through our daily practice of working for many hours in artificial indoor environments with little awareness of the natural conditions outside, compounded by hurried and disturbed meal times. Most of us in the Western world of office jobs and long working hours suffer from stress, tiredness and endless minor ailments. We need pills to help us sleep and alarms to help us awaken. Add the unhealthy food, air and water that we consume, and it's a wonder that our bodies survive as long as they do. Of course, survival itself is not enough, since it is often achieved only at great cost to our emotional and physical health.

Honoring the Daily Cycle

We can affect the most powerful changes in our lives by adjusting to our own most basic biological clock, the daily one. The daily rhythm is the pattern that resonates into every other moment, so if we are careful to create our daily pattern according to its natural needs, we will make all other types of attunement much easier. It is essential to set for yourself a daily pattern that suits you, but is also adjusted to the flow of natural time. Here's how to make the very best of the daily solar rhythm.

Step 1: Wake up with a rhythm

The way the day begins is often the single moment that resonates into the rest of the day. Since our biological clock is constantly adjusted by light, we should wake up early each morning, at the same time. It may be more ideal to rise with the Sun or just before it, so in places where the Sun rises at a reasonable time all year long (between the tropics) we should rise in the hour before sunrise.

One way in which we radically upset our clocks is by rising later on weekends and holidays. It produces exactly the same effect as jet lag, and is probably the reason why so many people are tired after the weekend, why Mondays are so bad. At first, the thought of losing the lie-in is like losing your last luxury, but gaining the energy levels by losing the blue-Monday effect is a much greater reward. To enjoy the laziness of the weekend, you can lie in bed and read a book, as long as you *awaken* at the same time as on weekdays.

Rising with an alarm clock is a disturbance of the last dream cycle, and anyway, you don't need an alarm. The biological clock is perfectly capable of waking us, as long as we wake at the same time every day. You may think that you need your alarm clock, but everyone has a built-in timer: you just have to remember to use it.

It's the same with going to sleep: for the rhythm to work, we need to go to sleep at the same time each evening. Ideally, you would start by allowing eight hours, no more or less, for sleeping. Eventually you'll discover the sleep period that works best for you. Practice by telling your body what time to awaken, repeating this a few times in your mind just as you go to sleep. If you need to be sure, you can set an alarm for a half hour later so you won't worry.

Wake up earlier than you need to. It relieves stress and may even allow the luxury of a brief lie-in without guilt or consequences to your timeliness.

Step 2: Reserve the first hour to change the whole day

The first hour of the day is the time best reserved for daily exercises and for a period of meditation.

Breakfast should be very light, because your body is still in the elimination cycle that starts during sleep.

Many people benefit from introducing a daily ritual that honors the arrival of the Sun. This is a great way to involve the mind and spirit in the attunement process, and to literally identify with the heartbeat of the whole rhythm of our cycles. It could be a meditation, some yoga or stretching, or just watching the beauty of the sunrise.

This first period of the morning is critical. In all things, the beginning sets the tone for the whole. *You can radically change your experience of daily life by simply taking charge of the first hour of the day.* If you deliberately start every day on a calm, clear note, you will eliminate the experience of the bad day from your life. After an early morning hour of peace, inner contact and self-attunement, the hassles of everyday life truly become secondary. For some busy people this may mean awakening an hour earlier, but the reward will far outweigh the initial adjustment.

Step 3: Three priorities a day

One of the simplest ways to balance our lives is to properly distribute our different activities.

There are two basic types of daily activity: the type we call *work*, referring to what we do for a living or because of obligation and commitment, and generally *have* to do. Then there's the type of activity we call leisure, and we usually wish we had more of it.

Here's a thought: our circadian rhythm is tuned for eight hours of sleep a day, as we have been told since childhood. We were also taught that a working day is from nine to five. That's eight hours. If we have eight hours of sleep and eight of work, that leaves another eight hours a day.

These are your play hours. This is the time to do *your* thing. Indulge a few pleasures or desires, spiritual and personal needs. Spend a little time with your children. Imagine if you had eight of these hours!

Many people, reading the above words, sigh longingly, or laugh at the foolish idealism in this hectic world of ours. It's true, you probably do work many more than eight hours a day, and certainly get fewer than eight for pleasure periods.

Some of us guiltily reject the notion of eight hours of play. Culturally, we have been taught to feel guilty when we waste time or are self-indulgent in any way, and it's a form of programming that is difficult to overcome.

Why play is as important as work

Play is not a waste of time. It allows for self-development and expression. Remember, the self is the cycle of the Sun, so developing this self-expression allows the healthy development of attunement to the daily cycle. Children and animals do not play to pass the time, they play to learn and experience life in an enjoyable fashion. As adults we continue to learn, and play provides a nice alternative to learning through trauma and difficulty. Play really is constructive, even if it's pleasurable.

As adults, we tend to confine our play to weekends, and so see it as a very separate part of our lives. During the week, that playtime might be spent staring passively at a television for an hour or two a night.

Most of us eventually form the impression that life is a daily slog, that every day is more or less the same as every other, and, overall, things are tough. Obviously, we feel this mostly because things don't turn out the way we want, and unexpected events with very real consequences often happen. We feel that life is about learning the hard way.

Think about this: if we spent the other eight hours of the day playing, doing things we wanted to do because they give us joy or pleasure or meet a personal need, we would feel exhilarated and pleased at the end of that. If our days had an equal amount of work and play, we would form the overall impression that life has some good, some bad; we'd also be learning the fun and easy way, like children. Only the naive and the arrogant suppose that learning stops at the end of childhood, or indeed, that it ever stops.

At first it seems idealistic and even absurd to allow for eight hours of play. Realistically, they include your eating time and probably a few chores too, but you will soon discover the effect they have on the remainder of your time. You will seem to spend fewer hours working, but your productivity will increase noticeably.

Go ahead and see for yourself. See playtime for what it is. It will generate increased relaxation and a greater sense of being in touch with yourself. Putting a value on playtime makes all the difference in how you approach your work, and the results you get out of it.

Step 4: The finishing touch

Rising with the Sun is the simplest route to attunement to the daily rhythm. In the same way, acknowledging the sunset will reinforce this sense of connection with nature. Let it create a natural transition in your day, another moment with yourself, just as you had around sunrise, and a signal of change of focus and activity to your body and mind.

This is not only a spiritual moment: it helps adjust the biological clock. Activities during the few dark hours in which we are awake should be different from those of daylight. Finish the day's food soon after sunset, because your body will enter its elimination cycle at around 10 P.M. Of course, such a pattern should never become too rigid. Spontaneity and change are important, too, and the aim is to establish a baseline rhythm from which the rest of your life proceeds.

The Sun at the Center of It All

The cyclical view of time is rooted in the seasonal cycle. In ancient times, when everyone lived much closer to the land, this cycle was the fundamental determinant of the quality of life, being related to the weather and to the availability of food.

Everything in nature changes with the seasons, but as we civilized our world, we lost awareness of much of this change. It seems that civilization can be described as the process of making everything less natural.

Today, in Western countries, most foods are available all year 'round, through importation or cold storage, and the only experience we have of the changing seasons is the weather. Even that is largely controlled using indoor temperature regulation.

The seasons, of course, are directly related to the apparent motion of the Sun over the course of the year. Just as the daily cycle is based on the Earth's motion relative to the Sun, so is the yearly cycle. Because of the close relationship between these two solar cycles and the very nature of human existence, the Sun is the most important symbol in human religious traditions. Many ancient religions were a form of Sun worship, and even as they evolved into modern religions they kept elements of Sun worship.

Of course, the Sun is quite literally the source of life on the planet, and our precise distance from it is often cited by astronomers and biologists as the very reason why life exists here and nowhere else in our solar system, at least, nowhere that we're yet aware of.

Whether we understand it from a religious or a biological point of view, the Sun is the most essential element of life on Earth, and its two cycles are the most fundamental aspects of our system of time measurement. Since mastery of your cycles is the principle of living in greater harmony with both nature and with time itself, there can be no more powerful way of doing this than by attuning to the solar cycles.

In astrological symbolism the Sun is the symbol for the self, the very center of the personality around which all the other personality structures are built. Your Sun sign is the most simple and basic outline of your character. The other aspects of personality orbit around the central self, which illuminates them and makes them individualistically our own. This is very similar to the physical shape of the solar system, with all the planets rotating around the Sun. Despite modern critics of astrology condemning it because of its apparent insistence on seeing the Earth as the center of the solar system, the symbolism of astrology clearly applies to the solar system as we know it.[1]

Honoring the Yearly Cycle

As we have seen, the daily solar cycle may be the single influence that changes our lives. Using it in tandem with the yearly solar cycle, we will gain the sense of power for which we strive. As civilized people, we believe that our control over natural forces makes us powerful. Of course, we do not control them at all; we actually mean our independence of natural forces when we say that. Ironically, in distancing ourselves from nature we *lose* power, and by attuning ourselves to nature, we gain power.

Step 1: The seasons

The simplest way to realign ourselves with the yearly rhythm is to admit the seasons back into our lives. This doesn't mean we have to turn off the heater in the depths of winter, but rather that we must re-attune to the way the whole planet is responding to winter.

In all living creatures, activities and diet change with the seasons. It's easy to take our cue from the natural world when adjusting our activities to suit the seasons, and many sports players are doing so when they play seasonal sports.

We can apply the simple principle of the four seasons to all our basic activities: springtime is the time for beginning things, while summertime is the time to expand all our projects; the time for involvement and action. In the autumn, we gradually tie up all our projects and reap their results, and in the winter we withdraw from initiating or growing activities and concentrate largely on strategizing for the following spring. In our hectic world we might not find it so easy to adjust, especially to the quiet winter, but as nature constantly demonstrates, this is the most efficient way to be productive.

Although in the short-term we have higher output in our summer-all-year-round approach to life, the stress imposed on our selves and on our entire way of life is enormous, leading to endless problems, and especially disease.

Many illnesses are a consequence of the body breaking down under external stressors. At the very least, stress makes us vulnerable to disease.

This natural seasonal cycle prevents these stressors from reaching the point where they can do physical damage. Think of a field that doesn't have a chance to lie fallow: it ends up producing years of inferior crops, finally becoming barren. In our modern world, just as we do with a barren field, we take chemicals like nicotine, caffeine, and sugar to keep us going, creating even more stress on our bodies.

An immediate way to improve your yearly rhythm is to learn to eat foods in their proper seasons. It is likely that this will have an enormous effect on your physical health, and as a result, your mental and emotional well-being. It also makes eating more interesting and creates more variety. Each month or two you are eating new fruits and vegetables and suddenly eating healthily doesn't look boring anymore.

Step 2: Happy birthday!

Actually, we do honor the yearly cycle in our culture, but in strange and inconsistent ways. While we are young, our birthday is the most important day in the year; we are special for one magical day, and we have a special ritual to celebrate it, the birthday party. Then, when we grow older, the day becomes less important, eventually being relegated to the list of childish fantasies along with Santa Claus and the tooth fairy.

While some adults continue to celebrate their birthdays, many prefer not to think about the fact that they are growing older. Of course, this is the ultimate form of denial and is a form of dishonoring of ourselves. We have forgotten that age means experience and wisdom. In recent times, the Western world has become obsessed with youth and beauty, and now only the physical dimension of aging is seen. With the degenerative diseases our unhealthy lifestyles tend to cause, we also have many real reasons to fear aging.

Once we have taken responsibility for our state of health, and reassume the power to make ourselves into more whole, attuned individuals, we can also rediscover the importance of the birthday.

Not only is honoring the solar cycle a valuable psychological and spiritual process, but it is an attunement to our personal seasonal cycle. The birthday is the day on which the Sun is in the same zodiacal (seasonal) position it was on the day of birth. This is like a renewal of the *personal* energy cycle, just as the Earth experiences it when the Sun returns to the position of the equinox to produce the next season.

The cycle of the Sun relates to the development of personal goals. These are not quite the same as business goals; they are more in the line of New Year's resolutions. In fact, your birthday is your personal New Year's Day, and you should treat it accordingly. Celebrate the renewal of your life-contract. Make your own resolutions, but not the January variety that usually end up as reasons to feel guilty. Most people fail at New Year's resolutions simply because it is the wrong time of the year to make them for those people who aren't born at that time.

Success is about timing. If we adjust ourselves to our own personal seasons, we'll find it much easier to understand and benefit from this natural cycle and achieve these goals naturally.

Step 3: The year planner

Just as the Earth has its own seasonal cycle based on the return of the Sun to the vernal equinox, each of us has our personal set of seasons from birthday-to-birthday. We can use our own seasons to plan our yearly goals.

For some, the personal goals may indeed blur into other areas, like work, so there are two criteria that personal-season issues must meet. First, they have a personal concern beyond the worldly or relationship goals; and second, they are the goals that could be achieved in less than a year. This is an important principle: you do not want things to carry on from year-to-year: it's a bit like a farmer trying to pass off last year's crop as fresh. (There are other cycles for the longer goals, as we'll see later.)

We find our own seasons by dividing the year between birthdays into four stages of three months each, with each stage representing one of the four seasons starting from spring at the time of your birthday. The dates that each personal season begins are the four "sun change" dates you marked on your worksheet.

Now, many people will find that their personal seasons are at odds with the natural seasonal cycles. Rather than competing with each other, these two rhythms function differently.

- The *actual seasons* are used to align ourselves to the world outside that exists in that year of our lives. These seasons also align us to everyday things: people, places, daily activities, foods, dealing with matters that come up, planning outings, or celebrations.

- The *personal seasonal cycle* is used for deliberately initiating personal goals that do not need the cooperation of the world around you. These may include changing habits, losing weight, learning a new language, and other goals that are about yourself rather than what your employer or others want from you.

Just as in the Earth's seasonal cycle, there are four critical periods of change during the year. (In seasonal terms, these are the equinoxes and solstices.)[2] If we learn to recognize these periods, lasting about a week or two each in the personal cycle, we will ensure that our yearly plans reach their goals more easily.

The goal is initiated on or just after the birthday, and three months should be allowed for it to be fully established in your life.

The first critical period occurs three months after the birthday around the second date in your "dates the sun changes" block, and is the week in which you should adjust your pursuit of your goals at that time. All goals need adjustment, because the plans that start in our minds and are then expressed in our actions do not consider the actual circumstances, which haven't yet happened. Once those circumstances do unfold and we are aware of them, adjustment must occur so that we can continue on the path to success. It's a little like a train: even though the track is there, the driver must still adjust the speed, otherwise the train will derail.

The sixth-month adjustment (the third date in your "dates the sun changes" block) is a little different. This is more like crossing those tracks: we need to pause and look around, but carry on in the direction we were going. This may include some of the same adjustments we needed to make three months earlier, but it represents a time by which we must have achieved the primary goals. Now we start reaping the rewards, entering the phase of working with those goals.

At nine months after the birthday (the fourth sun change date on the worksheet) another adjustment is made. It's rather like the one we made the first time around. Now we enter into the phase of letting go, of releasing the goal and dealing with what it has created in our lives. We will continue to be successful until six or seven weeks into the last stage, but then things do change.

Step 4: Wind down

We've all experienced the strange plateau that occurs before our birthdays. Nothing seems to work, energy is very low, and there's a feeling of meaninglessness.

Actually, it is a perfectly natural feeling. If you think about it in terms of the solar cycle, you can imagine the Sun pretty much exhausted at the end of the year's journey through the sky. Although that is a myth rather than the truth of the matter, the mythology is built out of our human experience rather than the relevance of what is physically happening to the Sun.

These last six or seven weeks are the wind-down phase, when we should do exactly that in every way. Remember that it's natural to feel a little depressed at this time: it's not the fear of aging but rather the experience of loss (and low energy). After all, the goal has been achieved and there's nothing more to work for.

Naturally, it's a great time to make plans for after your forthcoming birthday rather than judge all of life by this short phase during the year. So many people allow themselves to experience this as growing older rather than becoming quiet to prepare for the next growth phase. In this phase of preparation, spend more time alone, don't begin anything, and try to create a feeling of gestation, imagining yourself as a seed that waits for spring before trying to grow.

An example: Becoming healthier

A good example of a personal year goal is to take control of your health. Health is a solar concern because the Sun represents the source of all life and energy, and affects all other aspects of our lives. If you were to use the yearly plan as a way of regaining control in this area, it might run as follows:

First stage (up to three months): Initiating; use this period to plan and put into place your new health regimen. Learn about foods and exercise, and spend the period establishing your knowledge. Gradually, you introduce more of the healthy regimens into your life, but without obsessiveness or any extremes.

Critical phase at three months: A reassessment; spend a week or so looking back over what you have learned and done, and weed out the unnecessary and irrelevant.

Second Stage (three–six months): Growing; use this period to establish a regimen or discipline that employs your new eating and exercise habits. Don't spend too much energy on disciplining the old, bad habits. Work at establishing the new ones first and turning them into habits.

Critical phase at six months: Assess the benefits of the last three months' healthy living and use this as an inspiration and a challenge for the next three months, during which the new lifestyle must become fully established and achieved.

Third stage (six–nine months): Reward; start buying new outfits for the new social activities of this period. Learning *when* rewards are supposed to come in is the best way to benefit from them. Now, at six months, you should see clear results of your new lifestyle. This three-month phase should be used to identify so strongly with the new lifestyle that it becomes you. During this phase, start letting go of the more persistent bad habits, one at a time.

Critical phase at nine months: Reassessment; having reached the rewards and established a new lifestyle, assess how you can release the last remaining vestiges of the old lifestyle.

Fourth stage (nine–twelve months): Winding down; during this phase you eliminate the "no-longer-you" bad practices, and relax into your new lifestyle so that it becomes less of a discipline and more natural to you. By now it should be an integrated, new, good habit.

Critical stage (six weeks before birthday): Congratulate yourself and reinforce how able you are, so that these weeks don't seem so pointless. Plot your resolution for next year.

Throwing Light on Life

There is one further association of the solar cycle we should consider. By its nature, the Sun sheds light all around, having a tangible effect in the world outside of itself. This means that when our personal solar cycle is allowed to pulsate in its natural way, our personal energies are moved out into the world, and we can pursue goals and perhaps reap some rewards. At the same time, we interact with those around us, and are forced to make adjustments in order to reach our objectives.

If we take a one-sided approach to life, allowing the intellect and the ambitions to act without reference to their natural cycles, we will suffer in the world as we suffer in ourselves when we are out of attunement with our energy cycle. In our symbolic system, the Sun shines light onto all the planets (that's the only reason we can see them in the sky), and so the personal cycle is reflected in every other aspect of our lives. No wonder that being attuned to the present is the key to success!

The pulse of our everyday lives is the energy that drives us through the fascinating and often frightening world we experience. Work and play, romance and achievement, are tools by which we acquire that experience, but they are not the goals in themselves. By learning to operate with our natural personal rhythms, we learn a better way of coping with life and avoiding disillusionment. We learn to create the foundations for the greater cycles that also operate in our lives.

---

1. The astrological system of prediction is, in fact, based around the same principle of the solar cycle. Astrologers use the progress of each day after birth to symbolize each year after life, encapsulated in the simple astrological axiom of one day = one year. The real depth of this principle is plain to see, and is, in fact, also related to ancient knowledge encapsulated in the biblical text of Ecclesiastes. Clearly, this ancient wisdom is both a symbolic idea, as well as a scientific one, in that the science of our ancestors must have understood the correlation of the two solar cycles.

2. The 21st of September, December, March, and June are the spring equinox, summer solstice, autumn equinox, and winter solstice respectively in the southern hemisphere. The Sun is over the tropics and the equator during these days. These are the beginnings of the seasons, and are of course reversed in the northern hemisphere.

4

WHY DO I FEEL THIS WAY?
THE MOON'S CYCLE

Taking charge by doing things at the right time, while a powerful way to master our lives, is not enough. The daily cycle has taught us the importance of the day-by-day approach to life, but living in the present is easier said than done. Day-to-day living is filled with emotional fluctuations and events that trigger our reactions and play havoc with our neatly lain plans.

In this chapter

- Learning about the lunar cycle will help you understand emotional fluctuations and lead to mastery of the present, the "now."

- You will learn how the four basic phases of the moon's cycle can be used to successfully plan very short-term goals and understand the sensitive periods of the month.

- You will discover that the moon's regular changes through the twelve-stage cycle relate to everyday mood changes.

- You will learn about the best kind of activities for each stage of the cycle.

The Best Purpose for Each Day

One of the most useful things to do with astrological cycles is to use them to plan when best to do things. Analyzing existing cycles is helpful in understanding change, but knowing a cycle means knowing *when* to make change happen. This process of choosing when to do something is called "electional astrology," although traditionally it's based on many complicated rules, while in this book it is simplified to the basic use of cycles.

The Monthly Lunar Cycle and Its Phases

The month derives from the lunar cycle, in which the Moon takes about 29 days to regain its starting point. Although our months no longer reflect this cycle, the phases of the Moon allow us to continue to measure it.

The response of living creatures to the phases of the Moon is well documented. It has also been shown that animals do not respond to only the *appearance* of the Moon, but have biological clocks that tick at precisely the same rate as the orbit of the Moon.[1] It is well-known that the natural menstrual cycle has the same period as the moon, and it is often commented that since the body is around 70 percent water, it's likely to be subject to the tidal forces caused by the Moon, even if only on the smallest scale. Similarly, hospitals have long reported increased accident and injury rates around the time of Full Moon, giving credence to the ancient association of "lunacy" with the Moon.[2]

The lunar cycle is also a reflection of our own emotional cycles, subject to vacillation and phases. However, we have become so out of touch with our own emotions that we have learned to fear them, finding intense and painful emotion enormously difficult to deal with. We do everything in our power to change it as quickly as possible, thus not giving ourselves the proper opportunity to learn and grow from the experience. Once we understand that our emotions operate on a monthly cycle, though, it becomes much easier to manage all the fluctuations.

Using a Calendar Instead of the Worksheet

After the seasons, the lunar cycle is the clearest recognition of the four stages of a cycle that we see in our measurement of time. The four main phases of the Moon are marked in calendars even though most of us know of little use for this information. They are the same four stages of the cycle we measured in the other planets, although because it is such a rapid cycle it is not practical to provide a table for it here, which is why an almanac or calendar must be used. Almanacs are essentially books of natural cycles, largely lunar, that have long helped farmers to plan the proper planting and reaping times for their crops, and to catch fish at the right tides.

Find the lunar phases: each month, check in your calendar or almanac to see when the Moon is new, at first quarter, full and at last quarter. Your diary would be a great place to write down this information.

Giving Structure to the Month

The monthly cycle of the Moon allows us to deal with all the short-term projects in our personal and professional lives. The Moon cycle works best for the most personal of projects, things affecting our emotional lives. It also describes our reactions as opposed to our actions. Paying attention to the phases of the Moon can be one of the most powerful ways to structure a month.

Just as the year is divided into four, the month can be divided into the same four stages:

- The period from New Moon to the First Quarter should be used for initiating actions or plans.

- The second phase from First Quarter to Full Moon can then be used to nurture what has been initiated.

- The Full Moon represents the point at which everything has come to light, and it is a good time to act on what is known. The Full Moon is not such a great time to start things, because the Moon will wane from this stage, as will any progress made. As we shall see, the Full Moon has other effects in our lives that should be taken into account.

- The week following the Full Moon, until its Last Quarter, should be used to reap the results of what was initiated.

- The last week until New Moon is used to consolidate, complete, and strategize for the next cycle. Since the lunar cycle is best for very personal things, that last phase is best for reflection and contemplation, and for facing the darker side of our own emotional nature.

Dealing with the Full Moon

Few people would compare their moods with the phases of the Moon, but many more people are sensitive to the Moon than they realize. At each of the four main stages we are emotionally more changeable, although it is the emotional sensitivity that comes at Full Moon for many people that is the most disturbing.

Most of those who react to the Full Moon feel excitable or irritable, often having difficulty sleeping or even relaxing. Emotions may seem more intense and it often feels like one of those bad days.

Simply observing the phases of the Moon may quickly establish the correlation between the two cycles, helping the sensitive person adjust to them. If you know that you tend to become more sensitive and energetic at the Full Moon, take that into account. Important meetings and plans should not be undertaken at that time, and you can avoid the panic of sleeplessness by not even trying to sleep. Having a relaxing bath and lying in bed reading may be more relaxing. Even better, meditation, journaling or any other inner process undertaken at this time is very successful and a great way to really get in touch with the cycle. Most of us spend far too little time in this inner world.

The energy cycle is intimately connected to the lunar phases, and learning to work with the natural state of your energies is more rewarding than forcing your energies to suit whatever you happen to be doing.

Fine-Tuning the Cycle

As natural as lunar rhythms are to us, our emotional cycles are also affected by environmental conditions and even the kinds of food that we eat. This means that the correlation with the lunar cycle may seem not to work.

One way around this is to try and find your natural low or sensitive point yourself. Each month note the days when you seem to be particularly low or overly sensitive. The emotional low point in the month will recur every twenty-nine days, and can create a zero-point from which you can measure the four stages of the cycle at weekly intervals between each low point. After a while, you'll see just how your moods relate to the four stages and you can begin to use your personal lunar calendar as a planning tool.

Knowing the Moon's Own Cycle

We have seen that the cycle of the Moon can be directly correlated with our own cycles, but there is more to the lunar cycle than that.

We already know that every cycle has twelve stages. In the case of the Moon, each of these stages is two-and-a-half days long. As the Moon passes through each one of these twelve stages, there is an overall effect to be taken into account. This flow of "emotional energy" is visible in the growth of plants and even our own hair, as well as in our emotional shifts.

Remember, we don't know that the Moon *causes* these fluctuations in us; we only know that the Moon's period matches that of our own cycles. You can make further use of the lunar cycle dates noted in your diary to find the twelve stages of the cycle.

Each of the twelve stages is associated with particular types of activities. The Moon spends approximately two-and-a-half days in each of these stages. This is a guide to how the emotional cycle works, but you can refine and personalize it by following it for a month or two and recording your own reactions to events. This will help you understand your own emotional energy and adjust it to the rhythm described here.

Also, because of the approximation of half a day, allow for a day's variation as you learn to work with the cycle. Each stage lasts until the one that follows it.

- New Moon stage is best suited for high-energy activities, doing things alone, and starting things. Emotionally we are less sensitive and more secure.

- Two-and-a-half days later is a quieter time for enjoying the good things in life, and dealing with financial matters. Emotionally we are insecure and indulgent.

- The two-and-a-half days before First Quarter Moon is a good time for communication and is usually a very sociable time. Our emotions play a secondary role to our thoughts.

- At First Quarter Moon, sensitivity is high and energies are best directed toward domestic affairs. We are often insecure and needy.

- Two-and-a-half days later is great for parties, self-indulgence, entertainment, and romantic matters. Emotionally we feel more passionate, arrogant, and need a reaction, preferably a positive one.

- The two-and-a-half days before Full Moon should be used for organizing, paying attention to details, helping, and finishing things. We feel reserved and even a little withdrawn emotionally.

- The Full Moon is another period of sociable and romantic activities, in addition to those described above. Emotional fluctuation is common.

- Two-and-a-half days later moods are strong, often intense, and the period is good for intimacy, keeping secrets, or finding them out. Emotionally we are intense, withdrawn, but passionate. For many people this is the most sexually active time of the month.

- Two-and-a-half days before Last Quarter is a positive time for enjoyment, risk, and adventure. Sexual energy continues to run high, other people affect us less and reactions are strong.

- At Last Quarter the cycle enters a conservative phase, good for practical matters, business, hard work, and family matters. We may feel at an emotional low, even melancholy.

- Two-and-a-half days later is most individualistic, a time to do new and different things, be sociable, but also rebellious. We feel detached and unemotional during this phase, which is good for less personal connections.

- Two-and-a-half days before New Moon, the cycle enters a deep emotional and sensitive phase, good for meditation and other inner work, and for spending time alone. Emotionally we are oversensitive, our boundaries are weak and we are tuned to much deeper, inner impulses.

Naturally, these phases must be used in the way they best fit into your life, and how they fit in with the other, more personal cycles. Ultimately, your personal lunar phase should always have priority in helping you adjust to the present moment and understand your own reactions. The more you learn to adjust to the Moon, the more fully you'll be able to apply your knowledge and better attune yourself.

Everything Is the Present

We are about to move on and explore the many other cycles that enlarge the picture of ourselves and help us gain greater mastery over our experience of time. We need to remember that we started off this chapter acknowledging that in some way there is only the present, the now. That means that the conscious experience of the self at this present instant is the most important thing in the universe. It is, in fact, the only thing in the universe, and means that the only thing we can really ever come to know for sure is *ourselves*.

Understanding the solar and lunar cycles of the self goes farthest toward transforming the everyday experience of your life because the quality of your days adds up to the quality of your years. Now, let's move on.

1. Lyall Watson in the best-selling *Supernature* (as well as other scientists) has documented the opening and closing of oysters according to the daily rise and set of the
   Moon, and according to where the oysters are located. The Moon, through its
   monthly cycle, creates the ocean tides. Whether or not the Moon is visible, when the
   oysters are moved they will adjust their lunar clocks to suit the tides of the place they
   are moved to, even if there are no tides there (like in an inland tank). This shows that
   the oysters are in fact sensitive to the Moon itself, not merely to the inner clock. Just
   like the daily cycle, the visible planet and the invisible cycle work hand in hand.

2. *Luna* means Moon in the Latin languages.

5

EVERYDAY CYCLES:

MERCURY

Let's examine the facets of the human personality that are instrumental in defining who we are and determining the way we experience all the mundane, everyday experiences of life. After all, it is fine for us to use solar and lunar cycles to plan our daily lives, but life has a way of making the best-laid plans look foolish.

In this chapter

- The cycles of Mercury will allow us to understand why some days are better than others and why small things sometimes repeatedly go wrong.

- You will learn about Mercury retrograde and how to know when to make decisions and take action.

- The context for the mind cycle of Mercury will be explored and we will attempt to put the ego in its place.

The Ego's Assistants: the Mind and the Values

Of the five visible planets, two are closer to the Sun than we are, and three are farther out. Later we'll see how the farthest planets, Mars,

Jupiter and Saturn, represent our experience of the outer world. The two inner planets, Mercury and Venus, are always seen close to the Sun because their orbits are within our own.

Working with the rhythms of these two cycles so close to the solar ego cycle can help us understand how fragile the ego really is, and how to accommodate its fluctuations in our life. Of course, like all the other cycles we experience, they also have practical, everyday manifestations.

In this chapter we will concentrate on Mercury, whose cycles reflect the most mundane of our everyday concerns.

Personal Mercury Cycles

Mercury's cycle is very similar to that of the Sun. In fact, astrologers themselves sometimes ignore the cycle of Mercury because it goes by so quickly. There are two types of Mercury cycles that have a strong correlation with our stress levels and our success in everyday matters. One of them is entirely related to our individual, personal cycles, and the other affects all of us at the same time.

It is particularly important to be aware of the critical turning points of the Mercury cycle, especially since the troublesome symptoms are themselves so characteristic of life in our hectic technological world that they often go unnoticed despite their destructive effects.

The personal Mercury cycle-changes match more-or-less those of the Sun, so in effect, Mercury's personal cycles give you additional information that is relevant to all your personal yearly cycles, especially those related to your interaction with others. This is not the same as our *relationships* with others, which are in a category all their own!

While the personal Mercury cycle, like the personal lunar one, cannot practically be tabulated in a book of this size, fortunately we can easily chart the less personal Mercury cycle that we all share, Mercury in its current position of its own cycle rather than where it is in relation to its starting point at your birth. Table 4, page 209, will show you how to determine the critical points in this cycle.

Mercury Retrograde

Like almost all planets, Mercury appears to go backwards in the sky (see chapter 1). Now even though this is merely an illusion, it turns out that it is of enormous significance to human affairs, and probably reflects a deeper correlation between how things work in this mysterious universe and the rhythm of the Mercury cycle.

The phenomenon is known as "Mercury retrograde," and it occurs about every four months, lasting three weeks each time. During these three-week periods many of the Mercury challenges occur for everyone, particularly misunderstandings, machines (especially computers and cars) breaking down or behaving oddly and, for many people, an endless catalogue of minor hassles adding up to a very frustrating period. Since Mercury deals with numbers and words, communication and money are often subject to error and confusion.

Consult Table 4 (on page 209) for the critical Mercury periods. The first and last day of each of the three periods is generally the worst, and the effects are sometimes noticeable the week before they start. A good example of a recent Mercury retrograde period is the United States presidential election of 2000. November 7 of that year was the last day of a Mercury retrograde period, and the election was severely and historically marred by unprecedented technological problems related to ballots, counting, arguments, decisions being repeatedly reversed (retrograde), and an entire catalogue of Mercury retrograde woes.

Measuring Mental Cycles

Symbolically, Mercury is the archetype of the human mind, responsible for rationalization, thinking, communication, and the powers of thought and speech. Classically, it was also associated with the power of magic, which is a highly disciplined exercise of the will. Notice the remarkable symbolism that this physical planet provides for these ideas: as the planet closest to the Sun, it is almost impossible to distinguish one from the other. We cannot see Mercury with the naked eye because of its proximity to the Sun. Similarly, we identify so closely with our mind and our will that we fail to distinguish it from our sense of self. That's why so many people were influenced by Descartes' simplistic claim that thinking and being are the same thing ("I think, therefore I am.")

The metaphysical notion that thought creates all matter applies equally to the relationships between mind and self. Mercury is the fastest-moving planet and is perceived as slipping through one's fingers—this is why it gives its name to the elusive liquid metal. Our own experience is that the mind is equally rapid in its capacity for change, although this doesn't detract from its wilfulness.

The Mind's Excessive Power

The symbolism of Mercury is rich in contradiction, much like the mythological messenger of the gods whose name it bears. Mercury is often called the "trickster" because of its tendency to sudden change; just like the human mind. In mythology, it is the speedy movement and its proximity to the Sun (the king for whom it is the messenger) that gives Mercury its characteristic qualities. On the one hand, it bears the will of the king (that is, the will of the ego) and on the other, it has an agenda of its own, just like the human will. Embodied in this dual role is the conflict between the will of the lower self—wilfulness, stubbornness, rationality—and the will of the higher self, the one the magicians attempted to invoke, the true *sense* of self.

This perfectly reflects the planet itself, moving so quickly that one minute it is to one side of the Sun and soon after it is so close to the Sun that it is completely obscured by the brightness.

Although the ego is not the true self, in the Western, mind-oriented culture that fails to make the distinction between lower and higher self this ego commands enormous authority. The spiritual, unconscious and dark parts of the self are acknowledged in most cultures to be at least as important as the ego, yet in modern times they have very little conscious form of expression. As a result, they emerge in the worst aspects of our culture: crime, drugs and extremes of violence in children's games and entertainment, among other things.

The ego is increasingly allowed to believe that it is in total control and should whip the self into shape. The poor self suffers enormously from this cultural pressure, perhaps becoming egotistical but more likely developing a lifetime's worth of psychoanalyst's couch material.

Protecting the Ego

Nowadays, much of the mind's work is designed to help the ego in this enormous task. It shows in its reaction to the simplest efforts of the inner self to express itself—failure to remember dreams. Why do we fail so consistently to remember our dreams? The answer is that in our culture we place no value on dreams; we often fear them, and so the mind works to forget them.

Take meditation. When most people start learning to meditate, their mind becomes more active and their body starts to itch in all sorts of strange places. This is the mind doing everything in its power to re-establish conscious control of the ego, returning our attention to the external world.

The mind is like a determined policeman, instantly snapping into action the moment ego loses control. Now think of the image of the planet Mercury, the symbol of this mind. It orbits close to the Sun, shooting around it in only 88 days on guard, moving fast, and always ready to be there when the ego is threatened.

Most of us have experienced the mind as both friend and foe. It seems to have the power to turn against us, especially in conflict with the heart. Mind and heart are two different selves vying for expression: they are the two separate cycles of Mercury and Venus and we must learn to meet the needs of each if we expect them to cooperate with one another.

It is not only the heart that struggles against the authority of the mind. Astrology has recognized the connection between mind and body, and although they are often also in conflict, it is Mercury who is given the rulership of the body's state of health.[1]

Our state of health has a lot to do with the mind. Although we know the body has a fantastic physical defense system, we have discovered that the immune system seems to serve the whims of the mind. When we fear illness or believe we have it, we often produce the very symptoms we fear. We get ill more often when we are unhappy or stressed, when the mind is worrying and negative. Viewed astrologically, the mind is not in conflict with the body. Rather, it seems that mind/body conflict is a modern development. In reality the mind, as the ruler of health, is capable of creating a perfectly healthy body as long as the mind's own needs are satisfied.

In other words, the heart, body, and mind do not *necessarily* have conflicting needs. In modern times we have managed to separate them and even to cause conflict between them; by knowingly eating bad foods and smoking, for instance, all the while using our own rational mind to convince ourselves that no ill effects will ensue. Since we are deliberately fooling ourselves in the face of all reason, this is not a natural conflict between mind and body. It is more natural for the mind to act in the body's interest, a principle that is vital in our use of Mercury's cycle in our lives.

Mercury's Message

By linking health to the mind, astrology shows that many health issues are essentially stress issues. The health rulership of Mercury is derived from the fact that Mercury's association is *the immediate environment.* Since all things we interact with are stressors on our systems, whether for better or for worse, the body's relationship with stress may eventually produce physical reactions. Food is a stressor, traffic is a stressor, so are excitement, fear, conversation, argument, anticipation, hard work, and just about everything else. It takes its toll, it causes wear and tear, so it is a stressor.

Although it is the Mercury aspect of ourselves that deals with all of this, helping us to rush around our busy lives like the hurried god for whom the archetype is named, it is also the messenger who brings communications from the ego as well as from the higher self. When the stress is too much, Mercury will start sending messages; first in mental things, like irritation, communication problems, hearing, or comprehension problems, and lots of things going wrong. If we persist in not listening to the messages, we finally develop physical illness.

Considering the fact that Mercury is the first planet beyond the self, the Sun, it is the critical link to the self and working with its cycle can lay the foundation for attunement to all the other archetypal aspects of our everyday lives and ourselves.

Working with the Mercury Cycle

Knowing when Mercury is retrograde is just as important as knowing about personal cycles. The landmark points in the personal Mercury cycle are so similar to the Sun's cycle that they are practically impossible to distinguish, although if you get more serious about cycles you might want to learn how to plot your specific Mercury changes. It's not possible to provide personal tables for Mercury in a book of this size, but you'll find the Mercury retrograde table very useful.

It is sometimes possible to time your Mercury projects so that the four landmark points occur around the same time as Mercury retrograde. This will ensure that all the challenges are contained within the same one-month period, and the remaining approximate nine months of the year will be more successful. If projects are begun immediately after a Mercury retrograde period, the landmark periods will occur around the same time as Mercury retrograde. This means that the critical turning points are somewhat longer (about a month) but more contained. Otherwise, you'd have to account for the four turning points as well as the three retrograde periods during the year.

Getting a Bigger Picture

Notwithstanding the relevance of Mercury to the minutiae of our everyday lives, and the correlation of Venus to the critical issue of self worth and relationships, it is not the small yearly cycles that make all the difference. It often seems that a thousand problems are going on and that a year is a long time, but usually very little importance is achieved in one year. Certainly, things happen and goals are reached or dropped, but in terms of the evolution of our own life, our own journey, each year is simply a stepping stone.

Learning to attune yourself to the Sun, Moon, and Mercury is useful and certainly worthwhile, but it is by understanding the larger, slower movements in our lives and how they relate to these smaller cycles, that we can master our strange relationship with destiny. When we examine the really major changes and issues in our lives, we discover they are a *combination* of cycles rather than one individual, changing cycle. Remember, learning to tell the time involves being able to understand not only the individual hands of the clock, but also how they relate to each other.

---

1. "Rulership" is the ancient term that reflects our ancestors' belief that the planets symbolized actual gods, but nowadays it means "is associated with." Rulerships were largely developed out of empirical observation and everyday experience, which is characteristic of all the cycles. It was a way of identifying that a particular event belonged to a particular cycle. We could similarly say that the long hand on your watch rules the minutes, while the short hand is the ruler of the hour. They do not physically measure time as an odometer measures distance by touching the road. Rather, they move along at the same rate as hours and minutes and so they can easily be associated with time.

6

LOVE, SEX, AND MONEY:
VENUS AND MARS CYCLES

There is no aspect of the human experience that cannot be measured as a cycle. Still, there is one particular reason that most people visit astrologers: to know what on Earth is going on in their romantic lives. So many people feel that this aspect of their lives is totally out of their control, either because they can't meet the partner they've been dreaming of or because their relationship is not going as they desired.

In this chapter

- We will examine how the Venus cycle relates to romance and money, and how abundance is cultivated.

- The more sensitive issues of values will be related to the Venus cycle.

- We will examine the nature of love and see how the Venus cycle helps us discern the relationship between self-worth, luck, and romantic success.

- The cycle of Mars will be introduced and used to understand sexual needs.

- You will see how the cycles of Venus and Mars work together to reveal our romantic needs and how we try to meet them.

- You will see why some relationships work and some don't, and how to understand our own needs in order to attract the right kind of people into our lives.

- The Venus cycle will be used to predict love and money changes.

- We will use the Venus and Mars cycles to understand and predict compatibility between people.

Using the Worksheet

Take note of the years in your Venus column when one of the other planets crosses your Venus cycle. These important changes in your relationships and finances are discussed in this chapter.

Your drives, especially the sex drive, experience changes in the years that other planets cross your Mars cycle.

You will also use the box on the bottom of your worksheet that compares your numbers against those of your partner.

Venus and Values

Venus, that other constant companion to the Sun, is is the archetype of the human heart. As such we associate it with matters of love and passion, with relationships, and the people and things we love. After all, Venus is the mythological goddess of love and beauty.

Venus is our heart's desire, but it is also our value system. Because of this, Venus is intimately connected with our sense of self. It's in our relationships that we really put ourselves on the line to others, and ultimately expose ourselves at deep levels. This inevitably involves issues of self-worth, and in fact, much of the process of whether or not to become involved with someone is more about how we value ourselves than about fate or opportunity.

Contrary to the cliché, beauty is not only in the eye of the beholder, it is in our own inner eye. Common experience teaches us that physical attractiveness is more often a result of self-confidence than good genes.

Matters of self-worth, those inner security issues, are really the most fundamental issues of self. In the same way that Mercury's proximity to the Sun makes the mind a servant to the ego, so Venus' proximity makes the sense of our own value another ego slave.

We constantly measure and adjust our self-worth according to the successes we have in life, but this becomes an erratic and unstable way to establish self-worth and security. Rather, we need to establish a value system that allows us to value ourselves no matter what fluctuations are taking place in our material lives.

For most of us, Venus represents the types of success that contribute most to our self-worth: success in money and success in love. When we are doing well at love or with money we feel rewarded and that life is harmonious. When these fundamental issues are not working, we feel insecure and powerless, as though we've lost control over our own destiny.

Venus does not represent a great cycle of destiny; these are everyday matters, however important they seem to us. But the reason they *are* important, the very reason why money is in fact such a big deal for us, is that they actually address the question of self-worth. Now you begin to understand why love and money are so powerful in our lives. Their power lies not in their strength, but in our own weakness.

Working with the Venus Cycle

Although Venus is the planet that deals with relationships, we tend to be concerned about our relationships only when they are going wrong. In reality, although the cycles of Venus reflect that aspect of ourselves, we usually deal with those crises at times of our *trauma and challenge* cycle-changes (like Saturn, Uranus, and Pluto cycles, which we will examine later) rather than our Venus cycle-changes. However, since the whole point of knowing your cycles is to manage them effectively and minimize the trauma, understanding the cycle of Venus can go a long way to avoiding those traumas in the first place.

Venus cycles are not as easy to estimate as other cycles, because its highly elliptical orbit means that it won't neatly divide into four stages.

As it happens, though, experience has taught us that the cycle change-points of Venus are particularly subtle. This is because our self-worth is not noticeably cyclical itself. Self-worth crises are strongly related to other problems that arise in our lives, so observing the cycle of Venus will not be very helpful. We must learn how changes in other cycles affect matters of self-worth and our romantic lives.

The Venus tables will be used in conjunction with other cycles and you will see how powerful these cycles really are. You can experiment with using the Venus cycles (in Table 3, page 189) in the same way as other cycles, checking your date of birth and then checking when your number recurs every three-to-six months, but you may not find any effect.

Despite this, there is still a powerful way to work with Venus to transform your own self-worth issues, and to get your romantic life working as you'd like it to. Relationship issues are some of the most powerful lessons we face, and being so powerful they involve much more than just Venus. In the next two chapters we will learn how to discover our own relationship patterns and how they relate to other cycles.

Luck and Romance

It is not surprising that people find this very important part of life to be outside of their control. Most people believe that relationship success depends on luck—luck in the sense of chance as well as good fortune. The strange thing about this expectation is that these very same people know that career success is usually a factor of how hard you work, with luck playing only a very small role. Why then do we expect relationship success to happen all on its own? What makes us believe that once we have found the right partner and established a relationship, the relationship will stay sweet? No aspect of life behaves this way and it's quite remarkable that we continue to believe that this all-important area of our lives requires no more than this static and superstitious approach.

Perhaps it's not so mysterious when we look at how our culture depicts matters of the heart. We have come to believe that we have a perfect partner somewhere out there in the world, and that the forces of destiny will help us meet this person. More important, because this is our ideal partner or soulmate, we assume that the simple fact of these two souls re-uniting is all that is necessary to establish a deep bond. We believe that because a relationship is meant to be, the details will take care of themselves.

Consciously and logically we know these beliefs are unrealistic and naive, yet, still, we experience profound disappointment when the relationship or the loved one behaves according to the rules of real life rather than idealized romance. We all know in theory that a relationship requires work, but even while undertaking this work we complain that if the relationship was really the right one it wouldn't really need all this effort. What a strange idea! The rest of life's experience shows us quite simply that the harder we work the better the results, that there is no profit from little effort; yet a proven fact of life evaporates in the glow of romance.

Even that word "romance" has come to mean an idealized state of relationship, when in fact it really refers to a *fictional* state of relating. The word originally meant "a work composed," that is, a work of fiction. Why do we prefer fiction to reality? Perhaps we want to avoid all that hard work, or perhaps our expectations are created by the mysterious circumstances under which relationships often begin.

Chance Encounters

It is well known that until comparatively recent times, relationships that ended in marriage were usually relationships that *started* with marriage. The parents of the couple who would marry arranged the marriages, and despite the fact that the partners never knew one another, a successful relationship would often evolve.

This is not to say that romantic attachments did not exist. Of course they did, as did all the variations common today: relationships based on sex, money, power, or something that was beneficial to one or both parties.

Romantic attachment was usually based on idealized courtly love, doubtless the source of our classic version of romance, in which a knight might have a relationship with a married woman of noble birth. This passionate affair was sanctioned because it did not threaten the legal and religious bond of marriage, and faithlessness between the adulterous lovers was considered a greater sin than their adultery. It might also be remembered that the great tradition of courtly love practically demanded that the relationship end in tragedy.

With the trappings of our medieval past removed, relationships that are characterized by passion and love increasingly became a matter of chance. Nowadays, with arranged marriage having almost entirely fallen away, we depend on chance encounters. Friends and social occasions provide opportunities to meet others, but most people believe that meeting the right person depends entirely on a stroke of fate. This also fosters the belief that there is a "right" person out there somewhere.

When things go wrong in a relationship, we assume we've met the wrong person. After all, it was a chance encounter, so perhaps the right one is still out there. This also reinforces the idea that a relationship doesn't require work if you love someone. All that's required is that you meet the right person. In a world of some six billion souls, this approach is riskier than depending on winning a lottery to pay your bills, but it remains the primary belief system of most people who look at their unhappy relationships and wonder "why?"

What Love Is

Philosophers and artists have debated the nature of love since ages past and undoubtedly will continue to do so for ages to come. From the viewpoint of cycles and the philosophy of astrology a few useful characteristics of love help us define some of its most essential ingredients, the ones responsible for the forces of attraction and the likelihood that the relationship will last.

Earlier in this chapter we examined the cycle of Venus, the archetype of the human heart. We defined this archetype as the value system, identifying its important role in protecting the integrity of the ego. We know Venus to be the mythological goddess of love, so this tells us that romantic love is a function of our value system. We also learned that the value system is built around how we value *ourselves*. This means that romantic love is a function of self-worth.

How we perceive and value a potential partner—how we determine if they are Mr. or Ms. Right—depends entirely on how we value ourselves. Although we might have a pre-established idea of the right looks, job or Sun sign, our response to them, like much else we do, is more a matter of projection than anything else. We might even say that Mr. or Ms. Right is the image of ourselves idealized, as we wish to be.

When we are confident of ourselves, we project a more powerful image. We are seen as having our lives "together" and we will be perceived as physically attractive. This will naturally attract people who have a certain self-confidence themselves. Similarly, when we are at our lowest and imagine ourselves to be useless and unattractive, if we attract anyone at all it's almost bound to be the kind of person who reinforces this image of ourselves. For example, it might be someone who abuses or takes advantage of us, or who has very little to contribute to our growth. Unconsciously we are saying, "This is all I am worth."

Romantic idealism is based on what you imagine yourself to be worth, your sense of security and your value system in general. For example, if your value system is that money is an important resource, the physical beauty or stunning personality of a prospective partner may not be enough to attract you: you'd need to see their bank balance first.

Not the Right Person, But the Right Time

Once again, we need to look beyond our fragile ego and understand our natural cycles to get a better picture of how our relationships are evolving, because we know that romanticism is part of the cycle of self-worth and value systems—the Venus cycle that we briefly examined earlier. It should not be surprising to discover that since our self-worth fluctuates according to a natural rhythm, so do our relationships. This means that relationship changes, and even the beginnings of relationships, will happen along with changes in these cycles.

Like everything else, it's all a matter of timing. Astrologically speaking, there is no right person out there; there is only a right moment, and knowing when these changes occur makes it very much easier to understand and deal with relationship changes.

Money Is a Relationship

The way we experience money is remarkably similar to our experience of romance, another apparently external factor somewhat beyond our control. We tend to believe that we need luck to accumulate any real quantity of money, and we invest it with all sorts of emotions like guilt, greed, pride, and many others. These are the same feelings that our personal lives stir up, and all of them have a great deal to do with feelings of self-worth.

The difficulties that many of us have with financial matters also stem from problems of self-worth. The most common consequence of undervaluing yourself is to accept less money, whether in terms of a salary or direct payment for a service that you are providing. Then there is the equally common experience of money seeming to have a life of its own. No matter what you do to get your financial affairs in order, unforeseen expenses seem to undermine your gains. While we do understand the relationship between work and money, we often feel self-pity or victimized, when despite our hard work money seems to follow its own agenda.

It's not at all surprising, then, to learn that we have long associated the cycles of our financial life with those of the planet Venus. Just like our relationships with other people, the fluctuations in our finances directly relate to the fluctuations in our feelings of worth.

One of the mistakes that many people make in trying to accumulate large sums of money is to believe that hanging on to it as tightly as possible will help to make them wealthy. As the story of Scrooge in Dickens' *A Christmas Carol* illustrates, it might make you technically wealthy, but to retain this tight grip on money you need to be tight-fisted, and therefore selfish, greedy, and ultimately disappointed.

Projecting Abundance

More and more people are discovering the wisdom that has been handed down since ancient times: put money out into the world and it will keep on returning to you, multiplying itself each time. This has become known as "the law of return." It might sound like feel-good New Age philosophy with no real foundation, but it is the same issue as self-worth in relationships: what you project into the world is what you attract back to yourself. In this case, it is abundance that you project by being generous or loose-handed with money, ensuring that abundance comes right back to you.

Most important, you can't project abundance unless you feel that you are worthy of acquiring lots of money. This is another reason why so many people, despite even this generosity, still do not attract money back to themselves.

With the return of spiritual values into our personal value systems, many people assume that these are at odds with material values. They feel guilty about acquiring money, believing that it means they are materialistic and not spiritual, and so their generosity is often about pushing away the dirty money rather than actually projecting abundance, since abundance is assumed *not* to include material abundance. This conglomeration of contradictory ideas projects only confusion and unworthiness into the world and the outcome is obvious: no money.

It is a false assumption that material abundance and spiritual abundance are mutually exclusive. Abundance is indiscriminate; it has a quality of more, not less, and so predefining what fits into that abundance will limit it and go against its very nature. If you believe you are worthy of having everything that you need or want, you must accept that this includes material abundance.

The age-old struggle between spirituality and materialism is not a struggle with money itself. Ancient wisdom (in this case the Bible) does not say that "money is the root of all evil," but rather that "the *love of money* is the root of all evil." Money itself, though, is a means to an end, and if you need abundance in this real world it is unlikely you will achieve it without money. The proper relationship with money is to see it as a means, neither allowing it to become the goal itself nor seeing it as being in competition with that goal.

Predicting Love and Money Changes

Both love and money are aspects of our self-worth, which is correlated with the cycles of the planet Venus, so it's not difficult to anticipate changes in these feelings of worthiness. Invariably, these changes also lead to changes in relationships. For example, a radical change to marriage may be precipitated by the realization "I deserve better than this." This really means "I am *worth* more than this" and it reflects a change in the area of self-worth. Similarly, a surprise increase in salary makes us feel rewarded because it reflects something about our own abilities and value: it confirms or increases our self-worth.

Of course, we also experience shifts in the other direction: loss of self-worth. In these cases too, self-worth, material resources and the regard others have for us are all changing at the same time.

As we have seen, fluctuations within the Venus cycle do not seem to reflect such profound changes in our lives even if they are related to subtle shifts in our feelings of self-worth. Since Venus represents such personal resources, it is not going to manifest as dramatic external change.

The only way any change will happen is when one of the other cycles overlaps or synchronizes with the Venus cycle. In fact, because self-worth and money seem to be such fragile issues in our lives, the changes that these areas experience at times of crossings from other cycles are often very dramatic and noticeable.

Your Venus Crossings

Let's interpret the times you have found on your worksheet when other planets cross over your Venus cycle, then consult the table to get an idea of the type of cycle change that may be expected.

Remember to check back to dates in the past when you experienced significant relationship or financial changes.

You can also do a little extra work on the worksheet to find more detailed information:

- For close-ups on particular relationships or times in your life, use Table 6 (page 213) to see what month Mars crosses your Venus number. (These crossing are frequent, so you need only look at the current period to get a close-up on important months.)

- Use Table 1 (page 149) to see when in the year (every year) the Sun is the same as your Venus number for a small boost.

- Use Table 7 (page 227) to interpret crossings of the Venus Cycle.

The Symbolism of Mars

Mars is outside the Earth's orbit and is the first planet beyond the Earth. Naturally, it is a candidate for representing our drives and actions, which are the first steps outside of ourselves and toward the demands and rewards of the outside world.

Think about the Sun and Moon as *within* the Earth's orbit: the Sun is at the center of it and the Moon sticks close to us all the time. Mars is outside of this closed system, symbolizing how our inner needs and feelings must be translated to drives and actions out there in the world.

Mars was so named because of its association with action, aggression, and all the masculine output drives that people of both genders share.

In our modern language, drives govern our goal-seeking or ambition, and naturally our sexual behavior. We will examine Mars' relationship with goals and energy levels more closely in the next chapter, but for now its connection to the sex drive will be helpful in understanding relationships.

The Sex Drive

There is a debate about sex that has gripped the imaginations of experts in human psychology as well as everyday people. This is not surprising, since sex is undoubtedly the most popular talking point throughout the ages, despite whatever taboos may be imposed at different times in history. The debate attempts to resolve the question of whether the sex drive can be completely divorced from the emotional drive. Sometimes, this debate takes the form of an inquiry into the differences between men and women, but in any form it boils down to two questions: can there be romantic love without sex? And more important, can there be sex without love?

In the liberated era in which we live the debate seems less significant, because in the Western culture sex has increasingly taken on a role that leaves love and romance way behind (for example, its use as a marketing device). But since we know that everything is cyclical, we are doubtless merely witnessing the pendulum swinging to one of its extremes, and it will head back in the other direction eventually.

From the viewpoint of astrological archetypes, sex and love are clearly two separate things, but that does not make them mutually exclusive. We know Mars to be the symbol for all our outwardly directed drives, including the sex drive. As we have seen, the symbol for the romantic form of attachment is Venus. Now, these are indeed two separate cycles, but they have a great deal to do with one another. Mythologically, of course, Venus as the goddess of love and Mars as the god of war were lovers, but not husband and wife. Perhaps the myth is pointing out that neither romance nor lust make for a lasting relationship. Astrologically, we must use both of these cycles to determine the permanence of a relationship.

Our Primal Instincts

There can be no doubt that sex is one of our most primal, animal instincts, and some would argue that it is such a powerful one that it circumvents all the higher faculties like the rational and emotional ones. This may be partly true, but the sex drive also has a great deal to do with how we view ourselves and how we believe others see us.

In the astrological map of the human psyche, sexuality falls into the area associated with our worth *in the eyes of others* and stands directly opposite the area associated with our self-worth. Opposites are considered as two parts of the same thing and, thus, astrologers can never really talk about the cycles of Mars without taking into account the cycles of Venus. As much as these two things are diametrically opposed, they are also totally interdependent. (Perhaps this is astrology's answer to the great debate.)

In fact, the sex drive is at least partly about projecting our self-worth (Venus) into the world with the expectation that it will be recognized. We dangle our Venus like bait in the hope that somebody will become attracted to it, and then we hook him or her with our passionate Mars.

It is no coincidence that the planet Venus is the planet of femininity, beauty and attraction, and is represented by the symbol of circle-over-cross ($\venus$), which has become the recognized symbol for female. Similarly, Mars is clearly the planet of masculine energies, drives such as aggression, sexuality and ambition, and its symbol is the circle surmounted by the cross or arrow ($\mars$), which has become the recognized symbol for male. Of course, since all of us have both Venus and Mars cycles, we are not referring to gender differences, but rather to archetypal male and female energies possessed by both genders. They are the archetypes Jung referred to as "animus" and "anima" respectively.

Since we all engage in the process of projection, attraction and capture, we all use both the masculine and the feminine principles in finding a partner. Similarly, since we all have both Venus and Mars cycles, we continue to use both within our relationships.

Certainly there are differences between the genders. However, since projection is such a key process in relationships, we also need to project the qualities of the *opposite* gender to attract a member of that gender or to awaken the opposite archetype in someone else. For example, a heterosexual male might project Venus in order to allow a woman to see his softer side (her own Venus responds), while a homosexual male might project Venus to allow another man's Mars (masculinity) to respond. That means that we all project both Venus (self-image and our personal archetype of the feminine), and Mars (sexual desire and our personal archetype of the masculine).

Using Mars Cycles to Understand Sexual Needs

Changes in the way we express our sexual desire are to be expected during the course of a relationship. In most cases, our basic approach is well-established during our early years, and an astrologer looking at the pattern of the planets at your birth can explain the nature and meaning of that basic pattern. But we all go through phases of wanting sex or not being interested in it at all, and the fluctuations in the patterns of sexual expression may be confusing and damaging in a relationship that is not prepared for them. When one partner's Mars is snubbed, it is their Venus that reacts because it is usually self-worth that is affected, and these issues can mushroom into confusion and misunderstanding between partners.

Understanding fluctuations within our Mars cycle and synchronizations to it from other cycles can help attune us to our own sexual rhythms and avoid miscommunication in our relationships.

Interpreting Changes in the Mars Cycle

In the next chapter, you will learn how to find all the phase changes in our Mars cycle for the current period, so as to understand how your drives relate to the pursuit of your goals. You can use the same cycle changes to understand changes in your patterns of desire.

More useful for now are the crossings of other planets over the Mars cycle. Since we know Mars to be connected to all our drives, the Mars synchronizations in this table are also used to understand more about the professional and other outwardly oriented drives in our lives. As with the Venus cycles, these changes affect such basic issues in our lives, so they are often very noticeable.

- Use Table 7 to interpret synchronizations to your Mars cycle.

- Also use this Mars information to add to what you learn in the next chapter about goal cycles.

- Check back to dates in the past when you experienced significant relationship, work or goal changes.

In and Out of Bed with Madonna

- Her reputed high-school years of sexual experimentation occurred while Uranus and Saturn crossed her Venus position in 1972–1975.

- Pluto and Saturn crossed Venus, the planet of heart's desire in the 1983–84 period of her rapid rise to fame.

- Pluto crossed Mars in 1989, the year of her divorce and the final end of a tempestuous marriage.

- Her relationship with Warren Beatty ended when Saturn crossed both her Venus and her Mars in 1991–92.

- The relationship with Guy Ritchie began after Neptune *came off* her Venus (read about Neptune crossing Venus earlier in the chapter) and Saturn arrived there in 1999. Saturn and Uranus were also crossing Mars at the same time, and of course that was the year of the great big Uranus and Neptune midlife crisis for her.

Using Mars and Venus to Understand Compatibility

There is one more very powerful tool that these two critical cycles offer us—an understanding of compatibility between partners at fundamental levels, such as the timing of sexual desire. This section will show you a whole new way to use the cycles of these planets.

Quite simply, you compare your Venus and Mars cycles with those of your partner to get insight into some of the similarities and differences you experience. What you really see is the difference between your basic cycle patterns for each of these cycles and how far out of phase they are from one another.

You'll compare each of the cycles against the other person's cycle for the same planet, and also compare one person's Venus against the other person's Mars.

To do this, use the Venus and Mars numbers you listed for yourself and your partner at the bottom of the worksheet. Then, use the following table to compare them.

One partner has	The other partner has	What you can expect
Venus between 0 and 29	Venus between 0 and 29	You both have similar values, although you might be a little competitive. You may make incorrect assumptions about your part ner; try to understand his or her needs.
Venus between 0 and 29	Venus between 30 and 59	Your values are different in many ways and may often seem at odds. Compromise is difficult.
Venus between 0 and 29	Venus between 60 and 89	Values are highly compatible even though they are somewhat different. Easy to understand the other's ways.
Venus between 30 and 59	Venus between 30 and 59	Your values are largely similar, yet you both have a strong need for security and are unwilling to adapt to the other's ways. Be careful that stubbornness or unwillingness to change does not cause a problem.
Venus between 30 and 59	Venus between 60 and 89	Your values are different in many ways and may often seem at odds. Compromise is difficult.

One partner has	The other partner has	What you can expect
Venus between 60 and 89	Venus between 60 and 89	Your values are probably similar, yet even where they aren't it is easy to adapt to each other. It is easy to grow together. Don't allow change or inconsistency to make you grow apart.
Mars between 0 and 29	Mars between 0 and 29	Your drives are similar but often in competition. You both try to take the initiative. It may be easy to anger the other, but sexual compatibility is good. Find ways to make the partnership equal and create a goal for the relationship.
Mars between 0 and 29	Mars between 30 and 59	Your drives are different and often at odds. You'll usually experience desire at different times and express it in different ways.
Mars between 0 and 29	Mars between 60 and 89	Drives are highly compatible although somewhat different. One takes the initiative and the other goes along with it. Easy to fit in with the other's ways.

One partner has	The other partner has	What you can expect
Mars between 30 and 59	Mars between 30 and 59	Your drives are similar, however, you are both stubborn and somewhat aggressive in expressing them, leading to differences. Neither wants to yield to the other. Competitiveness can be destructive, but a common goal can make for powerful sexual energy.
Mars between 30 and 59	Mars between 60 and 89	Your drives are different and often at odds. You'll usually experience desire at different times and express it in different ways.
Mars between 60 and 89	Mars between 60 and 89	Your drives are highly compatible, although you both tend to fluctuate. It is easy to adapt to the other. Be careful that lack of initiative or aggression doesn't allow the relationship to fade into a lack of energy between you.
Venus or Mars between 0 and 29	The other planet between 0 and 29	A highly compatible combination. Strong attraction, easy to have fun together. Don't get hung up on your differences.

One partner has	The other partner has	What you can expect
Venus or Mars between 0 and 29	The other planet between 30 and 59	Needs and drives do not seem to overlap or compete. You could have a quiet and gentle relationship, but there is not much fire between you.
Venus or Mars between 0 and 29	The other planet between 60 and 89	Highly compatible. Your needs and drives interpolate easily, although you might sometimes need to do something to increase excitement.
Venus or Mars between 30 and 59	The other planet between 30 and 59	A highly compatible combination. Strong attraction, easy to have fun together. Don't get hung up on your differences. Beware of frustration.
Venus or Mars between 30 and 59	The other planet between 60 and 89	Needs and drives do not seem to overlap or compete. You could have a quiet and gentle relationship, but there is not much fire between you.

One partner has	The other partner has	What you can expect
Venus or Mars between 60 and 89	The other planet between 60 and 89	A highly compatible combination. Strong attraction, easy to have fun together although you might sometimes need to do something to increase excitement.

An Ongoing Process

Venus and Mars are the tools we need to help us understand our relationships and to make them work. Once we understand these cycles, we must apply the same rules for all the others: they are an ongoing process. There is no point at which you can say: "I have learned the hard stuff, done the work, and now I can expect a peaceful relationship." The cycles do not end; we continue to face the challenges of the turning points and of other cycles that cross these cycles.

Each turn or crossing is an opportunity to take a relationship to a new place: for example, if Saturn crosses your Venus cycle it is not Fate saying, "That's it, I'm afraid, the relationship is over." It is simply a point where a relationship reaches a challenge, one that may lead you to decide to end the relationship or to deal with feelings of isolation or separation and take courageous action to ensure that the relationship *doesn't* end.

Mars and Venus are the most important tools we deal with in our everyday lives. These cycles are the key to much of what occupies us and what we consider important. Although their focus is values and drives, these areas cover all that is important to us. Learn these two cycles well: they are the key to self-mastery through everyday life.

7

PLANNING FOR SUCCESS:

MARS AND JUPITER

For most of us, the really important cycles relate to how and when we pursue our goals. Most people are willing to believe that they should endure repeated problems and patterns when it comes to their relationships, but when things go wrong with goals, this is usually seen as bad luck. Learning more about Mars will help make things go right.

In this chapter

- You will learn how the cycles of output and reward can be timed and synchronized to make the most out of out short- and medium-term goals.

- You will learn why many of us create a pattern of failure.

- You will use the Mars cycle to see how your output and success go through cycles and how to use your energy more effectively.

- You will learn how to find the best time to start any project or goal.

- You will learn how to use the timing of the Jupiter cycle to begin a project so that the best possible results can be achieved.

- You will learn a powerful way to combine the Jupiter and Sun cycles to predict greater successes.

Using the Worksheet

The "turning point" years you filled in for your Mars cycle are current, so you can look immediately to see when your Mars cycle changes. For practical purposes, the turning points for individual goals are more useful, so you can fill in some dates for your most pressing current goals using the Mars and Jupiter cycles:

Finding the Best Starting Time for a Goal

- Use Table 2 (page 155) to find the date closest to the start of your project, business, investment or risk. Look up the number in the column headed "Jupiter" and remember that you can interpolate numbers to get closer to the actual number. Fill in the name or keyword for your project at this date in the worksheet.

- Moving forward in the table, check from about three-and-a-half years past the start date for the recurrence of your number plus or minus two. Check this date and fill it in on the worksheet.

- Scan over the following nine months or so from that date to see your number plus or minus two occurs again. It doesn't have to be the same number as the previous step (as long as it's within two of the starting number), and fill it in.

- You have identified a period when growth will occur and when projects may be more successfully undertaken.

Finding the Turning Points for a Goal

- Turn to Table 6, which lists the approximate positions in the Mars cycle from 1990 onward.

- Find the date closest to the date of the beginning of the projects. You can also use the cycles to estimate numbers for dates not listed. For example, if the cycle lists Mars at position twenty on the fifth of the month, and position twenty-eight on the tenth, you could safely use the number twenty-four if the date you want is the seventh or eighth of the month.

- Note the Mars cycle number for this date.

- Scan forward in the table over the next two years, noting all the approximate dates when Mars is again at the same number, or the closest number to yours listed. These are the Mars turning points. You can go further than twenty-two months, remembering that the cycle of four starts over again. In fact, the two-year turning point, when Mars starts again, is a very powerful boost point for a longer project.

Before you analyze when the cycle changes are for your project, you need to understand how timing must be synchronized with success.

Work and Reward Are Directly Linked

When we repeat mistakes in our own lives, no matter how undesirable and even unfair we think they are, we somehow sense that we ourselves are responsible. But when it comes to work we often believe that because we try hard and work hard, we *ought* to have good results every time. It's true that our hard work will produce good results, but only with an understanding of the cycle of output and reward.

The principle of "whatever you put out is what comes back to you" is at the heart of our understanding of how reward happens. In recent times it's become a major principle of the understanding of karma. While it seems like a very New Age kind of thought, it's really ancient and fundamental. For example, the Bible is a source of such proverbial wisdom as the idea that we end up reaping the results of the seeds we sow.

It's interesting that in China work was considered to be part of the natural flow of the Tao, reality or universal energy, whereas in Judaeo-Christian culture it was at first believed to be punishment sent by God. In modern times, capitalist economies have linked work and reward more strongly than ever. Now, work can be connected to our personal needs as well as our eventual goals. More than ever, work can lead to reward and can be refined to do so more successfully.

Timing Leads to Success

Two principles are common to all cycles, and indeed to all human activities: balance and moderation. The principle of cycles is based on the idea of balance and rhythm, and timing is not the only thing required to get this right. If you think of a cycle like a railroad track going up and down over hills, it becomes apparent that the train driver must cope with two conditions. He must time his accelerations and decelerations so that he can easily ascend hills without flying off the tracks when going downhill on the other side. Second, his load must be limited, or hill climbing will be extremely difficult, and going down the other side may be fatal.

In the same way that timing leads to success, when it comes to output and input, the principles of timing must be further extended to manage the load itself. The balance means that in order for our goal cycles to work properly, we must apply the proper amount of energy.

For example, if it will take one year to reach a goal, assuming a working day of eight hours, then working sixteen hours a day is not likely to make you reach the goal in six months. The nature of the cycle is that it takes a certain amount of time to reach fruition, like any gestation period. It may be possible to shave off a few weeks or even a few months by doubling the hours per day, but the most significant effect will be massively increased stress. This will make the work more error-prone, will create other problems and end up taking the full amount of time anyway, simply because of stress-related complications.

A Pattern of Failure

Sometimes, through haste, we end the work before the end of the cycle is reached. In the nature of cycles this premature ending means that the full potential of the work was never reached and there is an unnatural gap between the apparent end of one cycle and the beginning of the next. Imagine reaping a crop before it is ready. Usually, the pressure of the need for reward (income) might also mean that the following cycle is begun prematurely, and the entire series of work cycles is thrown out. This leads to long periods of difficulty and a pattern of failure, frustration, or something equally unrewarding.

Achieving Balance

Cycles are intrinsically about balance and about appropriateness. To use them properly, we must adjust to their natural rhythms; we must learn to be more comfortable with the flow of time rather than feel as though we are fighting a battle against it. If we worked only eight hours a day, and planned our output according to natural cycles, we would never feel that we were fighting a losing battle because we would have a clear sense of what should be happening at any given time. We would know which results to expect and when to expect them. We would even eliminate a good deal of our stress, solving not only many of our goal-related issues, but also, probably, most of our health issues as well.

The way to re-establish the balance is relatively easy:

- If you work more than eight hours a day, set a goal to reduce your daily working hours by one hour within the next year.

- With a year to do it, it's easier than you imagine. Challenge yourself by trying it again the next year, aiming to reduce the work hours by a second hour.

- With the hundreds of hours you start gaining in your life, do something you really love or want to do.

- If your rhythm or job requires that you can never get down to less than twelve hours a day, try eliminating one day per week within the year. Do wonders for yourself by having a personal weekend day when you can do what you like.

Output: The Cycle of Mars

While mental and emotional factors are internal, as is our sense of values, drives are deliberately directed toward things outside of ourselves.

As we grow and take on the world, our first and most enduring relationship with it is through our output. The expenditure of energy in all its forms, the use of hands and head, these are the stuff of everyday life. So many things are about drives—even having a cup of tea! Much of the time our thoughts are of planning, and our actions are the execution of our plans, such as drinking that tea or becoming the president of a company.

Appropriate Use of Energy

Any good general will tell you that the way to win a war is certainly not by relentless and endless assault, but by carefully planned strategies and strikes at key moments. Heavy artillery is capable of winning wars, sometimes, but not without extraordinary levels of unnecessary destruction.

In today's world, the stress created by the demands of society has led us into a drive pattern that is basically "apply as much as possible, whenever possible, and you're sure to get good results eventually." If we run our own engine, Mars, at high output all the time, we create an enormous amount of stress within the body, just like a car that's constantly run at the highest revs. We'll break down sooner and probably more dramatically than if we were not so over-stressed.

Working with Your Mars Cycle

Working with Mars is like learning to tune your engine perfectly. Goals are not only about doing, they are about planning. After all, they are based on an intended outcome, which means that some anticipation of the future is involved. The cycle of Mars teaches us when to act, when not to, and how to plan our goals over a period of time. Knowing when to expect results improves our chances of success.

The cycle of Mars is almost two years in length; twenty-two months, more precisely, with the reward point occurring from twelve to eighteen months into the process. From this we learn that while our *personal* goals and lives go through one-year stages, our *professional* goals should be extended over eighteen months, even over two years.

In fact, this point immediately identifies one of the problems in many instances of unrealized goals, or of people losing impetus halfway. Certainly, many one-year professional goals will succeed, especially since one year is indeed a significant point along the cycle. However, most goals need the longer period, although we often don't know that in the beginning. Our experience with one-year goals teaches us to expect ful-fillment after a single year for everything we do, and in these cases we are going to be disappointed at least half the time. This is exacerbated by the fact that the calendar tends to make us parcel our lives into January-to-December chunks, and it is very unlikely that everything will actually fit into this artificial way of looking at time.

Of course, the distinction between personal and professional is often very vague. Since we pursue many goals that are not related to our pro-fession, but that are similar to professional ones, how do we make the proper choices for the Mars cycle?

Goals may be defined as ambitions and intentions that aim to ac-complish something in particular, and require us to gather and use re-sources along the way. A distinguishing feature of Mars goals is that they are essentially about the world out there. The recognition or re-wards acquired by the pursuit of Mars goals usually come from the world out there too.

The landmark stages along the way of the Mars cycle occur every five to six months. These strategic points along the way help us mea-sure our progress thus far, and make adjustments for the next cycle. Al-though you can keep this period in mind when working with the cycle, remember to check the worksheet, because sometimes these stages come much earlier or later than expected.

- The turning points of your own Mars number show your natural output energy fluctuations;

- The numbers you have found for a specific goal or project develop over a twenty-two-month period.

- The first step in synchronizing with rewards is to imagine each stage as consisting of three substages of equal length.

What Happens Over Twenty-Two Months

Here is a basic structure that shows you what to expect from this cycle. In reality, the stages will vary in length according to your worksheet. Once you've found out how long each of your four stages is for any goal, divide that by three to find the length of the three substages of each major stage. For example, if a stage is six months its three substages are two months each.

Stage One: Months 1–6

- After a goal is put into action (and to be even more precise you may employ an astrologer to help you decide the best time to begin something using electional astrology) it should take slightly less than two months, which is the first substage, for you to start seeing just what you are dealing with.

- Allow for another one-and-a-half months (the second substage) to get the project working the way you want, but don't start looking for results.

- Only during the last two months of this phase (the third substage) will you finally establish the circumstances you need for your project to grow. The overall goal during this stage is to have an established project by the time the first critical point is reached.

- A crisis is usually reached at around five or six months, when it becomes apparent that the method or even the goal itself does not quite gel with the situation at hand. Decisions need to be made at this point, resulting in adjustments. Now that you know the circumstances in which your goal finds itself, adjust the goal, making allowances for reality. Do not attempt to adjust reality itself! This is not the time to change the world; it is your method that needs a change. This is the process of weeding, during which you should take a firm look at the situation and eliminate the inessentials and those methods that are not working.

Stage Two: Months 6–11

- This is the major working period for any project or goal. When this period starts, accept that the existing conditions are the ones you are going to need. While for the first month and a half to two months it's possible to add or start new things, avoid this if possible. Certainly, by the time you are into the third month of stage two, nothing new must be added at all.

- Stage two is for growing what you already have, and allowing your project to take hold. Your goal now is not to finish the project, but rather to reach the high note by the end of about eleven months (or preferably at the time the tables show your number around nine to fourteen months after the start of the project).

- Shorter-term projects can be closed at the end of this stage, but true success takes a little longer. The overall goal now is to bring the project to fulfillment, so results should be apparent by the next critical point.

- Critical turning point at around eleven months: This mid-cycle critical point is very challenging. Apart from the fact that a goal point is reached, levels of frustration and irritation tend to rise dramatically. This is the time to take a vacation. Allow at least two weeks to ensure that you manage to wind down and let off steam. There should be a clear sign that results and rewards are imminent, but the last adjustment must be made. It's almost as if there's an accumulation of Mars energy and you must be sure to release it.

- Remember, excess Mars energy often leads directly to health problems, and more often to conflict. Part of the release of Mars energy at this time is a necessary process of re-examining the entire project or goal, and adjusting direction so that you are more clearly aimed at the fulfillment of the goal. This is not a *change* of direction, as it was at the previous critical point, but more like a modification of method so that the last stages can deal with reaping rewards or simply achieving the results you are after. During this time, and at the beginning of the next stage of the cycle, eliminate as much as possible of the inessential, and make clear commitments and choices about how you are going to handle the next stage.

Stage Three: Months 11–15

- The beginning of this stage is a little like a new year, which makes it even more appropriate to cleanse away the old ways and resolve upon some new ones. This entire stage is a process of gathering rewards, but the idea is not to get as much as you can as fast as you can. You still need to stay attuned to the time it takes the cycle to play itself out naturally. The best way to strategize the fulfillment period is to divide it into the same three one-and-a-half to two-month stages that you used in the previous stages.

- For the first of these periods, concentrate only on those things that are already at the fulfillment stage, and gradually expand towards gathering results and rewards wherever possible by the second period. During the last period, you can work on those aspects of the project that are the most long-term.

- Critical point at around sixteen months: Medium-term goals measured by the Mars cycle have achieved most of their results by this stage, and this last critical phase should be used to tie up the final loose ends. Like all critical periods, this is potentially stressful, so it is important to take an attitude of ending and closing to this phase.

Stage Four: Average 16–22 months

Although the goals have been met, in our four-stage system we still have a full quarter of the cycle remaining. You may wonder why this phase is not used to bring the project to completion.

Since the concept of the four-stage cycle is very closely linked to the seasons this fourth stage is something like the winter of the goal period. In the natural cycle, winter allows for the death of the old and the opportunity for the fertile Earth to take a break, and undergo the same death-and-rebirth process as the life that it supports.

In our fast-paced, achievement-oriented world, we seldom allow time for lying fallow between projects, and so we build stress that contributes to the breakdown of our personal lives and our health. As a farmer will tell you, in the short term you may not see the effect of never giving a field a break, but eventually that soil will produce inferior crops.

In the winter of a goal cycle, we need to let go and move away not only from the goal and its circumstances, but even the attitude and intention that created that goal in the first place. Use this winter phase to contemplate what we gained and learned by pursuing that goal, not only in terms of the direct rewards it produced. This way we can gain even more, and succeed in letting go of the drive that brought us to the goal. If we constantly operate on the same drive, we are just going around and around the same track without really getting anywhere.

So, on the one hand we can let go of the old goal that has been accomplished, or has achieved as much as it can, and has no potential to be a longer-term goal. On the other hand, we can start thinking towards the next goal. This is not a time of strategy; it is a time of *incubation* of the new ideas and goals. Allow them to come and go, stir them occasionally, and you'll find that ideas tend to flourish when not pressurized. This five-month phase is a rare period when the pressure is off. What's more, by the end of it you are ready and eager to tackle the next goal without the relentless, obsessive drive from one to the next that characterizes our modern world.

Of course, you're not sitting around doing nothing: you will have a few other goals with their own twenty-two-month cycles that you're busy tracking, as well as being at other stages of one year goals and the demands of everyday life.

Looking up numbers for a new goal is preferable than to approximate the turning points of a cycle, which tend to be so uneven in length. Best of all is to actually plan a cycle to begin at the best possible time.

Getting the Extra Boost

You may need a bit of a push to get the goal on the road or the confrontation out of the way, be it through inspiration, ambition or situational demands. Here's an extra trick that the cycles can teach you:

Using the Mars table (Table 6, page 213), try to start a project or face up to things when the Mars number is the same as the personal Sun number on the worksheet. You'll see the difference in the results.

As you'll see later, combining two cycles in this way has all sorts of potent implications.

The Best Time to Start Something

Working with your goals is more than simply knowing when to make adjustments. If you plant something at the wrong time of the year, you may make all the right adjustments at the right time—like pruning and watering—but the plant will still die.

As with everything else in nature, there is a best time to start something, a time when all the circumstances are harmonious and success will follow. Naturally then, true success with goals means starting them at the right time. We use the three-stage cycle of Jupiter to find this time.

The Three Basic Stages

The three-stage cycle has a rhythm connected to *flow* as opposed to the four stage one of *change*. This is so useful that it was said to be the basis of both British and German astrological investigations during World War Two, using Jupiter as a measure of it. The ancient Chinese, who were advanced in their development of art, medicine and technology millennia ago, based their entire astrological system on Jupiter. In modern times, astrologers have shown that the three-stage Jupiter cycle is directly linked to the success of political, financial and even personal endeavors.

While transition through four stages is obvious because changes tend to happen at each of the stages, just as they do in nature, transition through *three* stages is subtler and needs to be taken advantage of shrewdly. In the example of the three stages of a season mentioned earlier, the change from early summer to high summer is a less precise, more personal perception than the one from summer to autumn.

Jupiter Measures the Smooth Change Cycle

Jupiter is the symbol for gains of all kinds, including negative ones like excess. Jupiter is associated with beneficence, brightness and hope. For our purposes, we are interested in its powerful association with the cycle of reward. Jupiter even describes what types of reward suits you best:

If your Jupiter number is	Your reward type is
Below 30	You have Jupiter in the fire element and need recognition
30–59	You have Jupiter in an earth element and need status
60–89	You have Jupiter in an air sign and need appreciation from your peers
90–119	You have Jupiter in a water sign and need security

If the four major season changes require us to make an adjustment, and they certainly do, judging by the weather, then the three stages of each season (early, high, late) are more subtle and pleasing in their change. They represent the evolution of an existing thing, not the change from one thing to another. There is a smooth flow from one to another, not a break and transformation. Although it's subtle to detect, the cyclical clock of Jupiter makes it easy to find.

When the structure of the cycle's smooth flow is examined in stages, each one is approximately four years in length (three stages of four years each to one full twelve-year cycle). On one hand, this means that every four years there is an evolutionary shift in something, and it also means that you can start something successfully every fourth year, once you know where to start counting.

Using the Jupiter Cycle

Jupiter's association with hope and beginnings explains why its cycle was thought of as the luck cycle. Since luck is the result acting at the right time with the right attitude, whether chance or divine intention provide the moment, the observation of the four-year flow is a recognition of a periodic perfect moment to act to get rewards.

This means that long-term undertakings will show significant growth somewhere around every fourth year, although of course the Jupiter numbers in the table of cycles will show the precise times when growth can be expected. Remember, though, that it is more than just growth. The Jupiter turning points can be used to plan growth points, additional ventures (like further changes) or any change that requires a really good outcome and in which a little luck would be most welcome!

Notice that the Jupiter numbers are unlike other cycles; they cycle from 0 to 119. This is because we are measuring a three-part cycle rather than a four-part cycle. The four-part cycle of Jupiter can be useful, but it tends to indicate periods of waste rather than of growth!

The J's on your worksheet represent the three-part stage of Jupiter. Every fourth year you have a natural "good flow" year, where you have a J marked, and every twelfth year your circled Jupiter indicates a year that tends to be more rewarding on the whole—you personal "good luck" year. This is when your personal Jupiter cycle returns to its starting point.

An Even More Powerful Jupiter Cycle

The cycle that has attracted all the research is not, in fact, the one you have just worked with. Reward is such a personal thing—like satisfaction—that it must be connected with a basic personal cycles, like that of the Sun (for the self).

When the Jupiter number matches the Sun's number by the three-part harmonic, an enormously successful beginning may be expected. Many winners of presidential campaigns, tenders, and many successful businesses have begun (some inadvertently) under just such cycles. Although it may not work every time, since there are other factors to consider, it certainly produces its rewards most of the time.

In keeping with the special three-part nature of this cycle, we need to establish the Sun's starting point in three-part terms, not four-part as before. We need to find a new Sun number: *you can't use the one you found earlier.* Check the position of the Sun on your birthday in the column marked Sun-Jupiter in Table 1.

Starting from today's date, check the position of Jupiter in Table 2. Scan forward until it is as close as possible (within two) of the Sun number that you found in step 1. Note this date.

Keep scanning ahead over the next few months to see if the position recurs. Note every time you are within two of your special Sun number you found in step 1.

Try starting projects on these dates, even looking out for turn-arounds in your favor in unexpected areas of your life. You can certainly enhance your success and your apparent luck by working with this particular aspect of the Jupiter cycle—just try it. You can also look up the special Sun number in Table 1 of any project's beginning and use the Jupiter number from Table 2 to find the luck cycle for each individual project. Remember, though, that your own Sun number is always the more important one.

PART THREE

MASTERING THE LONG-TERM
WITH THE CYCLES OF LIFE

8

LONG-TERM CYCLES:
ADJUSTING TO YOUR AGE
WITH SATURN CYCLES

For most people the real meaning of time is age. Despite the everyday pressures of time and the clock and calendar deadlines, our real experience of time is witnessing ourselves, our loved ones and our projects grow older. The critical decisions that affect our everyday lives are certainly significant, but as time rushes by so quickly it is the bigger picture that counts more.

In this chapter

- You will learn how the cycle of Saturn relates to long-term cycles.
- You will discover the meaning and use of the well-known seven-year cycle.
- The twenties and thirties are explained in detail and you will learn how to use Saturn to get the best from them.
- The critical Saturn Return at age twenty-nine is explained.
- You will learn how Saturn's limitations help us to understand karma and lead to spiritual growth.

Changes Happen with Age

Aging is probably one of the most exciting and most daunting experiences that we will have. It needn't be.

Although the cycles of the slower moving planets take much longer to play themselves out than the ones we've used so far, they offer us an understanding of how we mature. Learning when age changes happen will help us more successfully face the challenges of adulthood and beyond. In particular, Saturn's cycle measures the seven-year stages of growth, maturity into adulthood and even some deeper lessons of the soul.

Finding Age Changes on Your Worksheet

- The main aging stages are the S's you marked in your Saturn column. You'll see that these changes are seven years apart in your life.

- Stop to think back over a few of the years marked this way and remember significant developmental stages in your life—accepting difficult changes, making choices that still reflect in your adult life, even some difficult experiences.

Attunement to Shorter Cycles Is Not Enough

The changes associated with aging make us fearful, and for some reason we need to feel purpose and meaning in our lives. No matter how good we get at mastering the small stuff, trauma still happens, and when it does most of our sense of control and attunement flies straight out the window.

It is our growth over longer cycles that allows us to attune ourselves properly to time. Things move so quickly these days that we expect changes to happen dramatically and immediately. We perceive time as passing very fast and that millions of things are happening. In retrospect we recall only few important things each year, and both those and the more trivial ones add up to gradual developments that experience clear, cyclical points of change.

The Seven-Year Itch

Seven is the most unsurprising number in our culture. It comes up everywhere, from the days of the week to the seven notes in a musical scale. The seven-year cycle is particularly familiar, from the days of the Pharaoh's dreams in the story of Joseph, to the sabbatical taken by the professor every seven years as relief from teaching.

Most familiar of all is the seven-year itch, seen when one or both partners in a relationship feel stuck and restless every seven years. In fact, that very pattern of restlessness often causes changes in work, residence or image according to the same seven yearly schedule.

Saturn Measures the Aging Cycle

When we look at Saturn's cycle we can understand why time seems to go so clearly through these stages. Saturn is the ruler of time and of limitations, ultimately the limitations of the physical world itself.

Saturn takes around twenty-nine years to complete one full period—about the same amount of time originally attributed to the meaning of "generation" in modern human life. Once we apply the seasonal principle of four main stages to this period, each season of Saturn is seen to last a little over seven years.

The turnaround year is therefore about every seventh year, the year we need to adjust to keep track with the progress of time and growth in our physical lives. Saturn has long been associated with karma and personal responsibility, as well as with growth itself.

It is easy to divide human life into seven-year stages: The age regarded as the completion of the formation part of the cycle is seven years, the beginning of growth of the individual who has been formed. Around fourteen, growth starts maturing with the onset of puberty, and at twenty-one we are released like wild seeds to discover our freedom and begin to find who we are in the world. Only by twenty-nine or thirty years of age are we finally adult.

Finding Your Seven-Year Turning Point Years

Although you might respond in a variety of ways, Table 5 can help you identify one or two of the main issues that tend to arise, especially at the age of twenty-nine.

Remember that you may find significant events for each of the three dates that you find every year; it is the whole period they cover that describes the seven-year change of cycle.

Working with the Saturn Cycle

When we see our limitations against the natural constraint of time, we begin to operate within our own growth rhythm. In the same 30 years, individuals grow at different rates and to different extents, but the pulse of that growth retains its seven-year resonance. Adjusting to this cycle is not a question of slowing down: the rate of growth will come naturally once the cycle is honored. Growth, by definition, is a function of time.

In practical terms we can learn to deal consciously with adjustment issues every seven years; particularly in our relationships but in all other areas of life, too. Think about it when your relationship or job is seven, fourteen, or twenty-one years old. Of course, every seventh year of your life there is the major adjustment period that usually affects more than one area. These changes are never dramatic and are often internal issues rather than crises.

The Key to All Processes

Saturn moves very slowly, so there are several different stages and parts of its cycles that are useful when working with long-term goals. Here is a basic structure of time according to Saturn:

- The nature of obstacles, limitations and difficulties changes every two-and-a-half years (one third of the seven year season);
- Strategies and methods must change every three-and-a-half years (halfway point);
- Reorganizing and even breakthroughs occur every five years (two-thirds);

- A turning point is reached at seven years that requires reassessment; often change of direction, and sometimes a decision to bring something to a close. The quarter-cycle crisis that occurs at this point can represent a crisis of "what form should this take" or "what is the real purpose or meaning of this?" This is the confrontation with limitations that forces us to refine our motives and methods and thus be successful. See how powerful limitation is?

This is a key to all processes, and knowing it can help you master many things in your life.

The Importance of Limitation

Many of us are daunted by our limitations and live in fear or resentment because of the obstacles that stand in the way of our smooth progress. So much of our life is controlled by impossibilities and "if only" that disillusion is driven home at a very personal level. When it comes to alternatives, we are offered few signposts to the middle path between getting on with things and becoming driven, ill and unhappy.

The path to wholeness and to purpose is not achieved by cowering before our obstacles, nor is it done by relentlessly beating against such impersonal forces.

When a river encounters a mountain it does not suffer; it adjusts and turns, and reaches its destination by solving the problem of the mountain. In time, the river will conquer the mountain and erode it peacefully. Both river and mountain will have changed very much over those years.

Limitations may be the greatest gift we have. They are necessary for us to be able to achieve a goal by following a path. There are many paths to any destination, but unless we limit ourselves to one of them we'll never reach that destination. Some paths may indeed be more challenging, but they get there in the end. If we keep starting new paths, we'll always be at the beginning, even if they're easy paths. If we learn to work with limitations rather than against them or not work with them at all, we master the longer-term cycles that define our lives as a whole and create for ourselves a sense of meaning and purpose.

Limitation allows definition of things, of oneself, and allows energy to be accumulated and directed. The power of the river is achieved precisely through its containment by banks and mountains. Its power would dissipate if the river spread unbounded over the plains. It would be the same with ourselves. As the *I Ching* says: "Unlimited possibilities are not suited to man; if they existed, his life would only dissolve in the boundless."[1]

Limitation is really a part of these same old cycles, and we can understand it by looking at the longer-term cycles and, like the river, learning to flow with them rather than against them. Time is the function of limitation, so we can look at the cycle that represents time itself and get straight to the core of the matter.

The Twenties: Finding Your Place in the World

Physical maturity is complete by the early twenties, and so we are officially adults. Despite the fact that teenage life has proved that physical maturity is well ahead of emotional adulthood, at the age of twenty-one we are launched into the world as though we have the full capabilities of an emotionally mature or experienced person.

Now, there is nothing inherently wrong in that, because we will learn very quickly from experience. The real problem is that we become burdened with responsibilities ahead of their time because maturity is assumed. For example, many people begin a career that will become the primary determinant of their daily life and their goals when they have only just been given the freedom to have any of their own goals in the first place.

The key we are given at this tender age should not be one to an office, but rather as it was originally intended: the key to freedom. This is not freedom without consequence or responsibility; it is the freedom to discover what we like or don't like, what we can or can't do, and what will satisfy us in life. After three seven-year seasons of formation, we can relax and be ourselves, lie fallow for a while. We should avoid being pressurized into undertaking long-term responsibilities, especially with regard to career choices and commitments. Sure, some lucky individuals have a clear and self-defined sense of purpose at this time, but too many have it inculcated by the force of peer or parent.

The twenties are the time to explore and experiment, with the youthful, rash courage to learn the hard way. In the twenties, we finally discover ourselves . . . for the second time. We discovered ourselves physically earlier in life, and will rediscover ourselves many times in the decades ahead. The naive sense of invincibility common at this time is not useful for much more than that courage, but the courage to learn allows an incredibly high intellectual and philosophical potential.

Our freedom of thinking and our willingness to learn allow breakthroughs in mental development. Many great geniuses have done their best work at this time in life. Einstein is a good example. Realistically, it may mean that we have to work as a waiter or clerk simply to pay the rent, but that also helps us with the experience we are trying to gather at this time.

Once we have a better plan for adulthood, aiming to be on our career path by the end of the twenties rather than the beginning, we feel less despair at the dullness of such work because we know it's not an endless treadmill ahead of us.

Turning Thirty: Adulthood

Although we're encouraged to believe that adulthood begins at twenty-one, we retrospectively discover that it's only *after* the twenties that we really feel grown up. Turning thirty has all sorts of resonance in our culture, not only because of the change of the digits (a compelling factor in itself) but because most of us endure a trial by responsibility during our twenty-ninth year, the Saturn year itself. This is the year Saturn returns to its starting position for any person and is called the Saturn Return.

Check for the Saturn Return on Your Worksheet

This important transition is marked in your Saturn column as the circled S at age twenty-eight or twenty-nine. If you are older than thirty, think about what happened to you during that year in your life.

This completion of the first full Saturn cycle in life is invariably challenging. In astrological terms, this is seen as the beginning of adulthood. Many people remember that new issues at that time set a pattern for years to come. Marriage, divorce and having children are common, but so are other undertakings and decisive moments. It is the completion of one full cycle of life, a generation of learning, and the beginning of a new cycle. Most people never forget their twenty-ninth year because of how hard it was. Still, it certainly helps explain why thirty feels so good in comparison.

Adulthood is something many young people look forward to with eagerness, believing that freedom will finally be achieved. As adults, we believe, we can do as we please and are not answerable to anybody, unlike the childhood years of parents and teachers. Ironically, for most people the opposite turns out to be true. Adulthood is the undertaking of responsibility, and appropriately so, because the execution of responsibilities is again the domain of Saturn, and, as we have seen, the way to deal with karma.

During the thirties most of us acquire the responsibilities of debts, mortgages, jobs and families. As we feel a greater sense of who we are and what we want from life, we feel increasingly opposed and bogged-down by the world. Time marches on relentlessly, and the situation only worsens.

By the late thirties, some people feel they are victims of processes beyond their control, and here is the true seed of disillusionment. Here, in everyday life experience, is what appears to be evidence that life is indeed out of our own control and acting against our own personal interests.

There is another side to turning thirty, which most also experience: the older we get and the more we grow, the easier everything becomes. There may be a great sense of relief somewhere during the 30th year, and despite the increased responsibilities, we feel as though something has been taken off our shoulders. There is clearly a trade-off: after all, life is not supposed to be any kind of punishment. Even though adulthood is not what we expected, it will teach us individuality through limitations rather than simply hand it over on a plate. This is a far more enriching and rewarding experience.

Case History: Accepting Limitations

Alan and Nadia had married when he was twenty-two and she was twenty-four. They came from traditional Jewish backgrounds and placed great value in their cultural values of large families and professional achievement.

At twenty-eight, Alan began to withdraw from Nadia, as Nadia's success as an executive increased while his low-earning accounting practice made him feel "less of a man." By age twenty-nine they had been trying to conceive a child for two years, but Alan's inexplicable low sperm count seemed to eliminate this possibility.

Alan and Nadia came to an astrologer because of how his growing depression and withdrawal was affecting their marriage. He felt emasculated and could not accept that he would never be a father since he believed that his religious imperative to "be fruitful and multiply" was literal. He couldn't "allow" his wife to work if they had a child as he had some pretty fixed ideas about that, too. It seemed that divorce was inevitable, a distinct possibility for a Saturn Return.

Alan's personal horoscope revealed an overpowering Saturn of category 1 in Table 5 which made him feel deeply obliged to his parents and in-laws to fulfill their expectations of grandchildren. This impossible task was creating stress that was destroying his work and home life.

In looking at his cycles, he began to understand that his current age was an end of the cycle of discovery that had begun at the time of his marriage (he entered the "freedom phase" at twenty-two) and that the next natural stage was to accept limitations. He learned that his resentment of Nadia's success and that his wholesale submission to his in-laws' expectations was blocking his own path forward.

This was a revelation to Alan. Working with Saturn's cycles, he came to understand the importance of taking responsibility for his life rather than blaming things on his wife's higher-paying job or his in-laws. By thirty, he had settled into becoming as successful an accountant as possible and enjoying the fact that his wife's success ensured that they could afford to take the next big step, adopting a child. He now knew that what he thought was a religious or parental disapproval was in fact his own "stuff" being projected onto them. Accepting this limitation gave him a route to fatherhood.

Working with Long-Term Goals

The completion of the twenties has long been acknowledged in our culture, even if sometimes rather subtly. It is sometimes still known by its proper astrological name, the "Saturn return."

While it certainly is the end of childhood, it must also be seen as the beginning of adulthood. Like all beginnings of a solid, long-standing edifice (we have many more years to live) a solid foundation must be built. If we were acting within our own natural rhythm, we would be consciously establishing responsibilities. Rather than try to avoid new ones, we can be selective and choose responsibilities willingly, with the knowledge that we are in the *planting* stage of the new twenty-nine-year cycle.

Goals and investments can be plotted with this in mind. A certain amount of growth and reward may result within the initial seven years but it's a long-term process. People are in such a rush to get it all done, expecting to achieve most things in their thirties. They give little thought to what good that will do if they have many more decades to live. It is no accident that insurers use age tables that start drastically working against you once you end the twenties.

To many, conceptualizing a cycle as twenty-nine years in length is impossible, even disheartening. Because we feel a strong need to know who we are and just what we are supposed to be doing with our lives, we expect identity and purpose to arrive automatically long with adulthood. Childhood only gives us the tools to find these things, and, if we are lucky, a vision of what they might be.

It is during adulthood that they must unfold. It's not natural to be able to know what is at the end of that long thirty years, and we should allow the full cycle for true development of ourselves as adults and to complete as much of our foundation as possible.

In our twenties we are still in the phase of growing and establishing our identity despite the fact that physically and legally we are adults. Adulthood is about responsibility and undertakings, so we can expect much of it to be challenging. We should work at establishing solid roots to help weather the difficult years ahead. By no means will things stay the same for the full thirty years, and we need resources to deal with the changes and see us through to the end.

Analyze Your Limitations Simply

It is an interesting and valuable exercise to analyze any limitation in your life by asking yourself "How is this connected to time or material things?" There are very few obstacles that don't fall into these categories.

Knowing Your Age

It might be surprising to discover that very few of us act appropriately for our age. But once you appreciate how little awareness we have of our cycles, it becomes clear that our notions of time and age are distorted. Despite the incredible advances that have almost doubled the human life span in just a few hundred years, we have not adapted our goals and behavior to suit the longer time we spend on Earth. As a result, we are rushed into careers and relationships in our early twenties as if we were to die in our forties, as many of our ancestors did.

In days gone by, people had less free choice; they were born into a social class and sons almost invariably followed the professional footsteps of their father. The girls had little choice but to follow the domestic, maternal duties of their mother. Marriage was far more of a social contract than a romantic one, and had a great deal to do with the desires and wishes of the parents (particularly the father) of the bride, and sometimes of the groom too—his wife would be his devoted servant.

As a result of persistent social expectation, most people feel increasingly pressured during their twenties and even more so in their thirties, if they are unmarried and not settled into a profession or "purpose in life." This culminates in a crisis by about forty, and despite it happening to almost everybody, we are largely unprepared for it.

This crisis is akin to the literal death our forebears experienced around this time in their lives—and through the painful changes that often occur at this age our old lives die and a new phase begins, giving credence to the cliché-cum-adage that life begins at forty. (In fact, as we'll see in the next chapter, there is a planetary cycle that explains where that idea may have come from.)

Acting our age means understanding our seven-year rhythm and deliberately adjusting our goals accordingly. You needn't be a particularly goal-oriented person to do this, nor should you be daunted by the idea of thinking so far in advance. For most of us, knowing our age is not a matter of specific planning. It is the art of adjusting ourselves to the tempo of events and opportunities so that we feel more in tune with what is happening, less surprised by the unexpected and able to make wiser choices and decisions.

The Thirties: Establishing Your Place in the World

There's no doubt that we recognize thirty as more than a number, especially in the twenty-first century, as we readjust to the natural cycle and experience relationships and child-rearing during the thirties. The success of the television show that turned "thirty-something" into common currency reflects our cultural desire to establish our lives during the thirties. It also leads us to the assumption that by the end of the thirties we should have achieved many of our goals. Admirable, and perhaps in some ways it is true, but we rarely stop to wonder in *which* ways that may be. Invariably, it is reduced to a financial goal: the proverbial million, and many expect that in their thirties.

So we spend the thirties industrious and excited, often still confused, and often worried about the achievements we are supposed to have reached by now. Cultural pressure is enormous at this stage, because we are no longer in a position to be supported by our parents and we have mounting financial demands from the world out there. On top of all of this, the generations who are in their twenties and thirties in the early 21st century have parents who experienced their own age cycles very differently. Most of those parents had full-sized families and long-held jobs by the time they entered their thirties, something that is simply no longer true (and as we have seen, appropriately so).

These parents struggle to relate to the slow maturity of their off-spring, who confront them with further financial burdens, while young people are *aware* of the process of maturing.

The young people live in an age of information, of processing the self and seeking more answers. They understand the role of their parents, the expectations of society, and the fact that the old answers no longer work.

By the later thirties we have loads of responsibilities and have manifested much of the stuff of adulthood: "The world is too much with us." We start wondering if this is all there is to life, and we gradually slip towards a plateau where nothing more seems to be gained. Perhaps, just as purpose is sensed, it slips away into frustration.

Somewhere during the thirty-sixth year another seven-year cycle turns and we shift into a new stage. Remember how the four stages of Saturn work: since the first full cycle at twenty-nine, we have just completed a seven-year cycle of establishing something: adulthood. By thirty-six or thirty-seven, it is well and truly established, and suddenly it seems that we are going to be stuck with this. We feel trapped and start realizing that many of the dreams we had for ourselves are turning out to be untrue. No wonder we feel bored and somewhat disillusioned.

As we'll see, other cycles are also winding down at this time, and it will take all the way until thirty-nine to react and shift things enough to get out of the trap. Often those final years of the thirties are filled with challenges that previous generations experienced somewhat later as their mid-life crisis. It is not unusual to have quite traumatic experiences in these years if you were born in the 1960s and 1970s—they come during the forties for those born in the 1950s, 1980s, and 1990s. We'll examine this cycle more closely in the next chapter.

Madonna's Seven-Year Turning Points

In Madonna's case, there are Saturn cycle changes in 1966, 1972–73, 1979–80 and the big deal Saturn return in 1987. The one around 1980 is when she started writing her own songs, breaking away from an unsuccessful song-writing partnership of two years; posed naked for photographs and made her first film, a soft-core porn movie. That's the breakaway cycle at age twenty-one.

Her Saturn return in 1987 coincides with her first world tour, her first major image change and the beginning of the end of her marriage to Sean Penn. The Press called 1987 "Madonna's Year."

Big career moves continue to happen every seven years for Madonna. In 1995 (her next Saturn change) she begged for and got the part of Evita. Significantly, for the first time in her life she underwent rigorous singing instruction, which had a permanent effect on her subsequent work.

Finding a Sense of Soul

When we adopt this cyclical approach to these longer life cycles, we are adopting a more objective view and aligning ourselves with what is often considered to be karma. This often-misused Sanskrit term (meaning "action") refers to the limits we impose on ourselves through our own actions and choices, particularly through the attachments we make. So it is not surprising that in a more spiritual approach to astrology, Saturn is assigned the role of the Lord of Karma.

In those worldviews that see limitation as karma, Saturn takes on the role of representing the ageless, spiritual aspect of the self usually called soul. In this view that relates karma to responsibility for actions in other lifetimes, Saturn also represents learning and experience that is gained by the soul's difficult passage through many lifetimes. Saturn's role as the link between time, responsibility, limitations and learning is even more clearly seen.

In the long run, alignment to the "soul perception" of time and growth is both more rewarding and more satisfying. It allows us to discover what is truly appropriate for our age, rather than remain trapped in inconsistent cultural beliefs about time.

Saturn's cycle teaches us to work naturally with the limitations of our time and space exactly as the river does, and, with time, achieve more extraordinary growth. This alignment will not magically make obstacles disappear. Rather, it will help us read the signs of our environment, our time and place, and adjust to obstacles appropriate to existing conditions rather than to supposed future conditions.

---

1. Richard Wilhelm translation, by Cary F. Baynes, Book I, Hexagram 60.

9

AGING WITH MASTERY:
SATURN IN LATER LIFE

The foundations laid by the early Saturn cycles serve well to establish us in life, but are soon shaken up by the "midlife crisis" and the new demands that the peak adult years will bring.

In this chapter

- You will examine the ongoing pulse of Saturn's cycles beyond the age of forty.

- You will learn why difficulties repeat themselves despite our past experience.

- We will take a closer look at what maturity is all about by looking at the key transitions of ages forty, fifty, and sixty. (Since the midlife crisis is such an important transition point, we will give it a chapter of its own after this one.)

- We will examine the proper role and responsibility of seniority.

- Timing the need to find purpose and continue to grow in later life is shown.

Finding the Years in the Worksheet

- The cycles we examine in this chapter continue in your Saturn column.

- The S around age forty-three represents putting the midlife crisis behind you; at fifty it represents a new-found freedom, and at fifty-eight it is circled again to indicate the second Saturn Return.

- If you are over forty, consider some of the key developmental stages since then. How do *you* think you've matured—what do you do differently from when you were younger, and what aspects of your youth have returned?

Does Life Begin at Forty?

The common cultural idea that "life begins at forty" is often taken as a panacea for growing older. By then we've supposedly learned our lessons once and for all, and can look forward to fewer unexpected surprises. Trauma is bound to happen, but there is no need to endlessly repeat all those lessons again. Life after forty allows for "been there, done that, don't need to do it again" thinking. This is a great tool for organizing your priorities and saving yourself lots of the trauma, but can it really mean that all those old circumstances don't return? Are we finally free of repeating those same old disastrous relationship patterns? Life certainly doesn't seem to automatically get any less challenging at forty.

Why We Repeat Our Lessons

By now we know that cycles go up and down, but they always return. After all, life *begins* at forty—it doesn't end there! There's a point to learning life's hard lessons: we are going to have the opportunities to use them. If we learned each lesson once or twice and then put it behind us, we would be novices in all areas of life, the classic "Jack of all trades and master of none." We master something in order to use it.

A basic law of battle is not to get the enemy behind you. If it's behind you, you won't see it coming. Rather than aspiring to put difficulties behind us, we should strive to have them under our feet—something we have mastered but which is still present in our lives. If it stirs, we're ready to deal with it.

When you want to become highly skilled at something, you do it over and over again, just as an apprentice does, or someone studying for a university degree. Practice makes perfect; it prepares you. If practice is to be useful, it must relate to the challenge for which you are preparing yourself, or something very similar. Practicing Mozart in order to play difficult pieces does not make the difficult pieces any less difficult; it simply makes them easier for the master to play. Masters, after years of mastering their craft, go on to spend most of their life doing the very thing they have mastered. It would be pointless to put behind us the things that we've mastered.

So we needn't clasp our brows when the same old thing rears its head again; we should look upon it as a familiar tool. Mastery of our cycles is like mastery of tools, the tools with which we shape the experience of our lives. Our lessons become our tools, and we continue to use these same familiar tools to master our lives. Working with all the previous changes and experiences helps make such a tool easy to use, but it remains a complex tool. There would be no point in abandoning a tool once we had mastered it, because the need for the tool would remain. We learn to thrive on the challenges life offers, coming from a new place in our fifth decade when all the planetary cycles are finally familiar and ready for use.

The transition into the forties is often painful, exciting and challenging. We will examine the special one-off cycles that happen at that time in the next chapter. But even still, the relentless march of time and seven-year cycles continues.

Forty-Three to Fifty: The Seven-Year Cycle Continues

Around forty-three years old, the second seven-year Saturn cycle completes itself, often finalizing the changes we have wrought through the experience of all those forty-year cycles. This is the first S you checked for this chapter. This is a halfway point on the Saturn cycle: the last time we were in such a position was around the age of fourteen. That's when we became ourselves, putting aside childhood and moving into the throes of adolescence. We feel powerful in our teenage years.

For a while, a bright and energetic self pushes into the world. This is the familiar rush of success that often accompanies the forties, when we finally do what we really want to do. Once again foundations are being laid that will take another fourteen or so years to build upon; this is the time to commit yourself to the things you really believe in.

The Fiftieth Birthday

It's becoming clear that the significance of the "decade age" changes is not simply psychological. There was one at twenty-nine, one at forty, and now, seven years after the foundation was laid, the seven-year cycle again turns between the ages of fifty and fifty-one. This is the seventh seven-year cycle, a significant change of course because of it being the "Saturnth" (seventh) Saturn cycle. Remember the biblical tale of walls crashing down in Jericho on the seventh set of seven trumpet calls?

Fifty-One to Fifty-Eight: Release from Responsibility

This cycle, the fourth seven-year cycle since we had the twenty-nine-year return, is most similar to the one some 30 years earlier at the beginning of the twenties. For many, the twenties is "liberation," but now in the fifties this is liberation of an altogether different kind and much more akin to the breaking down of walls. Adulthood has largely been an edifice of responsibility and status. Our status in the world and our responsibilities as adults severely hamper the freedom we imagined our adult lives would provide.

During the fifties, an increasing number of responsibilities fall away. Many will pay off their mortgages at this time. Since many people in their fifties have children in their early twenties, the parallel cycle of the youngsters gradually releases the parent of responsibilities as the children take responsibility for more of their own life.

Of course, many parents find this phase fraught with difficulty. The habits of decades must change, and power must be lost as the children become independent. Letting go, which is the lesson that all parents know must come, is the first challenge. At the same time, younger people begin to take the more powerful roles in a familiar working environment, and we have to let go of the feeling of status and authority in much of our work.

This might take all of the next seven years to unfold, so many of us will also enter into an almost frenzied phase as we deliberately, sometimes defiantly, display our energies and abilities. As we shall see when we look further into aging, much of this feeling probably comes from the attitude our society displays towards its elderly members.

All these responsibilities were what gave us our sense of meaning and purpose in the world, especially as parents of growing children. As the walls fall down, however, and we are freed of these responsibilities, we begin to remember that meaning and purpose must come from something more permanent, more transcendent.

While the drive towards spiritual growth has many high points during our lives, the spurt that may occur at the beginning of the fifties is often the strongest and the most successful. We may make it more difficult by wanting answers at once, by wanting to know which path to take to answer these questions. It seems that so little time is left and that so much has been wasted.

This is far from the truth. We are now more capable of confronting our spiritual issues with the experience life has given us, and after all, there are probably a few more useful decades to come.

The fifties must be approached like the twenties, and fortunately many people really do feel young again at this time. It's a time for new discoveries, for finding your own sense of purpose and meaning, rather than accepting what society has been telling you. Just as we should not finish our twenties too quickly, benefiting more by taking the whole decade to explore our new potential, so we must not rush the marvellous process that happens during the fifties. It is once again a point where our identity changes. In fact, if we take things at their proper pace, we will stretch our souls to their fullest, glorious height and stay a bit longer on Earth to get it all done. But only in the *next* decade can we really have the chance to do something with it all.

Seniority Is Authority

Entry into the sixties is a line firmly demarcated in Western culture. For many, this is retirement age, entitlement to social pensions and concessions of various sorts. How quickly we have forgotten the true role of elders in our society. Even though we retain the words "senior citizens," these citizens have few of the rights of their seniority. It is not concessions the elders should receive, but privileges.

Entry into seniority is marked by the culmination of the second full Saturn cycle around the age of fifty-eight. Remember, the cycles are twenty-nine-years long, so this is the second Saturn return. Just as the first one ended childhood and initiated adulthood, now adulthood ends and seniority begins.

The Saturn cycle is the cycle of age and now that we are reaching our Saturnian years of seniority, it really comes into its own. Saturn's cycles also have a strong association with the past and thus have a significant bearing on ancestry, tradition and ancestral memory. It seems as though these have little value in twenty-first century society, although there are early signs that we are realizing the drastic mistake we have made in ignoring these traditions and memories. With productive living now extending into the seventies and eighties along with our ever-increasing life spans, there is a good chance we will indeed return to valuing the elders and their ways.

So seniority is a time to reassert our real status and start acting with the authority we possess by right of seniority. It is a simple fact that acting with authority produces results all on its own: just try it.

Of course, it's not always so simple. We need to deal effectively with the issues that the Saturn cycle presents, to prevent ourselves unconsciously "taking them on." Saturn "taken on" is belligerent and even bitter old age, the hardening in response to challenge instead of the adapting and growing that allow us to experience this transition with grace.

Working with the Saturn Return . . . Again

Your second Saturn return is the circled S around age fifty-eight and fifty-nine. It is often much easier to deal with the Saturn cycle the second time around, especially if you have spent your fifties letting go of all the baggage that adult life accumulates. It's never pleasant to end up surrounded by baggage in a tiny apartment with only a pension. Letting go will make space for many new things in life that may well last for decades to come.

This is not to say there are no trials: many people do find this period difficult simply because change is more unsettling at this age, and the Saturn return will bring change. The more we resist the changes this cycle end brings, the more difficult we make our lives. We are challenged to let go of our adult identity and move into the third phase of life, a challenge that is easier issued than met. We must relinquish control over those things we, as adults, are accustomed to controlling—such as our children.

In some way, the Saturn lesson will relate back to the one learned twenty-nine years before, even if only by theme (see the list of examples in Table 5). It will probably be more about letting go than taking on, which it was before. Unlike the letting go of the midlife crisis, which is letting go of beliefs about ourselves, this time around it's the letting go of worldly concerns and the shift towards a more spiritual approach to life.

Because it's Saturn, there are also bound to be issues about aging, time, memory and family. If you bear in mind the nature of the cycle you are dealing with, rather than feeling as if the universe is out to get you and nobody appreciates your struggle through life, you can successfully release much of that struggle.

One of the challenging issues is that of understanding your children as adults and shifting your role of parent to that of co-adult, while asserting your status as an elder by becoming an advisor to the family as a whole. This role of advisor is strictly for matters that affect the family as a whole, rather than your perceived needs of your particular children and their nuclear families. You have no direct influence in their families, but you certainly are a clan elder. This is the role that has gone missing in Western culture. If you understand yourself as the spiritual head of the family from this point onwards, it is easier to make the shift.

Case History: Learning to Let Go

Margaret was the busy stay-at-home mother of two grown children. Her youngest child had been born when she was twenty-nine, and so she related to category 5 in Table 5. At forty-two, she had built her long-dreamt of seaside home. At fifty, responding to a cooling in her marriage, she finally pursued her long-awaited Master's degree (she had an undergraduate degree from her early twenties) and became a clinical psychologist a few years later.

During her fifties, as her life took off and filled with new and exciting things, her marriage quietly disintegrated. Then, at fifty-eight, it all came crashing down: her husband divorced her and left along with the seaside home, and her youngest child cut off ties with her. Like many people, she struggled through the entire period of her second Saturn return (the circled S often covers two years), having to let go of the child who sided with his father, and her house she had lived to build.

Margaret learned about cycles at this time. She learned that at fifty-eight she had an opportunity to build from scratch all over again. Although it may not have lessened the pain of the difficult transition, the fact that she had so clearly experienced all the required transitions showed her that the cycles could be relied upon to help her get through and make the most of the next phase. Now she is pursuing another dream—the book she always wanted to write. She plans to be done at sixty-five.

The Real Purpose in Life

Much of our adulthood is spent trying to discover our purpose in life, and should we be lucky enough to come up with an answer to that quest, we then have the problem of trying to fulfill it. A survey of my clientele at that age shows that relatively few people would say they have found and followed "purpose" by the time they reach their fifties.

Since we are now increasingly freed from the constraints of adulthood, we need to assert our status by finally following our true paths.

Only with life's experience can we know what we truly always wanted to do, and only with seniority's freedom is there the possibility of actually doing it. This is not the kind of purpose that involves becoming the leader in our field or achieving some status in the world. For the most part, these are personal endeavors rather than achievement-oriented ones. They may include the novel that was never written, the journey never taken, all the things we didn't do for ourselves. We spent our youth being taken care of and our adulthood taking care of others. Now is the time to take care of ourselves, to put ourselves first without guilt.

With this knowledge, we must prepare for our seniority materially until society again acknowledges the status of the elders, and we must teach this to our children. We must teach them to look forward to seniority as the last phase of a rewarding life, not to dread it.

Life After Sixty

Life most certainly carries on, and in the real world there are still many challenges that face us. Once we have reached our sixties, we have reached out to the limits of the self, and it is these we explore when we acquire the wisdom and authority of this archetype. Saturn is also about limitations, though, and even with freedom from worldly responsibilities there are a number of limitations created by age itself, not the least of which is the body.

Physically, Saturn is also associated with the skin and bones and it is these that display the most visible signs of our age. The wrinkling of the skin and the increasing brittleness of the bones are not only signs of physical changes taking place, but also indicate that we are beginning to let go of the body.

Just as it took years to grow into the body, it takes years to grow out of it. This letting-go process is neither as difficult nor profound as it may sound. After all, those who become disabled by the effects of aging do not identify with their uncooperative bodies, for they *feel* no less able or strong than they always did. The spirit is as strong as ever.

Naturally, the seven-year cycles continue, and these often relate to physical issues such as the body, as well as issues of property and family. People who face the possibility of entering a nursing home often confront these issues on the turns of the Saturn cycle: age (approximately) sixty-five, seven-two, eighty, and eighty-seven, and so on. The Saturnian process of loss of calcium in the bones starts showing its consequences at this time—if we haven't thought ahead and ensured a healthy supply of calcium in the diet.

The period from fifty-eight to sixty-five is a beginning period in the set of four stages, similar to the beginning of the thirties and the very first seven years of life. A new life begins, with new adjustments. The personality shows signs of a new kind of maturity. Many people suddenly mellow out at this stage, amazing their children with their sudden tolerance and wisdom. This is why elders are the proper guides for the young: age and experience have moved them past the prejudices of the pride of adulthood. Of course, this is not always true; those who try to cling to the power of adulthood risk becoming bitter and frustrated.

Some of the liberating effects of the early sixties, the mellowing, are the final understanding of individuality. Our physical bodies and our place in the world have changed so radically that we are forced to let go of old ideas and beliefs and accept what we don't necessarily like about our own lives. Perhaps this is where the tolerance comes from, but it can certainly lead to a completely new level of self-acceptance. Many people learn to let others be themselves, especially their children, only after this cycle change.

From sixty-five to seventy-two, we find our place in this new age-bracket and thrive, reaching towards the true transformation as we enter the seventies. Many things are resolved at this time, and a new understanding of life settles into place. This may be a source of the biblical lifespan of "threescore and ten."

The years from seventy-two or seventy-three to eighty may be the years we finally appreciate being older and wiser. If we are indeed settled and able to finally sit in one place (but not literally), we do let go of the last lot of baggage. We should be able to live a deeply spiritual life without any of the loss of joy that comes with the possession-filled adult

years. We can finally understand much of the metaphysical and philosophical concepts that elude our younger friends, and we usually have
the wisdom to keep silent. The wisdom of silence is seldom learned before this period: even those in their sixties like to display their new-found
authority a bit too overtly.

We Keep On Learning and Growing

Of course, few of us age with the grace this idealized approach describes. In reality, most people face a great number of hardships associated with growing older. We must remind ourselves, yet again, that
while we have learned things, let go of them, and freed ourselves, *we are
presented with the same set of lessons over and over again.* Time does not
stop because we get older. Our task is to master the cycles of lessons so
that, despite the troubles of aging, we are able to see a bigger picture.
Mastery of the cycles simply means making the most of them no matter what the circumstances. We are old enough to know better than to
expect the world to become suddenly peaceful and harmonious just because *we* got older. With maturity, though, we should be able to handle
these same old challenges with fresh aplomb.

Cycles themselves are perpetual, always returning to their origin
point, and always continuing. They are the pulse of life, like the endless
waves of the ocean from which we first took our physical bodies. Even
Saturn returns again, around age eighty-seven, although by then there
are different kinds of challenges to deal with, and a whole new kind of
consciousness.

10

UNDERSTANDING AND PREDICTING CRISIS:
URANUS, NEPTUNE, AND PLUTO

The cycles of the visible planets which we have looked at so far give us a great understanding of the short and long-term processes we grow through and help us plan for the future. But we also live in a world that is fraught with challenges and changes inconceivable to the ancient astrologers who discovered these cycles.

In this chapter

- We will explore the exciting cyclical challenges of midlife and how they provide us with the tools to develop our individuality, spirituality and will.

- You will learn how the Uranus cycle measures the growth of individuality, how Neptune provides opportunities for spiritual maturity and how Pluto cycles teach through trauma.

- You will learn how to read three cycles together.

Once we know these cycles, we will use their crossings of all the other cycles as powerful predictors of significant changes throughout our lives.

Using the Worksheet

- To understand the growth process that the midlife period triggers, find the circled U in the Uranus column, N in the Neptune column and P in the Pluto column.

- Think of the time before the earliest of those dates, the time covered by the dates, and the time after the latest date. Can you see three somewhat different stages in your life then? It may be obvious or subtle, but the explanation in this chapter will help you see it and understand it.

- Now look in all the other columns on your worksheet where you find the letters U, N, or P. With what you have learned about the cycles so far, think of changes that have happened the aspect of your life measured by any cycle (column) that has one of those letters in it. In this chapter you will learn to understand what that change was about, and how to predict future changes.

Going Beyond Seven-Year Growth Stages

While Saturn's cycles clearly explain how experience and timing help lead to wisdom and greater success, it cannot account for our changing needs.

Many people reach their late thirties only to re-encounter early life frustrations—the feeling of not being in control, of not being recognized for who you are, of having to do things you don't want to do.

Redefining the Self

The discovery of the individuality, the self, is a bloody and painful experience symbolically akin to giving birth—and often, just as exciting. Coming in the middle of life, though, it is a process which often demands that we make radical changes to an already-established life.

Astrologically, the challenge of change at this time is described by three cycles which all reach a critical point within a relatively narrow span of time. The Uranus cycle is the challenge of individual will without the constraints of societal and parental expectation. The Neptune one is the challenge of meaning, the maturation of spiritual beliefs. Pluto's cycle challenges us, no matter what our beliefs, to deal with the fact that there are truly matters well beyond our control. (That unconscious thought is often a consequence of the first Uranus critical change at around twenty-one.)

Working with the Three Cycles of Adulthood

When viewed as a group of three, the cycles of Uranus, Neptune, and Pluto fill out the details of what the midlife crisis is really about.

Reminder: Notice in your worksheet that the time from the first circled P or U to the last circled N or P covers this "midlife" period for you.

Disillusionment and reorientation of power is the process by which we can at last truly know ourselves and complete the process of individuation. Freedom from the idealism and sense of infinite power of youth, while initially disconcerting, allows true power to emerge out of a realistic picture of our lives.

Although sometimes their actual turning points are separated by many years, the consciousness represented by Neptune and Pluto is part of the same issue. Nowadays we survive much longer than our ancestors, whose natural life-span would have ended at around the time of these cycles. Perhaps they never had a personal confrontation with such issues; perhaps this is one of the reasons why, in previous times, it was so much easier to accept the dogmatic spiritual meaning of others. It is only since the discovery of these planets, the exterior corollary of our changing consciousness, that we have lived so long.

To work with these deeper issues, we need to ask ourselves in the context of the specific issues:

What must I let go of?

What must I accept that I don't control?

Where have I lost power, or given it away?

Where am I clinging to old beliefs, old fantasies?_

Looking More Closely at the Three Cycles

What the three cycles have in common is that they require us to let go, to accept, and to redefine. They each do that in a different way.

Letting go is one of the most important lessons we can learn, and like so many lessons, it is best learned the hard way. This seems to be the way we grow best, and we have it in common with the entire natural world. It may seem peaceful, but all that natural beauty is a slow-motion war. For plants, losing a limb makes them grow two more. We're actually doing the same thing.

It is also important not to hastily substitute a new set of beliefs or behaviors to fill the gap left by the lost ones. We have to be patient, allowing the course of the cycles (usually lasting around three to five years) to give us the chance to learn new ways of being and thinking, appropriate to our newfound maturity.

For a better understanding of how the three cycles work together, we'll follow the changes that each one produces. Later, this knowledge will help us predict changes not related to the midlife crisis.

Uranus: Freedom and Individuality

Uranus, having an eighty-four-year period, will make its first challenge at twenty-one (one quarter of its cycle), which of course is the onset of "legal" individuality. Although we realize that we are not really adults at the time, this represents the beginning of our first taste of real freedom. Remember that Saturn also makes a pass by at twenty-one, introducing the fallow years of letting go, learning and having fun. Now we can see that it is the Uranus cycle that defines the twenties as having to do with freedom and independence, although this is merely the beginning of the path.

Can it be any surprise that the most important tick of Uranus' clock comes around the age of forty? It reappears at the critical half-way turning point of the planet's cycle, when the maturity crisis that occurs may indeed be a dramatic, often bloody birth, after which most people experience a re-start of life at a much more individualistic level. Many even get divorced just then, returning to a state of individualism.

Working with the Uranus Cycle

The Uranus column shows these changes around ages of twenty-one, forty, and sixty-two.

Although we recognize an individuation crisis at the end of the teenage years, we tend to think that it is all over by the time we're about twenty-one. How foolish we realize we were, once we are thirty. The twenties mark the real beginning of the individuation process, but we have nearly another twenty years to go before it ends. That makes Uranus much more relevant the second time around, particularly because that's when we have a life for it to change. Of course, the early twenties are filled with the confusion and excitement of the onset of the phase, but it will usually not bear comparison with the second cycle change at forty.

The age of twenty-one is the first beat of the same cycle that changes life at forty-odd, and it has great significance as the marker of our first stage of individuality. Twenty-one is certainly not trivial, it is simply that we are free to find ourselves, although we are not yet truly able to *be* ourselves. The expectations of our peers and the overwhelming need to be accepted, ensure that however individualistic we appear to be, it is, in fact, a strictly defined role.

In an ideal world, we would have prepared for the midlife cycle from about the age of twenty-one. If we, as young adults, understand the true meaning of that age and begin a process of self-discovery and experimentation, with a view to settling in the thirties and taking on our next challenges at forty, the midlife crisis would be much less of a crisis and the first half of life would probably be more satisfying.

As it is, though, the plateau towards the end of the thirties does help to prepare us, because by the time we are thirty-nine we are ready for almost any change, as long as *something* changes. The change may be traumatic because the expectations created at twenty-one implied that success should have already been achieved at forty. As we have seen, this is completely unrealistic, and forty simply represents the beginning of the next phase.

The way to deal with the change is by understanding that it is a time to let go of the program that was established by our early lives. Our identity as young adults is largely created by our early life circumstances (which is why psychoanalysts have such a field day later on in our lives). The only way a young child can begin to understand who he or she is comes from the feedback received from adults and peers: "You're a good boy," "You're a pretty girl," "You're so clever." And there are comments made to other adults in the presence of the child: "Maryanne is just so silly when it comes to art, it's like she has two left hands, but she's so helpful in the kitchen, aren't you darling?" These seemingly innocent remarks shape the child's picture of her worth: after all, what else is there to go on?

On top of this, the family itself has an identity that it needs to project into the world, and which it imposes on the children in the form of expectations and even "requirements" ("We Joneses don't do that"). The pressure of parental, cultural and societal expectation is tremendously strong all through childhood and well into the twenties. It's no wonder that an identity crisis must eventually arise, and it's clear that it's literally impossible for a young person to have a clear sense of identity at age twenty-one.

Knowing this, the midlife crisis may even be something of a relief, and it certainly makes a lot of sense as to why life may only begin at forty. This helps us establish the processes we need to work on to move successfully through this critical period of transition, as long as we concentrate on the basic issues:

If I had the choice, what would I not have in my life?

What do I feel the need to be free of?

What have I always wanted to do?

To many people it seems that their accomplishments are lost or snatched away during this time, but it is simply the loss of those things that don't reflect our true individuality. This is a time to deliberately remove from our lives behavior that is no longer working.

In practice, this is very difficult: it may even refer to our relationship or our job. Fortunately, it is difficult to go wrong: the cycle change is happening anyway, and if we don't willingly let go we just have to do so unwillingly. Simply put: we should be so lucky as to be able to miss our midlife crisis!

If it ever seems that fate is a reality in our experience, it is at this age. This is because three major cycles are all changing within a few years of each other, as you'll see when you read about the other planetary cycles in this chapter.

To work best with the Uranus cycle at this time, we must accept the inevitability of change, be willing to change as much as possible, and take responsibility for what we actually want; no longer what society tells us we want.

Madonna had her first Uranus change at only nineteen, in the 1977–78 period. In that year she moved to New York City to try her talents as a performer. It was the big breakaway, the move to the big city.

Uranus reappears in 1998–99. This is the midlife change cycle for Madonna at the age of thirty-nine. She embarked on two European tours at this time, sweeping the MTV music awards and meeting Guy Ritchie, her future husband. She became pregnant by him late that year. Another "new Madonna" was being born. She appeared in interviews at age forty as a suddenly mature, sexy, wise but wild-as-ever reincarnation of herself.

Neptune: Seeing Things in a New Way

The process of individuation is more than just a series of realizations about yourself; it is also a re-seeing of the world. The question "what is the meaning of life?" asked after years of experience, has more depth and more difficulty than when asked at the beginning of the journey, where we stand wide-eyed, optimistic, and confident.

In the battle-weary early forties, the process of *dis*illusionment needs to happen; a process of losing the illusion. Even though this is a coming-down in some ways, it eventually leads to a more meaningful way of understanding the world: and if you know your cycles, you can make it a much easier process.

This more transcendental aspect of the midlife crisis is not the sudden surprise of the Uranus cycle, but belongs to an aspect of ourselves even more recent than the rediscovery of freedom: personal spirituality.

Neptune, lord of the ocean, symbolizes qualities that are otherworldly, just as the ocean is. The watery quality of this world represents illusion but also vision, idealism and imagination. Humanity's greatest ideals are in this realm, although where there is illusion there is also disillusion.

The Neptune cycle, as we can see, is about reality and illusion, aspiration and disappointment. For these reasons, it is also about spirit.

The Spiritual Stage of the Midlife Crisis

Find the circled N in the Neptune column around age forty to forty-two.

At various stages of our lives, often marked by those Saturn cycles of seven years, we do indeed reshape our spiritual perspectives. It's not until the crisis of the forties, though, that we have the experience or the courage to define for ourselves our personal spiritual perspective. There may be little choice. Neptune's full cycle takes a plodding 164 years, meaning that it reaches its first turning point somewhere around the age of forty-one.

The Neptune cycle turning point thus occurs around about the time that the Uranus turning point is ending. Our own spiritual crisis is more than merely the issue of change; it is now a real question of meaning. Identity no longer means finding your place in the world, as it did when you were twenty-one, it now means *being* who you are and defining your own reality. For the first time, the soul is challenged to express itself more directly. Spiritual crisis is a fundamental part of the identity crisis that happens at this time. Although more subtle and slow, this cycle is probably the reason that so many people discover alternative spiritualities at this time. Neptune may be subtle, but that does not make it easy.

Neptune Feels Confusing

With Neptune as lord of the ocean, all of the symbolism of water may be applied to its cycle. On the one hand, water is the sustainer of life itself; on the other, its depths are impenetrable, filled with illusion and deception. Colors change under the ocean, objects appear closer to the surface than they actually are, and some even appear bent (like a pencil in a glass of water). Similarly, Neptune has associations with the soul itself, or the non-physical aspect of the human being. This includes the imagination and the world of dreams.

When the Neptune cycle comes along, the immediate effect is not generally vision and enlightenment, but long and unchanging confusion. Everything becomes vague and out of focus for a while. This is usually alarming, especially because the Uranus cycle may still be causing ripples of unease. Of course, the really alarming aspect is that the ego (the bright and clear solar cycle) feels severely threatened by suddenly not being in command of reality!

What appears to be confusion is really the emergence of a soul-level of perception. Now, this doesn't mean that we suddenly acquire the delightful ability to access the higher self, or whatever you may call it. It is not subject to our will, and so when it awakens in this manner we feel unable to understand or direct our lives. Naturally, those who are more comfortable with this state, and with their Uranian excitement, might actually enjoy this situation and experience it quite profoundly.

Since we are trying to shift into issues way beyond the scope of our egos, it is appropriate that this deeper self actually pushes the conscious self aside, so that it doesn't interfere. In the confusion of this period, it is rather like being in a boat on a lake without any oars. There is no danger, provided you don't rock the boat like a child trying to get a swing going. You'll only fall into the water that way. Eventually, you will drift ashore, because that is the nature of water and wind.

This destination is not one you would have chosen, but in retrospect it usually turns out to be the one that works out best for you. So it is that the higher self takes over from the ego to ensure that you reach a place you might not have found otherwise. It is from such a place in our lives and our thinking that we are able to confront successfully the issues symbolized by these grand cycles.

Working with the Neptune Cycle

At the time of our Neptune cycle turning point, we need to consider:

- What beliefs about myself and my world do I now realize to be false?

- How have I been fooling myself?

- What unnecessary sacrifices have I been making?

- What place does my spiritual life occupy in my life as a whole?

- Now that I'm older and wiser, what do I think is the meaning of life?

Not surprisingly, Madonna's Neptune cycles occur in the same 1998–99 period as her Uranus midlife change, signifying the deeper spiritual growth and dis-illusionment of life beginning again at forty.

Pluto: The Question of Will, Power, and Willpower

While the philosophical question of Free Will is a thorny enough one to have to worry about, it is our own everyday experience of "Will" that we must confront with Pluto. Will and Power are connected, as experience will have taught us. Experience has also taught us, though, that everything is not under our control, that willpower is difficult in an uncontrollable world.

The spiritual crisis is not simply a question of meaning of life, it's the question of "how much of this is really up to me?" And for many: "And if not me, then who?"

See where your circled P is in the Pluto column.

If it comes within five years of the other cycle it may be particularly significant, although its effects will be mixed up with Uranus and Neptune.

Check Table 5 to get an idea of some of the issues involved.

The Third Midlife Crisis Cycle: Thy Will vs. My Will

To the modern mind, the sense that we are not masters of our own lives is frequently difficult to accept. We struggle against it in the way that some of our biblical ancestors struggled against the authority of God. The notion of free will is so taken for granted nowadays that, for some, even the idea that God's will is greater is not easy to accept.

Pluto symbolizes the individual struggle with the forces of fate; the individual will having to act within the constraints of God's will (or destiny or any other word you prefer).

A Variable Change Point

Appropriately for such a transcendental symbol, Pluto's highly elliptical orbit changes the timing of this crisis from generation to generation. In many generations in the past this age was never reached. This is not true for our times.

With a cycle of 248 years it is a long time before we really get to confront it: a quarter of that is sixty-two years. Pluto's orbit is so far from circular that from our point of view the quarter cycle is often much shorter than that—as short as thirty-six years. For people born in the second half of the twentieth century, this period is close to forty years, and so it arrives right in the middle of Neptune's challenge, as well as during the fundamental Uranian midlife crisis.

Dealing with matters of power leads to the discovery of our own power, and thus to our individual sense of purpose. We must also finally accept that we are not all-powerful, as we felt in our youth, and the acceptance of this is another stage of removing illusions and discovering who we really are. What a relief to find that we only start getting a real sense of purpose in our forties. With the cultural pressures towards individuality that we experience, sense of purpose is often expected a lot earlier, and far too soon.

With Pluto We Learn the Hard Way

The first turn in Pluto's cycle may come well before either Uranus' or Neptune's clocks sweep by. It serves to provide dramatic external evidence that there are some things in our lives that are simply right outside of our control. This is how we experience the lesson of power, through circumstances that challenge our power over our own lives. They may even present us directly with power issues or feelings of powerlessness.

Pluto is rarely subtle. It may be hidden underground much of the time, but for many people it is something like an atomic bomb when it finally does act. Dramatic events may happen, the nature of which are pretty much dependent on where Pluto's cycle was at the time of your birth. But even without this specific information it's usually easy to identify it from the turn of events happening around us.

Pluto Issues Can Be Fundamental

Because the issues of will are such significant ones, the crisis that occurs may often strike at the very core of the self. Just as in a cycle of frequencies such as music, when one of the areas of the cycle is activated, many others may resonate in response. Beginning as a change in one or two fundamental issues of life, the need to transform eventually spreads through every aspect.

Case History: Working Out What You Want

Jeff seemed to have it all—a great marriage and two wonderful children as well as a high-paying position in advertising that he had worked twenty years to reach.

At thirty-eight he was overlooked for a promotion, and soon saw a younger man promoted to the head of his (Jeff's) department. Although hurt, his loyalty kept him going and he was sure that things would look up soon. Just as his Pluto cycle changed, he was laid-off.

Although devastated, he relied heavily on his family to keep his sanity. Yet over the course of the following year, as his Uranus cycle slowly completed and his Neptune one began, his relationship fell apart. His wife divorced him not long after his forty-first birthday.

Neptune changes at this time often take over two years to play themselves out (check your worksheet). During this time Jeff was depressed and almost suicidal. He managed to survive by moving into a small flat and reviving his youthful love of mountain walks in the scenic Table Mountain at the heart of the city of Cape Town.

While his depression paralyzed him for nearly a year, he emptied his savings. Then he started working for a tourist company and began a search for meaning in life. Initially visiting psychics and gurus, he finally found a source of inspiration close to his heart although different from his upbringing, and began introducing more and more meditation and contemplation into his life.

By the time Jeff was forty-four, he had recovered from his years of loss and confusion and had an opportunity to start his own business—as a mountain tour guide. He had reconnected with his spirituality and with his love of nature, although he had a way to go with his emotional life.

Most important, he learned that by being forced to let go of all he held dear, he rediscovered himself and his true passions. As he learned more about himself and gave his real needs more time, he realized how false his life at the top had been.

Jeff hadn't even been aware that he was unhappy in his job or what his actual passion was, but the powerful effect of the three cycles together helped transform his life and allowed him to fulfill his purpose in life—even despite himself.

How Pluto Changed Madonna

In Madonna's table we find the circled P in 1996. This is the year Madonna began her grand transformation that would end up with her midlife crisis. This was the year *Evita* was released, the film she most wanted to make, and her first child Lourdes was born. The out-of-wedlock birth of Lourdes and her publicized intent to have a child represented Madonna finally exercising her self-confidence and power (Pluto) in a mature fashion. She entirely took charge of her own life, strangely echoing the "Papa Don't Preach" song about such pregnancies in 1989.

Uranus and Neptune in Later Life

If you have filled your worksheet into your later life you will find another U around sixty-two and a circled one at eighty-four. There may be an N in the Neptune column around your eighties.

Refresh your memory of when the Saturn cycle changes around the same ages by checking the Saturn column.

Around the age of sixty-three we experience the third turn of the Uranian cycle of change. At twenty-one and at forty-two it brought us uncertainty and freedom at the same time. Now at around sixty-three these same matters arise, although we must look at it slightly differently. At twenty-one we ask how to adjust the way we are being ourselves to be more successful in the world; at forty-two we learn what we mean by "ourselves," and at sixty-three we ask how to release *inner* obstructions to being ourselves.

Uranus finishes one complete cycle at about eighty-four. Although it is not common for people to experience this complete cycle, those who do often experience a total renewal. I know two ladies who reached this age, both Scottish, perhaps not surprisingly. One took up climbing hills and small mountains and the other finally confronted her psychic abilities after developing physical paralysis.

Dramatic changes certainly can occur, but these examples may be more extreme than the average experience. Nevertheless, the Uranus cycle represents shifts in ways of perceiving, thinking and understanding well beyond those of early life.

Since Neptune can reappear in life around the eighties or nineties, another phase of spiritual growth and potential confusion is due. There is the potential for this to be a profoundly spiritual time of life, although, of course, the usual Neptunian experiences of confusion, loss and inspiration are likely to be the triggers for it.

Perhaps this sometimes emerges in an apparently delusional fashion, but I am sure that is simply from the point of view of everyone down here, in the pre-Neptunian way of seeing things.

Using Uranus, Neptune, and Pluto Now

We do not need to wait until the midlife crisis or our senior years to make use of these three cycles. In fact, their crossover points with all the other cycles in our lives produce many of the great changes, challenges and opportunities we face in our lives.

At the beginning of this chapter you identified cycle crossings on your worksheet. Work with the dates that cycles cross as you read the rest of this chapter.

Interpreting Overlapping Cycles

You now have an understanding of how all the basic cycles of life work and what they represent. You also know that these last three of them are not only life cycles but agents of change. To predict changes shown by overlapping cycles, all we need to do is add the principle of each change cycle to the principle of the cycle that it overlaps with.

As we did when we looked at Venus and Mars in chapter seven, we're combining the basic meanings of two cycles to predict a change. For example, Uranus = sudden changes, Venus = romantic life; Uranus crosses Venus = sudden changes in romantic life. When we looked at Jupiter crossing the Sun cycle earlier a similar principle was in operation (gain + self = gains to the self.) In fact, crossovers of the sun are particularly significant.

Of course, it will take time to really unlock this power, but you can start using these cycles to ensure greater success in all your undertakings, and even understand *why* things are happening to you at any particular time, even when you can't change them.

Accurately Predicting Change

Prediction is a thorny subject because it challenges our beliefs about fate and free will, and many twenty-first century people, including many astrologers, don't like to believe that prediction is possible.

Now you can decide for yourself, because this chapter is not composed of wild, theoretical claims but of factors you can test in your own life. You can find out in a few minutes if the system works, by testing it against events that have happened in your past.

A Primer on Overlapping Cycles

What follows is a brief guide to interpreting the overlapping of the remaining cycles. Bear in mind that the qualities of our individual cycles vary, although the principles remain the same. Each of us is unique and will express universal archetypes in a unique way. Your own experience will soon give you an idea of how these cycles work for you, because they tend to be similar each time they recur. For example, once you know the kind of thing that happens in your life when your Saturn cycle overlaps with your Sun, you can expect more or less the same kind of thing every time that happens.

Don't believe everything you read; test it for yourself. Check when planets have overlapped in the past and use the interpretation guide below to see what should have happened.

Use Table 7 as you did in chapter 7. In this table the first planet refers to the planet number in the **present or future** and the second planet refers to the planet number on **your birthday**.

Some examples from Madonna's cycles:

- Madonna has a number of Saturn crossings in 1962–64. The planet can be found in the columns of the Sun, Venus, Mars, Uranus, Neptune and Pluto. At this time her mother became ill and died of cancer.

- In 1976–78 Saturn and Uranus are very prominent. This is when she graduated from high school and set out to be a singer, meeting many of the people who become important in establishing her success.

- Uranus crosses her Sun in 1979–1980, the same period of her twenty-one-year old Uranus freedom cycle, the year she went to New York.

- In 1983–1985 Saturn again makes a group of crossings to the same series of planets (the patterns always repeat themselves.) At the same time, Pluto crosses Venus. At this time she made her first album, which contained her first hit. The film *Desperately Seeking Susan* was made and her image and career exploded into the world.

- She met and married Sean Penn in 1985, the year Saturn sat on her Sun and Pluto positions. As you may expect if you read about these combinations in the Primer, this was bound to be an explosive marriage. Madonna herself referred to her helicopter-infested wedding as "like Vietnam."

- She got divorced, changed her style with the shocking *Like a Prayer* album and video and met Warren Beatty in 1989. Pluto crossed her Mars and Uranus positions that year. Read about Pluto-Uranus and Pluto-Mars in the table and you'll see why this was happening.

- The seven-year Saturn crossing of all the other planets happened again in 1991–93, the years she released the controversial book *Sex*, the documentary *Truth or Dare/In Bed with Madonna,* and a couple of other disastrous-as-usual films. Pluto once again crossed her Sun at the same time.

EPILOGUE
GENERATIONS OF CYCLES

Mastering our own cycles that reflect the rhythms of our souls is only the first step in reconnecting ourselves with the cosmos. Once again we take our place as part of the great symphony of nature instead of snatching the conductor's baton and trying to control it all ourselves. Just as the cycles of nature embrace both the tiniest pulsation and the entire universe itself, so do our human cycles extend from the daily beat of the circadian rhythm to vast generational cycles that encompass the sweep of history.

In recent times, we have been plagued by our cultural obsession with the calendar. The arrival of the twenty-first century was heralded by a media frenzy that elevated the last year of the twentieth century, the year 2000, to the focus of all our efforts, errors, and predictions of the past.

Undoubtedly that mystical string of zeroes enchanted us, an enchantment that itself harks back to an earlier time when we understood the magic of how numbers show themselves in nature. However, that obsession also highlighted just how far we have detached ourselves from our natural rhythms, far enough to believe that an arbitrary calendar, incorrectly calculated by a minority culture and clearly related to specific religious beliefs, could somehow reflect a deeper force of nature. Many people genuinely believed that something on the scale of the end of the world would happen *just because of the calendar date.* This was a level of superstition unseen since the Dark Ages.

Perhaps in that very belief lies the hope that we will once again attune ourselves to something bigger. Perhaps our willingness to accept a string of zeroes as a determinant of destiny reflects a deeper memory, that there are indeed great cycles that slowly play themselves out as the fated events of history. For just as the daily, monthly, yearly and other human cycles reflect our deeper human processes, so do these slow rhythms of history itself.

The most familiar of these slow cycles is probably that of the great ages. These cycles of approximately 2,000 years have been discussed by many thinkers in many sources and are probably one of the contributors to otherwise-rational people's belief that the year 2000 could mean something greater. Most people have heard of the New Age or the Age of Aquarius, the common terminology for these great cycles of history. In fact, these are 2,160-year periods during which the vernal equinox point in the sky—the beginning of the zodiac—gradually moves backwards through one of the zodiac signs.

It has long been recognized that each of these transits of the vernal equinox backwards through an individual sign reflects an era in history somehow reminiscent of that sign. These periods of a little over 2,000 years are called "Great Ages." The appellation "Age of Aquarius" refers to the forthcoming Great Age. We stand at its cusp, although it may be another one or two hundred years before we actually enter that age.

These ages are used to explain great religious movements in history, among other things that last so long. The current age, the Age of Pisces, started at approximately the time of Christ's birth, and has been characterized by a religion based on compassion, belief in sacrifice, and use of the symbol of the fish (Pisces) as its own—the Christian religion. Compassion, sacrifice and fish are, of course, all symbols of Pisces.

The 2,000-odd years before that was the Age of Aries the ram. During this time, the Jewish religion was at its height, a religion that used as its symbol the ram's horn and sacrificed sheep. Genesis and Exodus are replete with God stating "I am" and emphasizing his exclusivity, which is not so dissimilar to the "I am" concept that, to this day, characterizes the sign Aries.

In the years prior to 2000 B.C. cattle worship dominated the planet, and this was of course the age of Taurus the bull. The biblical story of Moses burning the golden calf and asserting the might of the "I am" god is probably a cultural myth of the transition from Taurus into Aries.

Clearly, we need to look beyond our own personal cycles to understand our place in the larger scheme of things. What does this mean for the Age of Aquarius? Although none of us will live to see it, despite the hope and insistence of New Age faddists determined to usher in an era of peace and love, we do need to understand it better to understand our own place in history.

The appearance of people rejecting their past and trying to hasten the arrival of heaven on Earth is not unlike many other religions and eras of history, but has little to do with the Great Ages themselves. After all, at the time of Christ many believed the temple would be restored along with the Aries god of the Jews.

The Age of Aquarius will not be an age of universal friendship and equality (the idealized characteristics of Aquarius) any more than the Christian era was universally one of compassion and spirituality (the best of Pisces). We needn't be concerned that the current lack of focus, lack of spirituality and total disconnection from anything so characteristic of these end-of-age "New Agers" will characterize the next 2,000 years!

The Age of Aquarius will most likely be the age of technology and, like all the others, will undoubtedly have a major religion at its center. This religion will probably be connected to technology and will reflect the Aquarian ideals of universal equality as much as it will reflect the revolutionary and dramatic violence also characteristic of that sign.

Understanding these greater cycles helps us locate ourselves in the greater scheme of things, and helps us let go of the vanity that we are a last generation, an enlightened one that will transcend the difficulties of this Earth. It is a sad reflection of our too-materialistic culture that our concept of salvation has become the transformation of the physical body or the achievement of peace and harmony in the physical realm rather than in some spiritual form.

We do need to harmonize ourselves with these greater cycles just as we need to do with our own personal ones. There are cycles that are much shorter than 2,160 years, cycles that help locate us as part of a generation of our peers. Many of the cycles that have been discussed in this book describe periods that can help us understand more immediate history—for example, the overlap of the Saturn and Uranus cycle whose beginning points coincide every thirty-seven years, or of Uranus and Neptune, which start again together every 171 years. Research into types of social and political changes that occur at these intervals would reveal much more about history and its events than a study of textbooks biased by the justification of their eras.

Truly, we are creatures of spirit: in some way, this body and this Earth are something we use to engage our experience and learning. There is no need to liberate ourselves from the body or create a perfect Earth; it is the very pain and problems of the physical world that teach us the lessons we are trying to learn.

If we understand ourselves better, we understand ourselves to be part of the greater picture. It is through understanding our soul cycles that we can shake the dominance of our materialistic egos and see ourselves as a tiny but beautiful part of a much greater and more awe-inspiring picture.

As simple as the system of cycles is, this is only the beginning. There are many personal cycles that cannot be calculated with simplified tables such as the ones here; cycles that represent powerful and fundamental changes that happen in our identity, our domestic lives, our relationships and our professions. In fact, these are the main timing cycles for predictive astrology and the ones that give it the remarkable precision it has when working with accurately drawn horoscope charts. These are not in this book, but I hope this book has inspired you to consult an astrologer who can calculate these for you and help you synchronize your conscious self even more fully to the urges of those deeper pre-conscious forces that actually shape our destinies.

As I have indicated throughout this book, a proper understanding of astrology will give you a much more detailed and reliable picture. However, even then a lot will remain unknown. Because of the prejudices of history and the ever-changing fads of knowledge and belief, after thousands of years we still know very little about the relationship between the cosmos and ourselves. Astrology may well be the best way we have to study this relationship, but even so, it is a rudimentary tool in comparison to the marvels of the human being and of the cosmos.

Nevertheless, astrology is about ourselves, not about numbers and calculations. Once we take a conscious part in observing and understanding our cycles, we transcend the limitations of the human tools we use to measure them. We can learn to understand the nuances of our own cycles by a continual awareness of them, precisely the way we learn to understand other subtle things like dreams. Using them to control or predict your life is a little excessive, even if it seems possible eventually. The purpose is to learn to ride them like a surfer learns a wave: the wave has a force and direction of its own, which cannot be controlled, but which can be safely ridden by experienced riders to get where they want to go.

The cycles are the flow of your life, just like the aging of your body is its physical flow. It is a process of life, unchangeable and unavoidable, but one that can certainly be mastered. Learning to master this process would be a symbol for the mastery of life itself. So it seems that if we prioritize this lesson in our lives, it could give us a clear sense of purpose.

We experience a lack of purpose because we imagine that "purpose" should be on some kind of grand scale. We tend to think that our purpose must impact the world in some way. It is not so.

Our most common purpose is to master life itself: only in this way do we truly serve something greater than ourselves. To live, we must be brave and willing to master the process of life itself, to *be* ourselves as fully as everything else in nature seems capable of being. As each living thing lives according to its cycles, which give it an unfailing program for success, we have the potential to do the same.

Just as the butterfly emerges through a natural and cyclical process, so do we. We just have to drop all the stuff that we want and expect, to let go and allow things to happen. We need to observe, understand and react, but not control. This is our purpose, and this is why we need only understand our own cycles to be able to achieve something that fits into a larger purpose. The rose becomes a rose by being true to its nature, not by striving but by being.

Being our fullest selves, being human. In this way we will come to know ourselves, and in knowing ourselves we will not need to look outside of ourselves for answers, not even to the heavens above.

APPENDIX
CREATING YOUR OWN GRAPHICAL VIEW

If you are visually minded or even if you just want a new, holistic way to look at the flow of the worksheet, you can draw a graph similar to the one on my friends' fridge in New York. It allows you to synthesize everything you have learned.

The graph is at the back of the book with all the tables. It might look quite busy at first glance, but actually it's pretty simple. The graph is read from left to right and from top to bottom. From left to right are the years 2001 to 2010, and from top to bottom are the positions of each planetary cycle, numbered from 0 to 90 just as they are in the tables. Those strange curly lines crossing the chart from top to bottom are the planetary cycles; now you can see what they look like. You don't have to know too much to understand how to use them, just follow the step-by-step instructions and it will all become clear.

Optional Step: Filling in the Graph

- Starting with your Sun number, find this number on the scale that runs down the left-hand column of the graph. Now, using a red pen and a ruler, draw a straight line from this position on the left-

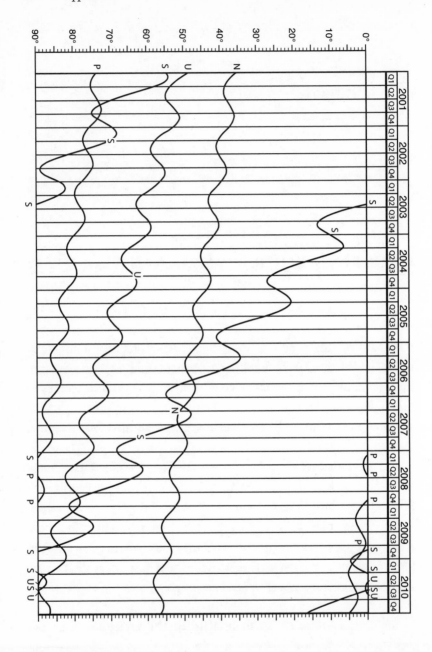

hand scale to the same position on the right-hand scale, and label the line "Sun."

- Do the same for each of your other numbers: Venus, Mars, Saturn, Uranus, Neptune and Pluto.

- Now look at each of the seven red lines you have just drawn. Each one is crossed a number of times by the printed black curly lines that represent the planetary cycles during the years 2001 to 2010. Every time a red line is crossed over by a black line, or by a little group of black lines, circle the crossing point. (Check the example chart that has been filled out if you are unsure of what to do.)

Each of those circled crossing points is an overlapping cycle. If you follow the curly black line to one of the edges of the graph, you'll see the planet name of the cycle. So, if the black line for Saturn crosses over the red line of your Sun at some point, that is a Saturn overlap of your Sun. When Saturn crosses over its own line, that marks a quarter-cycle change of the Saturn cycle.

You'll also notice that most crossings by one planet over another occur three times in close succession, because the curly black lines go up and down. This is that strange phenomenon of retrograde motion, and you can see it taking place by noticing how those black lines appear to move.

This graph has a number of advantages over a simple list: first, it allows you to look at the whole eight-year period in a single glance. Second, it allows you to see when many crossings happen simultaneously or close together in time. Circles crossings that are vertically in line with one another happen at the same time—a powerful indicator of multiple cycle influences. You can also see the sequence of time more clearly this way. It doesn't take long to get used to reading it, and it is quite amazing when you see how effectively it describes changes in your life.

Your graph is actually a simplified version of the graph that a professional astrologer would use and which shows twice as much information as this one. For that reason, some changes won't be reflected on this graph. In fact, the graph is the most powerful way to see the changes that overlapping cycles describe all in one place at one time. It is the tool you can use to unify all the information in one place, and this single piece of paper may be one of the most effective oracles.

---

1. Astrologers typically measure another four intermediate change points as well, using a forty-five-based system (the "eighth harmonic" aspects) rather than the ninety-based one presented here.

Table 1: Sun Cycle Numbers

Dates in this table appear day/month/year

Date	Sun - all	Sun - Jup	Date	Sun - all	Sun - Jup
1/1	10	40	8/2	49	79
2/1	11	41	9/2	50	80
3/1	12	42	10/2	51	81
4/1	13	43	11/2	52	82
5/1	14	44	12/2	53	83
6/1	15	45	13/2	54	84
7/1	16	46	14/2	55	85
8/1	17	47	15/2	56	86
9/1	18	48	16/2	57	87
10/1	19	49	17/2	58	88
11/1	20	50	18/2	59	89
12/1	21	51	19/2	60	90
13/1	22	52	20/2	61	91
14/1	23	53	21/2	62	92
15/1	24	54	22/2	63	93
16/1	25	55	23/2	64	94
17/1	26	56	24/2	65	95
18/1	27	57	25/2	66	96
19/1	28	58	26/2	67	97
20/1	29	59	27/2	68	98
21/1	30	60	28/2	69	99
22/1	31	61	1/3	70	100
23/1	32	62	2/3	71	101
24/1	33	63	3/3	72	102
25/1	34	64	4/3	73	103
26/1	35	65	5/3	74	104
27/1	36	66	6/3	75	105
28/1	37	67	7/3	76	106
29/1	38	68	8/3	77	107
30/1	39	69	9/3	78	108
31/1	40	70	10/3	79	109
1/2	41	71	11/3	80	110
2/2	43	73	12/3	81	111
3/2	44	74	13/3	82	112
4/2	45	75	14/3	83	113
5/2	46	76	15/3	84	114
6/2	47	77	16/3	85	115
7/2	48	78	17/3	86	116

Dates in this table appear day/month/year

Date	Sun - all	Sun - Jup	Date	Sun - all	Sun - Jup
18/3	87	117	26/4	35	35
19/3	88	118	27/4	36	36
20/3	89	119	28/4	37	37
21/3	90	120	29/4	38	38
22/3	1	1	30/4	39	39
23/3	2	2	1/5	40	40
24/3	3	3	2/5	41	41
25/3	4	4	3/5	42	42
26/3	5	5	4/5	43	43
27/3	6	6	5/5	44	44
28/3	7	7	6/5	45	45
29/3	8	8	7/5	46	46
30/3	9	9	8/5	47	47
31/3	10	10	9/5	48	48
1/4	11	11	10/5	49	49
2/4	12	12	11/5	50	50
3/4	13	13	12/5	51	51
4/4	14	14	13/5	52	52
5/4	15	15	14/5	53	53
6/4	16	16	15/5	54	54
7/4	17	17	16/5	55	55
8/4	18	18	17/5	55	55
9/4	19	19	18/5	56	56
10/4	20	20	19/5	57	57
11/4	20	20	20/5	58	58
12/4	21	21	21/5	59	59
13/4	22	22	22/5	60	60
14/4	23	23	23/5	61	61
15/4	24	24	24/5	62	62
16/4	25	25	25/5	63	63
17/4	26	26	26/5	64	64
18/4	27	27	27/5	65	65
19/4	28	28	28/5	66	66
20/4	29	29	29/5	67	67
21/4	30	30	30/5	68	68
22/4	31	31	31/5	69	69
23/4	32	32	1/6	70	70
24/4	33	33	2/6	71	71
25/4	34	34	3/6	72	72

Table 1   *151*

Dates in this table appear day/month/year

Date	Sun - all	Sun - Jup	Date	Sun - all	Sun - Jup
4/6	73	73	13/7	20	110
5/6	74	74	14/7	21	111
6/6	75	75	15/7	22	112
7/6	76	76	16/7	23	113
8/6	77	77	117/7	24	114
9/6	78	78	118/7	25	115
10/6	79	79	19/7	26	116
11/6	79	79	20/7	27	117
12/6	80	80	21/7	28	118
13/6	81	81	22/7	29	119
14/6	82	82	23/7	30	120
15/6	83	83	24/7	31	1
16/6	84	84	25/7	31	1
17/6	85	85	26/7	32	2
18/6	86	86	27/7	33	3
19/6	87	87	28/7	34	4
20/6	88	88	29/7	35	5
21/6	89	89	30/7	36	6
22/6	90	90	31/7	37	7
23/6	1	91	1/8	38	8
24/6	2	92	2/8	39	9
25/6	3	93	3/8	40	10
26/6	4	94	4/8	41	11
27/6	5	95	5/8	42	12
28/6	6	96	6/8	43	13
29/6	7	97	7/8	44	14
30/6	8	98	8/8	45	15
1/7	9	99	9/8	46	16
2/7	10	100	10/8	47	17
3/7	10	100	11/8	48	18
4/7	11	101	12/8	49	19
5/7	12	102	13/8	50	20
6/7	13	103	14/8	51	21
7/7	14	104	15/8	52	22
8/7	15	105	16/8	53	23
9/7	16	106	17/8	53	23
10/7	17	107	18/8	54	24
11/7	18	108	19/8	55	25
12/7	19	109	20/8	56	26

Dates in this table appear day/month/year

Date	Sun - all	Sun - Jup	Date	Sun - all	Sun - Jup
21/8	57	27	29/9	5	65
22/8	58	28	30/9	6	66
23/8	59	29	1/10	7	67
24/8	60	30	2/10	8	68
25/8	61	31	3/10	9	69
26/8	62	32	4/10	10	70
27/8	63	33	5/10	11	71
28/8	64	34	6/10	12	72
29/8	65	35	7/10	13	73
30/8	66	36	8/10	14	74
31/8	67	37	9/10	15	75
1/9	68	38	10/10	16	76
2/9	69	39	11/10	17	77
3/9	70	40	12/10	18	78
4/9	71	41	13/10	19	79
5/9	72	42	14/10	20	80
6/9	73	43	15/10	21	81
7/9	74	44	16/10	22	82
8/9	75	45	17/10	23	83
9/9	76	46	18/10	24	84
10/9	77	47	19/10	25	85
11/9	78	48	20/10	26	86
12/9	79	49	21/10	27	87
13/9	80	50	22/10	28	88
14/9	81	51	23/10	29	89
15/9	82	52	24/10	30	90
16/9	83	53	25/10	31	91
17/9	83	53	26/10	32	92
18/9	84	54	27/10	33	93
19/9	85	55	28/10	34	94
20/9	86	56	29/10	35	95
21/9	87	57	30/10	36	96
22/9	88	58	31/10	37	97
23/9	89	59	1/11	38	98
24/9	90	60	2/11	39	99
25/9	1	61	3/11	40	100
26/9	2	62	4/11	41	101
27/9	3	63	5/11	42	102
28/9	4	64	6/11	43	103

Table 1   153

Dates in this table appear day/month/year

Date	Sun - all	Sun - Jup	Date	Sun - all	Sun - Jup
7/11	44	104	5/12	72	12
8/11	45	105	6/12	73	13
9/11	46	106	7/12	74	14
10/11	47	107	8/12	75	15
11/11	48	108	9/12	76	16
12/11	49	109	10/12	77	17
13/11	50	110	11/12	78	18
14/11	51	111	12/12	79	19
15/11	52	112	13/12	80	20
16/11	53	113	14/12	81	21
17/11	54	114	15/12	82	22
18/11	55	115	16/12	83	23
19/11	56	116	17/12	84	24
20/11	57	117	18/12	85	25
21/11	58	118	19/12	86	26
22/11	59	119	20/12	87	27
23/11	60	120	221/12	88	28
24/11	61	1	22/12	90	30
25/11	62	2	23/12	1	31
26/11	63	3	24/12	2	32
27/11	64	4	25/12	3	33
28/11	65	5	226/12	4	34
29/11	66	6	27/12	5	35
30/11	67	7	28/12	6	36
1/12	68	8	29/12	7	37
2/12	69	9	30/12	8	38
3/12	70	10	31/12	9	39
4/12	71	11			

Table 2: Cycle Numbers for Jupiter to Pluto

Dates in this table appear day/month/year

Date	Jupiter	Saturn	Uranus	Neptune	Pluto
01/01/1940	1	24	48	86	32
21/1/1940	4	25	48	85	32
10/2/1940	8	26	48	85	31
1/3/1940	12	28	48	85	31
21/3/1940	17	30	49	84	31
10/4/1940	21	33	50	83	31
30/4/1940	26	35	51	83	31
20/5/1940	31	38	52	83	31
9/6/1940	35	40	54	83	31
29/6/1940	39	42	55	83	32
19/7/1940	42	43	55	83	32
08/08/1940	44	44	56	84	33
28/8/1940	46	45	56	84	33
17/9/1940	45	44	56	85	34
7/10/1940	44	43	56	86	34
27/10/1940	42	42	55	87	34
16/11/1940	39	40	54	87	34
6/12/1940	37	39	53	88	34
26/12/1940	36	38	53	88	34
15/1/1941	36	38	52	88	33
4/2/1941	38	39	52	87	33
24/2/1941	40	40	52	87	33
16/3/1941	44	42	53	86	32
5/4/1941	8	44	54	86	32
25/4/1941	53	46	55	85	32
15/5/1941	57	49	56	85	32
4/6/1941	62	51	57	85	33
24/6/1941	67	54	58	85	33
14/7/1941	71	56	59	85	34
3/8/1941	75	57	60	86	34
23/8/1941	78	58	60	86	35
12/9/1941	80	59	60	87	35
2/10/1941	81	58	60	88	36
22/10/1941	81	57	60	89	36
11/11/1941	80	56	59	89	36
1/12/1941	77	54	58	90	36
21/12/1941	75	53	57	90	35
10/01/1942	73	52	57	90	35
30/1/1942	71	52	56	90	35
19/2/1942	72	52	56	89	34
11/3/1942	73	54	57	89	34

Dates in this table appear day/month/year

Date	Jupiter	Saturn	Uranus	Neptune	Pluto
31/3/1942	76	55	58	88	34
20/4/1942	79	58	59	88	33
10/5/1942	83	60	60	87	34
30/5/1942	87	63	61	87	34
19/6/1942	92	65	62	87	34
9/7/1942	97	68	63	87	35
29/7/1942	101	70	64	88	35
18/8/1942	105	71	64	88	36
7/9/1942	109	72	65	89	36
27/9/1942	112	73	64	90	37
17/10/1942	114	72	64	90	37
6/11/1942	115	71	63	1	37
26/11/1942	115	70	63	2	37
16/12/1942	113	68	62	2	37
5/1/1943	111	67	61	2	37
25/1/1943	108	66	61	2	36
14/2/1943	106	66	61	2	36
6/3/1943	105	66	61	1	35
26/3/1943	105	68	61	1	35
15/4/1943	107	70	62	90	35
5/5/1943	109	72	63	90	35
25/5/1943	113	74	65	89	35
14/6/1943	117	77	66	89	36
4/7/1943	1	79	67	89	36
24/7/1943	5	82	68	90	37
13/8/1943	9	84	68	90	37
2/9/1943	14	85	69	1	38
22/9/1943	18	86	69	2	38
12/10/1943	21	87	69	2	39
1/11/1943	24	86	68	3	39
21/11/1943	26	85	67	4	39
11/12/1943	27	84	66	4	39
31/12/1943	27	82	66	4	38
20/1/1944	25	81	65	4	38
9/2/1944	22	80	65	4	37
29/2/1944	20	80	65	4	37
20/3/1944	18	80	65	3	37
9/4/1944	17	82	66	2	36
29/4/1944	17	84	67	2	36
19/5/1944	19	86	68	2	37
8/6/1944	21	88	69	1	37
28/6/1944	25	1	71	2	37
18/7/1944	28	4	72	2	38
7/8/1944	33	6	72	2	39

Table 2 157

Dates in this table appear day/month/year

Date	Jupiter	Saturn	Uranus	Neptune	Pluto
27/8/1944	37	8	73	3	39
16/9/1944	41	10	73	4	40
6/10/1944	45	11	73	4	40
26/10/1944	49	11	73	5	40
15/11/1944	53	10	72	6	40
5/12/1944	55	9	71	6	40
25/12/1944	57	8	70	6	40
14/1/1945	57	6	70	6	39
3/2/1945	57	5	69	6	39
23/2/1945	55	4	69	6	39
15/3/1945	52	4	69	5	38
4/4/1945	50	5	70	5	38
24/4/1945	48	6	71	4	38
14/5/1945	48	8	72	4	38
3/6/1945	48	10	73	4	38
23/6/1945	50	13	74	4	39
13/7/1945	52	15	75	4	39
2/8/1945	56	18	76	4	40
22/8/1945	59	20	77	5	40
11/9/1945	63	22	77	6	41
1/10/1945	68	24	77	6	41
21/10/1945	72	25	77	7	42
10/11/1945	76	25	77	8	42
30/11/1945	80	24	76	8	42
20/12/1945	83	23	75	9	42
9/1/1946	86	22	74	9	41
29/1/1946	87	20	74	9	41
18/2/1946	87	19	73	8	40
10/3/1946	86	18	74	8	40
30/3/1946	84	18	74	7	40
19/4/1946	82	19	75	7	39
9/5/1946	79	20	76	6	40
29/5/1946	78	22	77	6	40
18/6/1946	77	24	78	6	40
8/7/1946	78	27	79	6	41
28/7/1946	80	29	80	6	41
17/8/1946	83	32	81	7	42
6/9/1946	86	34	82	7	42
26/9/1946	90	36	82	8	43
16/10/1946	94	38	82	9	43
5/11/1946	99	39	81	10	43
25/11/1946	103	39	80	10	43
15/12/1946	107	38	80	11	43
4/1/1947	111	37	79	11	43

Dates in this table appear day/month/year

Date	Jupiter	Saturn	Uranus	Neptune	Pluto
24/1/1947	114	36	78	11	42
13/2/1947	116	34	78	11	42
5/3/1947	117	33	78	10	42
25/3/1947	117	32	78	10	41
14/4/1947	116	32	79	9	41
4/5/1947	114	33	80	9	41
24/5/1947	111	34	81	8	41
13/6/1947	109	36	82	8	42
3/7/1947	108	38	83	8	42
23/7/1947	108	41	84	8	43
12/8/1947	109	43	85	9	43
1/9/1947	111	46	86	9	44
21/9/1947	114	48	86	10	44
11/10/1947	117	50	86	11	45
31/10/1947	1	52	86	12	45
20/11/1947	6	52	85	12	45
10/12/1947	10	53	84	13	45
30/12/1947	15	52	84	13	45
19/1/1948	19	51	83	13	44
8/2/1948	23	49	82	13	44
28/2/1948	26	48	82	12	43
19/3/1948	28	47	82	12	43
8/4/1948	29	46	83	11	43
28/4/1948	29	46	84	11	43
18/5/1948	27	47	85	11	43
7/6/1948	25	48	86	10	43
27/6/1948	23	50	87	10	43
17/7/1948	20	52	88	10	44
6/8/1948	19	54	89	11	45
26/8/1948	19	57	90	11	45
15/9/1948	20	60	90	12	46
5/10/1948	23	62	1	13	46
25/10/1948	26	64	90	13	46
14/11/1948	30	65	90	14	47
4/12/1948	34	66	89	15	47
24/12/1948	39	66	88	15	46
13/1/1949	43	66	88	15	46
2/2/1949	48	64	87	15	45
22/2/1949	52	63	87	15	45
14/3/1949	56	61	87	14	45
3/4/1949	59	60	87	14	44
23/4/1949	61	59	88	13	44
13/5/1949	62	59	88	13	44
2/6/1949	62	60	90	13	44

Table 2   159

Dates in this table appear day/month/year

Date	Jupiter	Saturn	Uranus	Neptune	Pluto
22/6/1949	61	62	1	12	45
12/7/1949	58	63	2	12	45
1/8/1949	56	66	3	13	46
21/8/1949	54	68	4	13	47
10/9/1949	52	71	5	14	47
30/9/1949	53	73	5	15	48
20/10/1949	54	75	5	15	48
9/11/1949	56	77	5	16	48
29/11/1949	60	79	4	17	48
19/12/1949	64	79	3	17	48
8/1/1950	68	79	2	17	48
28/1/1950	73	79	2	17	47
17/2/1950	78	77	1	17	47
9/3/1950	82	76	1	17	46
29/3/1950	87	74	1	16	46
18/4/1950	90	73	2	16	46
8/5/1950	94	73	2	15	46
28/5/1950	96	73	3	15	46
17/6/1950	97	73	5	15	46
7/7/1950	97	75	6	15	47
27/7/1950	96	77	7	15	47
16/8/1950	94	79	8	15	48
5/9/1950	91	81	9	16	49
25/9/1950	89	84	9	17	49
15/10/1950	88	86	9	17	50
4/11/1950	88	88	9	18	50
24/11/1950	89	90	9	19	50
14/12/1950	92	2	8	19	50
3/1/1951	95	2	7	19	49
23/1/1951	99	2	6	20	49
12/2/1951	104	2	6	19	49
4/3/1951	108	90	5	19	48
24/3/1951	113	89	5	19	48
13/4/1951	118	87	6	18	47
3/5/1951	3	86	6	18	47
23/5/1951	7	86	7	17	48
12/6/1951	10	86	8	17	48
2/7/1951	12	86	10	17	48
22/7/1951	14	88	11	17	49
11/8/1951	14	90	12	17	49
31/8/1951	13	2	13	18	50
20/9/1951	11	4	14	18	51
10/10/1951	8	7	14	19	51
30/10/1951	6	9	14	20	51

Dates in this table appear day/month/year

Date	Jupiter	Saturn	Uranus	Neptune	Pluto
19/11/1951	4	11	14	21	52
9/12/1951	4	13	13	21	51
29/12/1951	6	14	12	22	51
18/1/1952	8	15	11	22	51
7/2/1952	11	15	11	22	50
27/2/1952	16	14	10	21	50
18/3/1952	20	13	10	21	50
7/4/1952	25	11	10	20	49
27/4/1952	30	10	11	20	49
17/5/1952	34	9	11	19	49
6/6/1952	39	8	12	19	49
26/6/1952	43	8	14	19	50
16/7/1952	46	9	15	19	50
5/8/1952	49	11	16	19	51
25/8/1952	51	12	17	20	52
14/9/1952	51	15	18	20	52
4/10/1952	50	17	18	21	53
24/10/1952	48	20	19	22	53
13/11/1952	45	22	18	23	53
3/12/1952	43	24	18	23	53
23/12/1952	41	26	17	24	53
12/1/1953	41	27	16	24	53
1/2/1953	42	27	15	24	52
21/2/1953	44	27	15	24	52
13/3/1953	48	26	14	23	51
2/4/1953	52	25	14	23	51
22/4/1953	56	23	15	22	51
12/5/1953	61	22	16	22	51
1/6/1953	65	21	16	21	51
21/6/1953	70	21	18	21	51
11/7/1953	74	21	19	21	52
31/7/1953	78	22	20	21	52
20/8/1953	82	23	21	22	53
9/9/1953	84	25	22	22	54
29/9/1953	86	27	23	23	54
19/10/1953	86	30	23	24	55
8/11/1953	86	32	23	24	55
28/11/1953	83	34	23	25	55
18/12/1953	81	36	22	26	55
7/1/1954	78	38	21	26	55
27/1/1954	77	39	20	26	54
16/2/1954	76	39	20	26	54
8/3/1954	77	39	19	26	53
28/3/1954	80	38	19	25	53

Table 2   161

Dates in this table appear day/month/year

Date	Jupiter	Saturn	Uranus	Neptune	Pluto
17/4/1954	83	37	19	25	53
7/5/1954	86	35	20	24	53
27/5/1954	91	34	21	24	53
16/6/1954	95	33	22	23	53
6/7/1954	100	33	23	23	53
26/7/1954	104	33	24	23	54
15/8/1954	108	34	25	24	55
4/9/1954	112	35	26	24	55
24/9/1954	116	37	27	25	56
14/10/1954	118	39	28	26	56
3/11/1954	90	42	28	26	57
23/11/1954	90	44	28	27	57
13/12/1954	119	46	27	28	57
2/1/1955	117	48	26	28	57
22/1/1955	114	50	25	28	56
11/2/1955	112	51	25	28	56
3/3/1955	110	51	24	28	55
23/3/1955	110	51	24	28	55
12/4/1955	111	50	24	27	54
2/5/1955	113	48	24	26	54
22/5/1955	116	47	25	26	54
11/6/1955	90	46	26	26	55
1/7/1955	4	45	27	25	55
21/7/1955	8	45	28	26	56
10/8/1955	12	45	29	26	56
30/8/1955	17	46	30	26	57
19/9/1955	21	47	31	27	57
9/10/1955	25	49	32	27	58
29/10/1955	28	52	32	28	58
18/11/1955	30	54	32	29	59
8/12/1955	31	56	32	30	59
28/12/1955	31	58	31	30	58
17/1/1956	30	60	30	30	58
6/2/1956	28	62	30	30	58
26/2/1956	25	63	29	30	57
17/3/1956	23	63	28	30	57
6/4/1956	22	62	28	29	56
26/4/1956	22	61	28	29	56
16/5/1956	23	60	29	28	56
5/6/1956	25	58	30	28	56
25/6/1956	28	57	31	28	57
15/7/1956	31	56	32	28	57
4/8/1956	35	56	33	28	58
24/8/1956	40	57	34	28	58

Dates in this table appear day/month/year

Date	Jupiter	Saturn	Uranus	Neptune	Pluto
13/9/1956	44	58	35	29	59
3/10/1956	48	59	36	29	60
23/10/1956	52	61	37	30	60
12/11/1956	56	64	37	31	60
2/12/1956	59	66	37	32	60
22/12/1956	61	68	36	32	60
11/1/1957	62	70	36	32	60
31/1/1957	61	72	35	33	60
20/2/1957	60	73	34	33	59
12/3/1957	58	74	33	32	59
1/4/1957	55	74	33	32	58
21/4/1957	53	74	33	31	58
11/5/1957	52	73	33	31	58
31/5/1957	52	71	34	30	58
20/6/1957	53	70	35	30	58
10/7/1957	56	69	36	30	59
30/7/1957	59	68	37	30	59
19/8/1957	62	68	38	30	60
8/9/1957	66	68	40	31	61
28/9/1957	70	69	41	31	61
18/10/1957	75	71	41	32	62
7/11/1957	79	73	42	33	62
27/11/1957	83	75	42	33	62
17/12/1957	86	78	41	34	62
6/1/1958	89	80	41	35	62
26/1/1958	91	82	40	35	62
15/2/1958	92	84	39	35	61
7/3/1958	91	85	38	35	61
27/3/1958	89	86	38	34	60
16/4/1958	87	86	38	34	60
6/5/1958	84	85	38	33	60
26/5/1958	83	84	38	33	60
15/6/1958	82	82	39	32	60
5/7/1958	82	81	40	32	60
25/7/1958	84	80	41	32	61
14/8/1958	86	79	43	32	62
3/9/1958	89	79	44	33	62
23/9/1958	93	80	45	33	63
13/10/1958	97	81	46	34	64
2/11/1958	101	83	46	35	64
22/11/1958	106	85	46	35	64
12/12/1958	110	87	46	36	64
1/1/1959	114	89	46	37	64
21/1/1959	117	2	45	37	64

Table 2   163

Dates in this table appear day/month/year

Date	Jupiter	Saturn	Uranus	Neptune	Pluto
10/2/1959	90	4	44	37	63
2/3/1959	2	5	43	37	63
22/3/1959	2	7	43	36	62
11/4/1959	1	7	42	36	62
1/5/1959	119	7	42	35	62
21/5/1959	117	6	43	35	62
10/6/1959	114	5	43	35	62
30/6/1959	113	3	44	34	62
20/7/1959	112	2	45	34	63
9/8/1959	113	1	47	34	63
29/8/1959	114	90	48	35	64
18/9/1959	117	1	49	35	65
8/10/1959	90	1	50	36	65
28/10/1959	4	3	51	37	66
17/11/1959	9	4	51	37	66
7/12/1959	13	7	51	38	66
27/12/1959	18	9	51	39	66
16/1/1960	22	11	50	39	66
5/2/1960	26	13	49	39	65
25/2/1960	29	15	48	39	65
16/3/1960	32	17	48	39	64
5/4/1960	33	18	47	38	64
25/4/1960	34	18	47	38	64
15/5/1960	33	18	47	37	64
4/6/1960	31	17	48	37	64
24/6/1960	28	16	48	37	64
14/7/1960	26	15	50	36	64
3/8/1960	24	13	51	36	65
23/8/1960	24	12	52	37	66
12/9/1960	25	12	53	37	66
2/10/1960	26	12	54	38	67
22/10/1960	29	13	55	39	68
11/11/1960	33	14	56	39	68
1/12/1960	37	16	56	40	68
21/12/1960	42	18	56	41	68
10/1/1961	46	21	55	41	68
30/1/1961	51	23	54	41	68
19/2/1961	55	25	53	41	67
11/3/1961	59	27	53	41	67
31/3/1961	63	29	52	41	66
20/4/1961	65	30	52	40	66
10/5/1961	67	30	52	40	66
30/5/1961	67	30	52	39	66
19/6/1961	66	29	53	39	66

164   *Table 2*

Dates in this table appear day/month/year

Date	Jupiter	Saturn	Uranus	Neptune	Pluto
9/7/1961	64	27	54	39	66
29/7/1961	62	26	55	39	67
18/8/1961	59	25	56	39	67
7/9/1961	58	24	57	39	68
27/9/1961	57	23	58	40	69
17/10/1961	58	24	59	40	69
6/11/1961	60	24	60	41	70
26/11/1961	63	26	61	42	70
16/12/1961	67	28	61	43	70
5/1/1962	71	30	60	43	70
25/1/1962	76	33	59	43	70
14/2/1962	81	35	59	43	69
6/3/1962	86	37	58	43	69
26/3/1962	90	39	57	43	68
15/4/1962	94	40	57	43	68
5/5/1962	98	41	56	42	68
25/5/1962	100	41	57	42	68
14/6/1962	102	41	57	41	68
4/7/1962	103	40	58	41	68
24/7/1962	102	39	59	41	69
13/8/1962	100	37	60	41	69
2/9/1962	98	36	61	41	70
22/9/1962	95	35	63	42	71
12/10/1962	93	35	64	42	71
1/11/1962	93	35	65	43	72
21/11/1962	94	36	65	44	72
11/12/1962	96	38	65	44	72
31/12/1962	99	40	65	45	72
20/1/1963	103	42	65	45	72
9/2/1963	107	45	64	46	71
1/3/1963	112	47	63	46	71
21/3/1963	117	49	62	45	70
10/4/1963	1	51	62	45	70
30/4/1963	6	52	61	44	70
20/5/1963	10	53	61	44	70
9/6/1963	14	53	62	43	70
29/6/1963	17	53	62	43	70
19/7/1963	19	52	63	43	70
8/8/1963	19	50	64	43	71
28/8/1963	19	49	66	43	72
17/9/1963	17	47	67	44	72
7/10/1963	15	47	68	44	73
27/10/1963	12	46	69	45	74

Table 2 165

Dates in this table appear day/month/year

Date	Jupiter	Saturn	Uranus	Neptune	Pluto
16/11/1963	10	47	70	46	74
6/12/1963	10	48	70	46	74
26/12/1963	10	50	70	47	74
15/1/1964	12	52	70	48	74
4/2/1964	15	54	69	48	74
24/2/1964	19	57	68	48	73
15/3/1964	23	59	67	48	73
4/4/1964	28	61	67	47	72
24/4/1964	33	63	66	47	72
14/5/1964	38	64	66	46	72
3/6/1964	42	65	66	46	72
23/6/1964	46	65	67	45	72
13/7/1964	50	64	67	45	72
2/8/1964	53	63	69	45	73
22/8/1964	55	62	70	45	73
11/9/1964	56	60	71	46	74
1/10/1964	56	59	72	46	75
21/10/1964	54	58	73	47	75
10/11/1964	52	58	74	48	76
30/11/1964	49	59	75	48	76
20/12/1964	47	60	75	49	76
9/1/1965	46	62	75	50	76
29/1/1965	47	64	74	50	76
18/2/1965	49	67	73	50	75
10/3/1965	51	69	73	50	75
30/3/1965	55	71	72	50	74
19/4/1965	59	73	71	49	74
9/5/1965	64	75	71	49	74
29/5/1965	68	76	71	48	74
18/6/1965	73	77	71	48	74
8/7/1965	78	77	72	47	74
28/7/1965	82	77	73	47	75
17/8/1965	85	75	74	47	75
6/9/1965	88	74	75	48	76
26/9/1965	90	72	76	48	77
16/10/1965	91	71	78	49	77
5/11/1965	91	71	79	49	78
25/11/1965	89	71	79	50	78
15/12/1965	87	71	80	51	78
4/1/1966	84	73	80	52	78
24/1/1966	82	75	79	52	78
13/2/1966	81	77	79	52	78
5/3/1966	82	79	78	52	77

Table 2

Dates in this table appear day/month/year

Date	Jupiter	Saturn	Uranus	Neptune	Pluto
25/3/1966	84	82	77	52	77
14/4/1966	86	84	76	52	76
4/5/1966	90	86	76	51	76
24/5/1966	94	88	75	50	76
13/6/1966	98	89	76	50	76
3/7/1966	103	90	76	50	76
23/7/1966	107	90	77	49	77
12/8/1966	111	89	78	49	77
1/9/1966	115	88	79	50	78
21/9/1966	119	86	81	50	79
11/10/1966	2	85	82	51	79
31/10/1966	4	84	83	51	80
20/11/1966	4	83	84	52	80
10/12/1966	4	83	84	53	81
30/12/1966	2	84	84	53	81
19/1/1967	90	85	84	54	80
8/2/1967	117	87	84	54	80
28/2/1967	115	90	83	54	80
20/3/1967	114	2	82	54	79
9/4/1967	115	4	81	54	79
29/4/1967	117	7	81	53	78
19/5/1967	119	9	80	53	78
8/6/1967	3	11	80	52	78
28/6/1967	7	12	81	52	78
18/7/1967	11	12	81	52	79
7/8/1967	15	12	82	52	79
27/8/1967	20	12	83	52	80
16/9/1967	24	10	85	52	81
6/10/1967	28	9	86	53	81
26/10/1967	31	7	87	53	82
15/11/1967	34	6	88	54	82
5/12/1967	35	6	89	55	83
25/12/1967	36	6	89	55	83
14/1/1968	35	7	89	56	83
3/2/1968	33	8	89	56	82
23/2/1968	31	10	88	57	82
14/3/1968	28	13	87	56	81
3/4/1968	26	15	86	56	81
23/4/1968	26	18	86	56	81
13/5/1968	27	20	85	55	80
2/6/1968	28	22	85	55	80
22/6/1968	31	24	85	54	80
12/7/1968	34	25	86	54	81
1/8/1968	38	26	87	54	81

Table 2   167

Dates in this table appear day/month/year

Date	Jupiter	Saturn	Uranus	Neptune	Pluto
21/8/1968	42	25	88	54	82
10/9/1968	47	25	89	54	82
30/9/1968	51	23	90	55	83
20/10/1968	55	22	1	55	84
9/11/1968	59	20	2	56	84
29/11/1968	62	19	3	57	85
19/12/1968	64	19	4	57	85
8/1/1969	66	19	4	58	85
28/1/1969	66	20	4	58	85
17/2/1969	65	22	3	59	84
9/3/1969	63	24	3	59	84
29/3/1969	60	26	2	58	83
18/4/1969	58	29	1	58	83
8/5/1969	56	31	90	58	83
28/5/1969	56	33	90	57	82
17/6/1969	57	36	90	57	82
7/7/1969	59	37	90	56	83
27/7/1969	62	38	1	56	83
16/8/1969	65	39	2	56	84
5/9/1969	69	39	3	56	84
25/9/1969	73	38	4	57	85
15/10/1969	78	37	6	57	86
4/11/1969	82	35	7	58	87
24/11/1969	86	34	8	59	87
14/12/1969	90	32	8	59	87
3/1/1970	93	32	9	60	87
23/1/1970	95	32	9	60	87
12/2/1970	96	33	8	61	87
4/3/1970	96	35	8	61	86
24/3/1970	94	37	7	61	86
13/4/1970	92	40	6	60	85
3/5/1970	90	42	5	60	85
23/5/1970	88	45	5	59	85
12/6/1970	86	47	5	59	85
2/7/1970	86	49	5	58	85
22/7/1970	87	51	5	58	85
11/8/1970	89	52	6	58	86
31/8/1970	92	53	7	58	86
20/9/1970	96	52	8	59	87
10/10/1970	100	52	10	59	88
30/10/1970	104	50	11	60	89
19/11/1970	109	49	12	60	89
9/12/1970	113	47	13	61	90
29/12/1970	117	46	13	62	90

Dates in this table appear day/month/year

Date	Jupiter	Saturn	Uranus	Neptune	Pluto
18/1/1971	1	46	14	62	90
7/2/1971	4	46	13	63	89
27/2/1971	6	47	13	63	89
19/3/1971	6	49	12	63	88
8/4/1971	6	51	11	63	88
28/4/1971	5	53	10	62	87
18/5/1971	2	56	10	62	87
7/6/1971	90	59	9	61	87
27/6/1971	118	61	9	61	87
17/7/1971	117	63	10	60	87
6/8/1971	117	65	10	60	88
26/8/1971	118	66	11	60	89
15/9/1971	90	67	13	61	89
5/10/1971	4	66	14	61	90
25/10/1971	7	65	15	62	1
14/11/1971	12	64	16	62	1
4/12/1971	16	62	17	63	2
24/12/1971	21	61	18	64	2
13/1/1972	25	60	18	64	2
2/2/1972	29	60	18	65	2
22/2/1972	33	60	18	65	1
13/3/1972	36	61	17	65	1
2/4/1972	38	63	16	65	90
22/4/1972	38	65	16	65	90
12/5/1972	38	67	15	64	90
1/6/1972	36	70	14	64	89
21/6/1972	34	73	14	63	89
11/7/1972	31	75	14	63	90
31/7/1972	29	77	15	63	90
20/8/1972	29	79	16	62	1
9/9/1972	29	80	17	63	1
29/9/1972	30	81	18	63	2
19/10/1972	33	80	19	64	3
8/11/1972	36	79	20	64	3
28/11/1972	40	78	21	65	4
18/12/1972	45	76	22	66	4
7/1/1973	49	75	23	66	4
27/1/1973	54	74	23	67	4
16/2/1973	58	74	23	67	4
8/3/1973	63	74	22	67	4
28/3/1973	66	75	22	67	3
17/4/1973	69	77	21	67	2
7/5/1973	71	79	20	67	2
27/5/1973	72	82	19	66	2

Table 2   169

Dates in this table appear day/month/year

Date	Jupiter	Saturn	Uranus	Neptune	Pluto
16/6/1973	72	84	19	66	2
6/7/1973	70	87	19	65	2
26/7/1973	68	89	19	65	2
15/8/1973	65	1	20	65	3
4/9/1973	63	3	21	65	3
24/9/1973	62	4	22	65	4
14/10/1973	63	5	23	66	5
3/11/1973	64	4	25	66	6
23/11/1973	67	4	26	67	6
13/12/1973	70	2	27	68	7
2/1/1974	75	90	27	68	7
22/1/1974	79	89	28	69	7
11/2/1974	84	88	28	69	7
3/3/1974	89	88	27	70	6
23/3/1974	93	88	27	70	6
12/4/1974	98	89	26	69	5
2/5/1974	101	1	25	69	5
22/5/1974	105	3	24	68	4
11/6/1974	107	6	24	68	4
1/7/1974	108	8	24	67	4
21/7/1974	108	11	24	67	4
10/8/1974	106	13	24	67	5
30/8/1974	104	16	25	67	6
19/9/1974	101	17	26	67	6
9/10/1974	99	18	27	68	7
29/10/1974	98	19	29	68	8
18/11/1974	98	19	30	69	8
8/12/1974	100	18	31	70	9
28/12/1974	103	16	32	70	9
17/1/1975	106	15	32	71	9
6/2/1975	110	13	32	71	9
26/2/1975	115	12	32	72	9
18/3/1975	90	12	32	72	8
7/4/1975	5	12	31	72	8
27/4/1975	9	14	30	71	7
17/5/1975	14	15	29	71	7
6/6/1975	18	18	29	70	7
26/6/1975	21	20	28	70	7
16/7/1975	23	23	28	69	7
5/8/1975	25	25	29	69	7
25/8/1975	25	28	29	69	8
14/9/1975	23	30	30	69	8
4/10/1975	21	31	31	70	9
24/10/1975	18	33	33	70	10

Dates in this table appear day/month/year

Date	Jupiter	Saturn	Uranus	Neptune	Pluto
13/11/1975	16	33	34	71	11
3/12/1975	15	33	35	71	11
23/12/1975	15	32	36	72	12
12/1/1976	17	30	37	73	12
1/2/1976	19	29	37	73	12
21/2/1976	23	27	37	74	11
12/3/1976	27	26	37	74	11
1/4/1976	31	26	36	74	10
21/4/1976	36	27	35	74	10
11/5/1976	41	28	34	73	9
31/5/1976	45	29	34	73	9
20/6/1976	50	32	33	72	9
10/7/1976	54	34	33	72	9
30/7/1976	57	37	33	71	9
19/8/1976	60	39	34	71	10
8/9/1976	61	42	34	71	11
28/9/1976	61	44	36	72	11
18/10/1976	60	45	37	72	12
7/11/1976	58	46	38	73	13
27/11/1976	55	47	39	73	13
17/12/1976	53	47	40	74	14
6/1/1977	51	46	41	75	14
26/1/1977	51	44	42	75	14
15/2/1977	53	42	42	76	14
7/3/1977	55	41	42	76	14
27/3/1977	59	40	41	76	13
16/4/1977	63	40	40	76	12
6/5/1977	67	41	40	76	12
26/5/1977	71	42	39	75	12
15/6/1977	76	43	38	75	11
5/7/1977	81	46	38	74	11
25/7/1977	85	48	38	74	12
14/8/1977	89	51	38	73	12
3/9/1977	92	53	39	73	13
23/9/1977	95	55	40	74	14
13/10/1977	96	58	41	74	14
2/11/1977	96	59	42	75	15
22/11/1977	95	60	43	75	16
12/12/1977	93	61	44	76	16
1/1/1978	90	60	45	77	17
21/1/1978	88	59	46	77	17
10/2/1978	86	58	46	78	17
2/3/1978	86	56	46	78	16
22/3/1978	88	55	46	78	16

Table 2   171

Dates in this table appear day/month/year

Date	Jupiter	Saturn	Uranus	Neptune	Pluto
11/4/1978	90	54	45	78	15
1/5/1978	93	54	45	78	15
21/5/1978	97	54	44	77	14
10/6/1978	101	55	43	77	14
30/6/1978	105	57	43	76	14
20/7/1978	110	59	42	76	14
9/8/1978	114	62	42	76	14
29/8/1978	119	64	43	76	15
18/9/1978	2	67	44	76	16
8/10/1978	5	69	45	76	17
28/10/1978	8	71	46	77	17
17/11/1978	9	73	47	77	18
7/12/1978	9	74	48	78	19
27/12/1978	7	74	49	79	19
16/1/1979	5	73	50	79	19
5/2/1979	3	72	51	80	19
25/2/1979	90	71	51	80	19
17/3/1979	119	69	51	80	18
6/4/1979	119	68	50	80	18
26/4/1979	90	67	50	80	17
16/5/1979	3	67	49	80	17
5/6/1979	6	68	48	79	17
25/6/1979	10	69	47	79	16
15/7/1979	14	71	47	78	17
4/8/1979	18	73	47	78	17
24/8/1979	22	75	47	78	17
13/9/1979	27	78	48	78	18
3/10/1979	31	80	49	78	19
23/10/1979	34	82	50	78	20
12/11/1979	37	84	51	79	20
2/12/1979	39	86	52	80	21
22/12/1979	40	87	54	81	21
11/1/1980	40	87	55	81	22
31/1/1980	38	86	55	82	22
20/2/1980	36	85	56	82	22
11/3/1980	33	84	56	83	21
31/3/1980	31	82	55	83	21
20/4/1980	30	81	55	82	20
10/5/1980	31	80	54	82	20
30/5/1980	32	80	53	82	19
19/6/1980	34	81	52	81	19
9/7/1980	37	82	52	81	19
29/7/1980	41	84	52	80	19
18/8/1980	45	86	52	80	20

Dates in this table appear day/month/year

Date	Jupiter	Saturn	Uranus	Neptune	Pluto
7/9/1980	49	88	52	80	20
27/9/1980	54	1	53	80	21
17/10/1980	58	3	54	80	22
6/11/1980	62	5	55	81	23
26/11/1980	65	7	56	82	23
16/12/1980	68	9	58	82	24
5/1/1981	70	10	59	83	24
25/1/1981	70	10	59	84	24
14/2/1981	70	9	60	84	24
6/3/1981	68	8	60	85	24
26/3/1981	66	7	60	85	23
15/4/1981	63	5	59	85	23
5/5/1981	61	4	59	84	22
25/5/1981	60	3	58	84	22
14/6/1981	61	3	57	83	22
4/7/1981	62	4	56	83	22
24/7/1981	65	5	56	83	22
13/8/1981	68	7	56	82	22
2/9/1981	72	9	56	82	23
22/9/1981	76	11	57	82	23
12/10/1981	80	14	58	83	24
1/11/1981	85	16	59	83	25
21/11/1981	89	18	60	84	26
11/12/1981	93	20	62	84	26
31/12/1981	96	21	63	85	27
20/1/1982	98	22	64	86	27
9/2/1982	100	22	64	86	27
1/3/1982	100	22	65	87	27
21/3/1982	99	20	65	87	26
10/4/1982	97	19	64	87	26
30/4/1982	95	17	64	87	25
20/5/1982	93	16	63	86	25
9/6/1982	91	16	62	86	24
29/6/1982	90	16	61	85	24
19/7/1982	91	16	61	85	24
8/8/1982	93	18	61	84	24
28/8/1982	96	19	61	84	25
17/9/1982	99	21	61	84	26
7/10/1982	103	24	62	85	26
27/10/1982	107	26	63	85	27
16/11/1982	111	29	64	86	28
6/12/1982	116	31	65	86	29
26/12/1982	90	32	67	87	29
15/1/1983	4	34	68	88	29

Table 2   173

Dates in this table appear day/month/year

Date	Jupiter	Saturn	Uranus	Neptune	Pluto
4/2/1983	7	34	68	88	30
24/2/1983	9	34	69	89	29
16/3/1983	11	34	69	89	29
5/4/1983	11	32	69	89	29
25/4/1983	10	31	68	89	28
15/5/1983	8	29	68	89	27
4/6/1983	5	28	67	88	27
24/6/1983	3	28	66	88	27
14/7/1983	1	28	65	87	27
3/8/1983	1	29	65	87	27
23/8/1983	2	30	65	87	27
12/9/1983	4	32	65	86	28
2/10/1983	7	34	66	87	29
22/10/1983	10	36	67	87	29
11/11/1983	15	39	68	88	30
1/12/1983	19	41	69	88	31
21/12/1983	23	43	71	89	32
10/1/1984	28	45	72	90	32
30/1/1984	32	46	73	90	32
19/2/1984	36	46	73	1	32
10/3/1984	39	46	74	1	32
30/3/1984	42	45	74	1	31
19/4/1984	43	44	73	1	31
9/5/1984	43	43	73	1	30
29/5/1984	42	41	72	1	30
18/6/1984	40	40	71	90	29
8/7/1984	37	40	70	90	29
28/7/1984	35	40	70	89	29
17/8/1984	33	41	70	89	30
6/9/1984	33	42	70	89	30
26/9/1984	34	44	70	89	31
16/10/1984	36	46	71	89	32
5/11/1984	40	48	72	90	33
25/11/1984	43	51	73	90	33
15/12/1984	48	53	74	1	34
4/1/1985	52	55	76	2	34
24/1/1985	57	57	77	2	35
13/2/1985	61	58	77	3	35
5/3/1985	66	58	78	3	35
25/3/1985	70	58	78	4	34
14/4/1985	73	57	78	4	34
4/5/1985	75	56	77	3	33
24/5/1985	77	54	77	3	33
13/6/1985	77	53	76	3	32

Table 2

Dates in this table appear day/month/year

Date	Jupiter	Saturn	Uranus	Neptune	Pluto
3/7/1985	76	52	75	2	32
23/7/1985	74	51	74	1	32
12/8/1985	71	52	74	1	32
1/9/1985	69	53	74	1	33
21/9/1985	67	54	74	1	33
11/10/1985	67	56	75	1	34
31/10/1985	68	58	76	1	35
20/11/1985	71	60	77	2	36
10/12/1985	74	63	78	3	36
30/12/1985	78	65	79	4	37
19/1/1986	82	67	81	4	37
8/2/1986	87	68	81	5	37
28/2/1986	92	69	82	5	37
20/3/1986	96	70	82	6	37
9/4/1986	101	69	82	6	36
29/4/1986	105	68	82	6	36
19/5/1986	108	67	81	5	35
8/6/1986	111	66	81	5	35
28/6/1986	113	64	80	4	35
18/7/1986	113	63	79	4	35
7/8/1986	112	63	79	3	35
27/8/1986	110	63	78	3	35
16/9/1986	107	64	79	3	36
6/10/1986	105	66	79	3	36
26/10/1986	103	68	80	4	37
15/11/1986	103	70	81	4	38
5/12/1986	104	72	82	5	39
25/12/1986	106	75	83	5	39
14/1/1987	110	77	84	6	40
3/2/1987	114	79	85	7	40
23/2/1987	118	80	86	7	40
15/3/1987	3	81	87	8	40
4/4/1987	8	81	87	8	39
24/4/1987	13	81	87	8	39
14/5/1987	17	80	86	8	38
3/6/1987	21	78	85	7	38
23/6/1987	25	77	84	7	37
13/7/1987	27	76	84	6	37
2/8/1987	29	75	83	6	37
22/8/1987	30	75	83	5	38
11/9/1987	29	75	83	5	38
1/10/1987	27	76	83	5	39
21/10/1987	24	78	84	6	39
10/11/1987	22	79	85	6	40

Table 2   175

Dates in this table appear day/month/year

Date	Jupiter	Saturn	Uranus	Neptune	Pluto
30/11/1987	20	82	86	7	41
20/12/1987	20	84	87	7	42
9/1/1988	21	86	88	8	42
29/1/1988	23	89	89	9	43
18/2/1988	26	90	90	9	43
9/3/1988	30	2	1	10	42
29/3/1988	34	2	1	10	42
18/4/1988	39	3	1	10	42
8/5/1988	44	2	1	10	41
28/5/1988	49	1	90	10	40
17/6/1988	53	89	89	9	40
7/7/1988	57	88	88	9	40
27/7/1988	61	87	88	8	40
16/8/1988	64	86	87	8	40
5/9/1988	66	86	87	7	40
25/9/1988	66	86	87	7	41
15/10/1988	65	88	88	8	42
4/11/1988	64	89	89	8	43
24/11/1988	61	1	90	9	43
14/12/1988	58	3	1	9	44
3/1/1989	57	6	2	10	45
23/1/1989	56	8	3	11	45
12/2/1989	57	10	4	11	45
4/3/1989	59	12	5	12	45
24/3/1989	62	13	5	12	45
13/4/1989	66	14	5	12	44
3/5/1989	70	14	5	12	44
23/5/1989	75	13	5	12	43
12/6/1989	79	12	4	12	43
2/7/1989	84	11	3	11	42
22/7/1989	88	9	2	10	42
11/8/1989	92	8	2	10	42
31/8/1989	96	7	1	10	43
20/9/1989	98	7	1	10	43
10/10/1989	100	8	2	10	44
30/10/1989	101	9	2	10	45
19/11/1989	100	11	3	11	46
9/12/1989	98	13	4	11	46
29/12/1989	96	15	6	12	47
18/1/1990	93	18	7	13	47
7/2/1990	91	20	8	13	48
27/2/1990	91	22	9	14	48
19/3/1990	92	24	9	14	48
8/4/1990	94	25	10	15	47

Dates in this table appear day/month/year

Date	Jupiter	Saturn	Uranus	Neptune	Pluto
28/4/1990	96	25	9	15	47
18/5/1990	100	25	9	14	46
7/6/1990	104	24	8	14	46
27/6/1990	108	23	8	13	45
17/7/1990	113	22	7	13	45
6/8/1990	117	20	6	12	45
26/8/1990	2	19	6	12	45
15/9/1990	6	19	6	12	46
5/10/1990	9	19	6	12	46
25/10/1990	12	20	6	12	47
14/11/1990	13	21	7	13	48
4/12/1990	14	23	8	13	49
24/12/1990	13	25	9	14	49
13/1/1991	11	27	10	15	50
2/2/1991	8	29	12	15	50
22/2/1991	6	32	13	16	50
14/3/1991	4	34	13	16	50
3/4/1991	4	35	14	17	50
23/4/1991	4	36	14	17	49
13/5/1991	6	37	14	17	49
2/6/1991	9	37	13	16	48
22/6/1991	13	36	12	16	48
12/7/1991	17	35	12	15	48
1/8/1991	21	33	11	15	48
21/8/1991	25	32	10	14	48
10/9/1991	30	31	10	14	48
30/9/1991	34	30	10	14	49
20/10/1991	37	30	10	14	49
9/11/1991	41	31	11	15	50
29/11/1991	43	33	12	15	51
19/12/1991	44	34	13	16	52
8/1/1992	45	37	14	16	52
28/1/1992	43	39	15	17	53
17/2/1992	41	41	16	18	53
8/3/1992	39	44	17	18	53
28/3/1992	36	46	18	19	53
17/4/1992	35	47	18	19	52
7/5/1992	35	48	18	19	52
27/5/1992	36	48	18	19	51
16/6/1992	38	48	17	18	51
6/7/1992	41	47	16	18	50
26/7/1992	44	46	15	17	50
15/8/1992	48	45	15	17	50
4/9/1992	52	43	14	16	51

Table 2   177

Dates in this table appear day/month/year

Date	Jupiter	Saturn	Uranus	Neptune	Pluto
24/9/1992	56	42	14	16	51
14/10/1992	61	42	14	16	52
3/11/1992	65	42	15	17	52
23/11/1992	68	43	16	17	53
13/12/1992	71	45	17	18	54
2/1/1993	74	46	18	18	55
22/1/1993	75	49	19	19	55
11/2/1993	74	51	20	20	55
3/3/1993	73	53	21	20	56
23/3/1993	71	56	22	21	55
12/4/1993	68	58	22	21	55
2/5/1993	66	59	22	21	54
22/5/1993	65	60	22	21	54
11/6/1993	65	60	21	21	53
1/7/1993	66	60	21	20	53
21/7/1993	68	59	20	20	53
10/8/1993	71	58	19	19	53
30/8/1993	75	56	19	19	53
19/9/1993	79	55	18	18	53
9/10/1993	83	54	18	18	54
29/10/1993	87	54	19	19	55
18/11/1993	92	54	19	19	55
8/12/1993	96	55	20	20	56
28/12/1993	99	57	21	20	57
17/1/1994	102	59	23	21	58
6/2/1994	104	61	24	22	58
26/2/1994	105	63	25	22	58
18/3/1994	104	66	26	23	58
7/4/1994	103	68	26	23	58
27/4/1994	100	70	26	23	57
17/5/1994	98	71	26	23	57
6/6/1994	96	72	26	23	56
26/6/1994	95	72	25	22	56
16/7/1994	95	72	24	22	55
5/8/1994	96	71	24	21	55
25/8/1994	99	70	23	21	55
14/9/1994	102	68	23	21	56
4/10/1994	106	67	22	21	56
24/10/1994	110	66	23	21	57
13/11/1994	114	66	23	21	58
3/12/1994	119	66	24	22	58
23/12/1994	3	67	25	22	59
12/1/1995	7	69	26	23	60
1/2/1995	10	71	27	24	60

Dates in this table appear day/month/year

Date	Jupiter	Saturn	Uranus	Neptune	Pluto
21/2/1995	13	73	28	24	61
13/3/1995	15	76	29	25	61
2/4/1995	15	78	30	25	60
22/4/1995	15	80	30	26	60
12/5/1995	13	82	30	25	59
1/6/1995	11	84	30	25	59
21/6/1995	8	85	30	25	58
11/7/1995	6	85	29	24	58
31/7/1995	6	84	28	24	58
20/8/1995	6	83	27	23	58
9/9/1995	8	82	27	23	58
29/9/1995	10	80	27	23	59
19/10/1995	14	79	27	23	59
8/11/1995	17	78	27	23	60
28/11/1995	22	78	28	24	61
18/12/1995	26	79	29	24	61
7/1/1996	31	80	30	25	62
27/1/1996	35	82	31	26	63
16/2/1996	39	84	32	26	63
7/3/1996	43	86	33	27	63
27/3/1996	45	89	34	27	63
16/4/1996	47	1	34	28	63
6/5/1996	48	3	35	28	62
26/5/1996	47	5	34	28	62
15/6/1996	45	6	34	27	61
5/7/1996	43	7	33	27	61
25/7/1996	40	7	33	26	60
14/8/1996	38	7	32	26	60
3/9/1996	38	6	31	25	61
23/9/1996	38	4	31	25	61
13/10/1996	40	3	31	25	61
2/11/1996	43	1	31	25	62
22/11/1996	47	1	31	26	63
12/12/1996	51	1	32	26	64
1/1/1997	55	1	33	27	64
21/1/1997	60	3	34	28	65
10/2/1997	65	4	36	28	65
2/3/1997	69	7	37	29	66
22/3/1997	73	9	38	30	66
11/4/1997	77	12	38	30	65
1/5/1997	80	14	39	30	65
21/5/1997	81	16	39	30	64
10/6/1997	82	18	38	30	64
30/6/1997	81	19	38	29	63

Table 2   179

Dates in this table appear day/month/year

Date	Jupiter	Saturn	Uranus	Neptune	Pluto
20/7/1997	80	20	37	29	63
9/8/1997	77	20	36	28	63
29/8/1997	75	20	36	28	63
18/9/1997	73	19	35	27	63
8/10/1997	72	17	35	27	64
28/10/1997	73	16	35	27	64
17/11/1997	75	14	35	28	65
7/12/1997	78	14	36	28	66
27/12/1997	81	14	37	29	67
16/1/1998	86	14	38	30	67
5/2/1998	90	16	39	30	68
25/2/1998	95	18	40	31	68
17/3/1998	100	20	41	32	68
6/4/1998	104	22	42	32	68
26/4/1998	109	25	43	32	68
16/5/1998	112	27	43	32	67
5/6/1998	115	30	43	32	66
25/6/1998	117	31	42	32	66
15/7/1998	118	33	42	31	66
4/8/1998	118	34	41	30	65
24/8/1998	116	34	40	30	65
13/9/1998	113	33	39	30	66
3/10/1998	111	32	39	29	66
23/10/1998	109	30	39	29	67
12/11/1998	108	29	39	30	67
2/12/1998	109	27	40	30	68
22/12/1998	111	27	40	31	69
11/1/1999	114	27	42	31	69
31/1/1999	117	28	43	32	70
20/2/1999	2	29	44	33	70
12/3/1999	6	31	45	34	71
1/4/1999	11	33	46	34	70
21/4/1999	16	36	46	34	70
11/5/1999	20	38	47	34	70
31/5/1999	25	41	47	34	69
20/6/1999	29	43	46	34	69
10/7/1999	32	45	46	33	68
30/7/1999	34	46	45	33	68
19/8/1999	35	47	44	32	68
8/9/1999	35	47	44	32	68
28/9/1999	33	46	43	32	68
18/10/1999	31	45	43	32	69
7/11/1999	28	44	43	32	69
27/11/1999	26	42	43	32	70

Dates in this table appear day/month/year

Date	Jupiter	Saturn	Uranus	Neptune	Pluto
17/12/1999	25	41	44	33	71
6/1/2000	25	40	45	33	72
26/1/2000	27	40	46	34	72
15/2/2000	30	41	47	35	73
6/3/2000	34	43	48	36	73
26/3/2000	38	45	49	36	73
15/4/2000	42	47	50	36	73
5/5/2000	47	50	51	37	72
25/5/2000	52	52	51	37	72
14/6/2000	56	55	51	36	71
4/7/2000	61	57	50	36	71
24/7/2000	65	59	50	35	70
13/8/2000	68	60	49	35	70
2/9/2000	70	61	48	34	70
22/9/2000	71	61	47	34	70
12/10/2000	71	60	47	34	71
1/11/2000	70	59	47	34	72
21/11/2000	67	57	47	34	72
11/12/2000	64	56	48	35	73
31/12/2000	62	55	49	35	74
20/1/2001	61	54	50	36	74
9/2/2001	62	54	51	37	75
1/3/2001	63	55	52	38	75
21/3/2001	66	57	53	38	75
10/4/2001	69	59	54	39	75
30/4/2001	73	61	54	39	75
20/5/2001	78	64	55	39	74
9/6/2001	82	66	55	39	74
29/6/2001	87	69	54	38	73
19/7/2001	91	71	54	38	73
8/8/2001	96	73	53	37	73
28/8/2001	99	74	52	37	73
17/9/2001	102	75	52	36	73
7/10/2001	105	75	51	36	73
27/10/2001	106	74	51	36	74
16/11/2001	105	73	51	36	74
6/12/2001	104	71	51	37	75
26/12/2001	101	70	52	37	76
15/1/2002	99	69	53	38	77
4/2/2002	97	68	54	39	77
24/2/2002	96	68	55	39	77
16/3/2002	96	69	57	40	78
5/4/2002	97	71	57	41	78
25/4/2002	100	73	58	41	77

Table 2   *181*

Dates in this table appear day/month/year

Date	Jupiter	Saturn	Uranus	Neptune	Pluto
15/5/2002	103	75	59	41	77
4/6/2002	107	78	59	41	76
24/6/2002	111	80	59	41	76
14/7/2002	116	83	58	40	75
3/8/2002	90	85	58	40	75
23/8/2002	5	87	57	39	75
12/9/2002	9	88	56	39	75
2/10/2002	12	89	55	38	75
22/10/2002	15	89	55	38	76
11/11/2002	17	88	55	38	76
1/12/2002	18	87	55	39	77
21/12/2002	18	85	56	39	78
10/1/2003	16	84	57	40	79
30/1/2003	14	83	58	41	79
19/2/2003	11	82	59	41	80
11/3/2003	9	82	60	42	80
31/3/2003	8	83	61	43	80
20/4/2003	8	85	62	43	80
10/5/2003	10	87	63	43	79
30/5/2003	12	89	63	43	79
19/6/2003	16	2	63	43	78
9/7/2003	20	5	62	42	78
29/7/2003	24	7	62	42	77
18/8/2003	28	9	61	41	77
7/9/2003	32	11	60	41	77
27/9/2003	37	12	60	41	77
17/10/2003	40	13	59	40	78
6/11/2003	44	13	59	40	78
26/11/2003	47	12	59	41	79
16/12/2003	48	11	59	41	80
5/1/2004	49	9	60	42	81
25/1/2004	48	8	61	43	81
14/2/2004	46	7	62	43	82
5/3/2004	44	6	63	44	82
25/3/2004	41	7	65	45	82
14/4/2004	40	8	66	45	82
4/5/2004	39	9	66	45	82
24/5/2004	39	11	67	45	81
13/6/2004	41	14	67	45	81
3/7/2004	44	16	67	45	80
23/7/2004	47	19	66	44	80
12/8/2004	51	21	65	44	80
1/9/2004	55	23	65	43	80
21/9/2004	59	25	64	43	80

Table 2

Dates in this table appear day/month/year

Date	Jupiter	Saturn	Uranus	Neptune	Pluto
11/10/2004	63	27	63	43	80
31/10/2004	68	27	63	43	81
20/11/2004	71	27	63	43	81
10/12/2004	75	26	63	43	82
30/12/2004	77	25	64	44	83
19/1/2005	79	23	65	44	83
8/2/2005	79	22	66	45	84
28/2/2005	78	21	67	46	84
20/3/2005	76	20	68	47	85
9/4/2005	73	21	69	47	84
29/4/2005	71	22	70	47	84
19/5/2005	69	23	70	48	84
8/6/2005	69	25	71	48	83
28/6/2005	70	28	71	47	83
18/7/2005	72	30	70	47	82
7/8/2005	74	33	70	46	82
27/8/2005	78	35	69	46	82
16/9/2005	81	37	68	45	82
6/10/2005	86	39	68	45	82
26/10/2005	90	41	67	45	83
15/11/2005	94	41	67	45	83
5/12/2005	98	41	67	45	84
25/12/2005	102	40	67	46	85
14/1/2006	105	39	68	46	85
3/2/2006	108	37	69	47	86
23/2/2006	109	36	70	48	86
15/3/2006	109	35	72	49	87
4/4/2006	107	34	73	49	87
24/4/2006	105	35	74	50	87
14/5/2006	103	36	74	50	86
3/6/2006	101	37	75	50	86
23/6/2006	99	39	75	50	85
13/7/2006	99	42	75	49	85
2/8/2006	100	44	74	49	84
22/8/2006	102	47	73	48	84
11/9/2006	105	49	73	48	84
1/10/2006	109	51	72	47	84
21/10/2006	113	53	71	47	85
10/11/2006	117	54	71	47	85
30/11/2006	1	55	71	47	86
20/12/2006	6	55	71	48	87
9/1/2007	10	54	72	48	87
29/1/2007	14	53	73	49	88
18/2/2007	17	51	74	50	89

Table 2   183

Dates in this table appear day/month/year

Date	Jupiter	Saturn	Uranus	Neptune	Pluto
10/3/2007	19	50	75	51	89
30/3/2007	20	48	76	51	89
19/4/2007	20	48	77	52	89
9/5/2007	18	48	78	52	89
29/5/2007	16	49	78	52	88
18/6/2007	13	51	79	52	88
8/7/2007	11	53	79	52	87
28/7/2007	10	55	78	51	87
17/8/2007	10	58	78	51	86
6/9/2007	11	60	77	50	86
26/9/2007	14	63	76	50	86
16/10/2007	17	65	75	49	87
5/11/2007	20	67	75	49	87
25/11/2007	25	68	75	49	88
15/12/2007	29	68	75	50	89
4/1/2008	34	68	75	50	89
24/1/2008	38	67	76	51	90
13/2/2008	42	66	77	52	1
4/3/2008	46	64	78	53	1
24/3/2008	49	63	80	53	1
13/4/2008	51	62	81	54	1
3/5/2008	52	62	81	54	1
23/5/2008	52	62	82	54	1
12/6/2008	51	63	83	54	90
2/7/2008	48	65	83	54	90
22/7/2008	46	67	82	53	89
11/8/2008	44	69	82	53	89
31/8/2008	43	71	81	52	89
20/9/2008	43	74	80	52	89
10/10/2008	44	76	80	52	89
30/10/2008	47	78	79	51	89
19/11/2008	50	80	79	52	90
9/12/2008	54	81	79	52	90
29/12/2008	58	82	79	52	1
18/1/2009	63	81	80	53	2
7/2/2009	68	80	81	54	2
27/2/2009	72	79	82	54	3
19/3/2009	77	77	83	55	3
8/4/2009	80	76	84	56	3
28/4/2009	84	75	85	56	3
18/5/2009	86	75	86	56	3
7/6/2009	87	75	86	56	2
27/6/2009	87	76	87	56	2
17/7/2009	85	78	87	56	1

Dates in this table appear day/month/year

Date	Jupiter	Saturn	Uranus	Neptune	Pluto
6/8/2009	83	80	86	55	1
26/8/2009	81	82	86	55	1
15/9/2009	78	85	85	54	1
5/10/2009	77	87	84	54	1
25/10/2009	77	89	83	54	1
14/11/2009	79	1	83	54	2
4/12/2009	81	3	83	54	2
24/12/2009	85	4	83	54	3
13/1/2010	89	5	83	55	4
2/2/2010	93	4	84	56	4
22/2/2010	98	3	85	56	5
14/3/2010	103	2	86	57	5
3/4/2010	108	90	88	58	5
23/4/2010	112	89	89	58	5
13/5/2010	116	88	89	59	5
2/6/2010	119	88	90	59	5
22/6/2010	2	88	1	59	4
12/7/2010	3	89	1	58	4
1/8/2010	3	1	90	58	3
21/8/2010	2	3	90	57	3
10/9/2010	90	5	89	57	3
30/9/2010	117	8	88	56	3
20/10/2010	115	10	88	56	3
9/11/2010	114	12	87	56	4
29/11/2010	114	14	87	56	4
19/12/2010	115	16	87	56	5
8/1/2011	118	17	87	57	6
28/1/2011	1	17	88	58	6
17/2/2011	5	17	89	58	7
9/3/2011	10	16	90	59	7
29/3/2011	14	14	1	60	7
18/4/2011	19	13	2	60	7
8/5/2011	24	11	3	61	7
28/5/2011	28	11	4	61	7
17/6/2011	32	10	4	61	6
7/7/2011	36	11	5	61	6
27/7/2011	38	12	4	60	5
16/8/2011	40	14	4	60	5
5/9/2011	40	16	3	59	5
25/9/2011	39	18	3	59	5
15/10/2011	37	20	2	58	5
4/11/2011	34	23	1	58	5
24/11/2011	32	25	1	58	6
14/12/2011	30	27	1	58	7

Table 2   *185*

Dates in this table appear day/month/year

Date	Jupiter	Saturn	Uranus	Neptune	Pluto
3/1/2012	30	28	1	59	7
23/1/2012	32	29	1	60	8
12/2/2012	34	29	2	60	9
3/3/2012	37	29	3	61	9
23/3/2012	41	28	4	62	9
12/4/2012	46	26	6	62	10
2/5/2012	50	25	7	63	9
22/5/2012	55	24	7	63	9
11/6/2012	60	23	8	63	9
1/7/2012	64	23	8	63	8
21/7/2012	68	23	9	63	8
10/8/2012	72	24	8	62	7
30/8/2012	74	26	8	62	7
19/9/2012	76	28	7	61	7
9/10/2012	76	30	6	61	7
29/10/2012	75	33	5	60	7
18/11/2012	73	35	5	60	8
8/12/2012	70	37	5	61	8
28/12/2012	68	39	5	61	9
17/1/2013	66	41	5	62	10
6/2/2013	66	41	6	62	11
26/2/2013	67	41	7	63	11
18/3/2013	70	41	8	64	11
7/4/2013	73	40	9	64	12
27/4/2013	77	38	10	65	12
17/5/2013	81	37	11	65	11
6/6/2013	85	36	12	65	11
26/6/2013	90	35	12	65	10
16/7/2013	94	35	13	65	10
5/8/2013	99	35	12	65	9
25/8/2013	103	37	12	64	9
14/9/2013	106	38	11	63	9
4/10/2013	109	40	11	63	9
24/10/2013	110	43	10	63	9
13/11/2013	110	45	9	63	10
3/12/2013	109	47	9	63	10
23/12/2013	107	49	9	63	11
12/1/2014	104	51	9	64	12
1/2/2014	102	53	9	64	12
21/2/2014	101	53	10	65	13
13/3/2014	100	53	11	66	13
2/4/2014	101	52	12	66	14
22/4/2014	104	51	14	67	14
12/5/2014	107	50	15	67	13

Dates in this table appear day/month/year

Date	Jupiter	Saturn	Uranus	Neptune	Pluto
1/6/2014	110	48	16	68	13
21/6/2014	114	47	16	68	13
11/7/2014	119	47	16	67	12
31/7/2014	3	47	16	67	12
20/8/2014	8	47	16	66	11
9/9/2014	12	49	16	66	11
29/9/2014	15	50	15	65	11
19/10/2014	19	52	14	65	11
8/11/2014	21	55	13	65	11
28/11/2014	22	57	13	65	12
18/12/2014	22	59	13	65	13
7/1/2015	21	61	13	66	13
27/1/2015	19	63	13	66	14
16/2/2015	16	64	14	67	15
8/3/2015	14	65	15	68	15
28/3/2015	13	65	16	68	15
17/4/2015	13	64	17	69	16
7/5/2015	14	63	18	69	15
27/5/2015	16	61	19	70	15
16/6/2015	19	60	20	70	15
6/7/2015	22	59	20	70	14
26/7/2015	26	58	21	69	14
15/8/2015	31	58	20	69	13
4/9/2015	35	59	20	68	13
24/9/2015	39	60	19	68	13
14/10/2015	43	62	18	67	13
3/11/2015	47	64	18	67	13
23/11/2015	50	67	17	67	14
13/12/2015	52	69	17	67	14
2/1/2016	53	71	17	68	15
22/1/2016	53	73	17	68	16
11/2/2016	51	75	18	69	16
2/3/2016	49	76	18	70	17
22/3/2016	47	76	19	70	17
11/4/2016	44	76	21	71	17
1/5/2016	43	75	22	72	17
21/5/2016	43	74	23	72	17
10/6/2016	45	73	24	72	17
30/6/2016	47	71	24	72	16
20/7/2016	50	70	24	72	16
9/8/2016	54	70	24	71	15
29/8/2016	58	70	24	71	15
18/9/2016	62	71	24	70	15
8/10/2016	66	72	23	70	15

Table 2   187

Dates in this table appear day/month/year

Date	Jupiter	Saturn	Uranus	Neptune	Pluto
28/10/2016	70	74	22	69	15
17/11/2016	74	76	21	69	16
7/12/2016	78	78	21	69	16
27/12/2016	81	81	21	70	17
16/1/2017	82	83	21	70	17
5/2/2017	83	85	21	71	18
25/2/2017	83	86	22	72	19
17/3/2017	81	87	23	72	19
6/4/2017	79	88	24	73	19
26/4/2017	76	87	25	74	19
16/5/2017	74	87	26	74	19
5/6/2017	73	85	27	74	19
25/6/2017	74	84	28	74	18
15/7/2017	75	82	28	74	18
4/8/2017	77	81	29	74	17
24/8/2017	81	81	28	73	17
13/9/2017	84	81	28	73	17
3/10/2017	88	82	27	72	17
23/10/2017	93	84	26	72	17
12/11/2017	97	86	26	71	17
2/12/2017	101	88	25	71	18
22/12/2017	105	90	25	72	18
11/1/2018	109	3	25	72	19
31/1/2018	111	5	25	73	20
20/2/2018	113	7	26	73	20
12/3/2018	113	8	26	74	21
1/4/2018	113	9	28	75	21
21/4/2018	111	9	29	76	21
11/5/2018	108	9	30	76	21
31/5/2018	106	8	31	76	21
20/6/2018	104	6	32	76	20
10/7/2018	103	5	32	76	20
30/7/2018	104	4	33	76	20
19/8/2018	106	3	33	76	19
8/9/2018	108	2	32	75	19
28/9/2018	112	3	32	75	19
18/10/2018	116	4	31	74	19
7/11/2018	90	5	30	74	19
27/11/2018	4	7	29	74	19
17/12/2018	9	10	29	74	20
6/1/2019	13	12	29	74	21
26/1/2019	17	14	29	75	21
15/2/2019	20	16	29	75	22
7/3/2019	23	18	30	76	23

Table 2

Dates in this table appear day/month/year

Date	Jupiter	Saturn	Uranus	Neptune	Pluto
27/3/2019	24	20	31	77	23
16/4/2019	24	20	32	78	23
6/5/2019	23	20	33	78	23
26/5/2019	22	20	34	79	23
15/6/2019	19	19	35	79	23
5/7/2019	17	18	36	79	22
25/7/2019	15	16	37	78	22
14/8/2019	15	15	37	78	21
3/9/2019	15	14	36	77	21
23/9/2019	17	14	36	77	21
13/10/2019	20	14	35	76	21
2/11/2019	24	15	34	76	21
22/11/2019	28	17	34	76	21
12/12/2019	32	19	33	76	22
1/1/2020	37	21	33	76	22
21/1/2020	41	24	33	77	23
10/2/2020	46	26	33	77	24
1/3/2020	50	28	34	78	24
21/3/2020	53	30	35	79	25
10/4/2020	56	31	36	80	25
30/4/2020	57	32	37	80	25
20/5/2020	57	32	38	81	25
9/6/2020	56	31	39	81	24
29/6/2020	54	30	40	81	24
19/7/2020	52	29	40	81	24
8/8/2020	49	27	41	80	23
28/8/2020	48	26	41	80	23
17/9/2020	48	25	40	79	22
7/10/2020	48	25	40	79	22
27/10/2020	50	26	39	78	23
16/11/2020	53	27	38	78	23
6/12/2020	57	29	37	78	23

Table 3: Mars and Venus Cycles 1940–1989

Dates in this table appear day/month/year

Date	Ven.	Mars	Date	Ven.	Mars	Date	Ven.	Mars
1/1/40	38	88	14/10/40	68	5	28/7/41	61	13
8/1/40	47	3	21/10/40	76	10	4/8/41	69	16
15/1/40	56	7	8/10/40	84	15	11/8/41	78	19
22/1/40	64	2	4/11/40	3	19	18/8/41	86	21
29/1/40	73	17	11/11/40	11	24	25/8/41	5	23
5/2/40	81	22	18/11/40	20	28	1/9/41	13	24
12/2/40	90	27	25/11/40	28	33	8/9/41	22	24
19/2/40	8	31	2/12/40	37	37	15/9/41	30	23
26/2/40	16	36	9/12/40	45	42	22/9/41	38	22
4/3/40	25	41	16/12/40	54	47	29/9/41	46	20
11/3/40	33	45	23/12/40	63	51	6/10/41	54	18
18/3/40	41	50	30/12/40	71	56	13/10/41	63	16
25/3/40	48	55	6/1/41	80	61	20/10/41	71	14
1/4/40	56	59	13/1/41	89	66	27/10/41	78	12
8/4/40	63	64	20/1/41	8	70	3/11/41	86	11
15/4/40	70	69	27/1/41	16	75	10/11/41	4	11
22/4/40	77	73	3/2/41	25	80	17/11/41	11	11
29/4/40	84	78	10/2/41	34	85	24/11/41	19	12
6/5/40	89	82	17/2/41	43	89	1/12/41	25	14
13/5/40	4	87	24/2/41	51	4	8/12/41	32	16
20/5/40	9	2	3/3/41	60	9	15/12/41	38	18
27/5/40	12	6	10/3/41	69	14	22/12/41	43	21
3/6/40	13	11	17/3/41	78	19	29/12/41	47	24
10/6/40	13	15	24/3/41	86	23	5/1/42	50	27
17/6/40	11	20	31/3/41	5	28	12/1/42	51	30
24/6/40	7	24	7/4/41	14	33	19/1/42	50	34
1/7/40	3	28	14/4/41	22	38	26/1/42	48	37
8/7/40	89	33	21/4/41	31	43	2/2/42	44	41
15/7/40	87	37	28/4/41	40	48	9/2/42	40	45
22/7/40	87	42	5/5/41	48	52	16/2/42	37	49
29/7/40	89	46	12/5/41	57	57	23/2/42	36	53
5/8/40	2	51	19/5/41	65	62	2/3/42	36	57
12/8/40	6	55	26/5/41	74	67	9/3/42	39	61
19/8/40	11	60	2/6/41	83	71	16/3/42	43	65
26/8/40	17	64	9/6/41	1	76	23/3/42	48	69
2/9/40	24	69	16/6/41	10	80	30/3/42	53	74
9/9/40	30	73	23/6/41	18	85	6/4/42	60	78
16/9/40	37	77	30/6/41	27	89	13/4/42	66	82
23/9/40	45	82	7/7/41	35	3	20/4/42	73	86
30/9/40	52	86	14/7/41	44	7	27/4/42	80	90
7/10/40	60	1	21/7/41	53	10	4/5/42	88	5

Table 3

Date	Ven.	Mars	Date	Ven.	Mars	Date	Ven.	Mars
11/5/42	5	9	15/3/43	22	35	17/1/44	77	65
18/5/42	13	13	22/3/43	30	40	24/1/44	85	66
25/5/42	21	18	29/3/43	39	45	31/1/44	4	67
1/6/42	29	22	5/4/43	47	51	7/2/44	12	69
8/6/42	37	26	12/4/43	55	56	14/2/44	21	71
15/6/42	45	31	19/4/43	64	61	21/2/44	29	74
22/6/42	53	35	26/4/43	72	66	28/2/44	38	77
29/6/42	61	39	3/5/43	80	72	6/3/44	46	79
6/7/42	70	44	10/5/43	88	77	13/3/44	55	83
13/7/42	78	48	17/5/43	6	82	20/3/44	64	86
20/7/42	86	52	24/5/43	14	87	27/3/44	72	89
27/7/42	5	57	31/5/43	22	3	3/4/44	81	3
3/8/42	13	61	7/6/43	29	8	10/4/44	89	6
10/8/42	21	65	14/6/43	37	13	17/4/44	8	10
17/8/42	30	70	21/6/43	44	18	24/4/44	17	14
24/8/42	38	74	28/6/43	51	23	1/5/44	25	18
31/8/42	47	79	5/7/43	57	28	8/5/44	34	22
7/9/42	56	83	12/7/43	63	33	15/5/44	42	26
14/9/42	64	88	19/7/43	69	38	22/5/44	51	30
21/9/42	73	2	26/7/43	74	42	29/5/44	60	34
28/9/42	82	7	2/8/43	77	47	5/6/44	68	38
5/10/42	90	11	9/8/43	80	51	12/6/44	77	42
12/10/42	9	16	16/8/43	81	55	19/6/44	85	46
19/10/42	18	21	23/8/43	79	59	26/6/44	4	50
26/10/42	27	25	30/8/43	77	63	3/7/44	13	54
2/11/42	35	30	6/9/43	73	67	10/7/44	21	59
9/11/42	44	35	13/9/43	68	70	17/7/44	30	63
16/11/42	53	40	20/9/43	65	73	24/7/44	38	67
23/11/42	62	44	27/9/43	64	76	31/7/44	47	72
30/11/42	70	49	4/10/43	65	78	7/8/44	56	76
7/12/42	79	54	11/10/43	68	80	14/8/44	64	80
14/12/42	88	59	18/10/43	72	81	21/8/44	73	85
21/12/42	7	64	25/10/43	76	82	28/8/44	82	89
28/12/42	16	69	1/11/43	82	82	4/9/44	90	4
4/1/43	24	74	8/11/43	88	81	11/9/44	9	8
11/1/43	33	79	15/11/43	5	80	18/9/44	17	13
18/1/43	42	84	22/11/43	12	78	25/9/44	26	18
25/1/43	51	89	29/11/43	20	75	2/10/44	35	22
1/2/43	60	4	6/12/43	27	73	9/10/44	43	27
8/2/43	68	9	13/12/43	35	70	16/10/44	52	32
15/2/43	77	14	20/12/43	43	68	23/10/44	60	36
22/2/43	86	19	27/12/43	52	66	30/10/44	69	41
1/3/43	4	24	3/1/44	60	65	6/11/44	77	46
8/3/43	13	30	10/1/44	68	65	13/11/44	86	51

Table 3   *191*

Dates in this table appear day/month/year

Date	Ven.	Mars	Date	Ven.	Mars	Date	Ven.	Mars
20/11/44	4	56	24/9/45	59	9	29/7/46	77	83
27/11/44	13	61	1/10/45	68	13	5/8/46	85	87
4/12/44	21	66	8/10/45	76	16	12/8/46	3	2
11/12/44	30	71	15/10/45	85	20	19/8/46	10	6
18/12/44	38	76	22/10/45	4	23	26/8/46	18	10
25/12/44	46	81	29/10/45	12	26	2/9/46	25	15
1/1/45	54	86	5/11/45	21	28	9/9/46	32	20
8/1/45	63	2	12/11/45	30	30	16/9/46	39	24
15/1/45	70	7	19/11/45	38	32	23/9/46	45	29
22/1/45	78	12	26/11/45	47	33	30/9/46	50	34
29/1/45	86	17	3/12/45	56	33	7/10/46	55	38
5/2/45	3	23	10/12/45	65	33	14/10/46	59	43
12/2/45	9	28	17/12/45	74	32	21/10/46	62	48
19/2/45	16	34	24/12/45	82	31	28/10/46	62	53
26/2/45	21	39	31/12/45	1	29	4/11/46	62	58
5/3/45	26	44	7/1/46	10	26	11/11/46	59	63
12/3/45	30	50	14/1/46	19	23	18/11/46	55	68
19/3/45	33	55	21/1/46	28	21	25/11/46	51	73
26/3/45	34	61	28/1/46	36	18	2/12/46	48	78
2/4/45	32	66	4/2/46	45	16	9/12/46	47	84
9/4/45	29	72	11/2/46	54	15	16/12/46	48	89
16/4/45	25	77	18/2/46	63	14	23/12/46	51	4
23/4/45	21	82	25/2/46	71	14	30/12/46	55	10
30/4/45	18	88	4/3/46	80	15	6/1/47	60	15
7/5/45	17	3	11/3/46	89	16	13/1/47	66	20
14/5/45	18	9	18/3/46	8	17	20/1/47	73	26
21/5/45	21	14	25/3/46	16	19	27/1/47	79	31
28/5/45	25	19	1/4/46	25	21	3/2/47	87	37
4/6/45	29	24	8/4/46	34	24	10/2/47	4	42
11/6/45	35	30	15/4/46	42	27	17/2/47	12	48
18/6/45	41	35	22/4/46	51	30	24/2/47	20	53
25/6/45	47	40	29/4/46	59	33	3/3/47	27	59
2/7/45	54	45	6/5/46	68	36	10/3/47	36	64
9/7/45	61	50	13/5/46	77	39	17/3/47	44	70
16/7/45	69	55	20/5/46	85	43	24/3/47	52	75
23/7/45	76	60	27/5/46	3	47	31/3/47	60	81
30/7/45	84	65	3/6/46	12	50	7/4/47	68	86
6/8/45	2	69	10/6/46	20	54	14/4/47	77	2
13/8/45	10	74	17/6/46	29	58	21/4/47	85	7
20/8/45	18	78	24/6/46	37	62	28/4/47	3	12
27/8/45	26	83	1/7/46	45	66	5/5/47	12	18
3/9/45	34	87	8/7/46	53	70	12/5/47	20	23
10/9/45	42	1	15/7/46	61	74	19/5/47	29	28
17/9/45	51	5	22/7/46	69	79	26/5/47	37	34

Table 3

Dates in this table appear day/month/year

Date	Ven.	Mars	Date	Ven.	Mars	Date	Ven.	Mars
2/6/47	46	39	5/4/48	61	48	7/2/49	31	56
9/6/47	54	44	12/4/48	68	49	14/2/49	40	62
16/6/47	63	49	19/4/48	74	50	21/2/49	48	67
23/6/47	71	54	26/4/48	81	52	28/2/49	57	73
30/6/47	80	59	3/5/48	87	54	7/3/49	66	78
7/7/47	88	64	10/5/48	2	57	14/3/49	74	84
14/7/47	7	69	17/5/48	6	59	21/3/49	83	89
21/7/47	15	74	24/5/48	9	62	28/3/49	2	5
28/7/47	24	79	31/5/48	11	65	4/4/49	11	10
4/8/47	32	83	7/6/48	11	69	11/4/49	19	16
11/8/47	41	88	14/6/48	9	72	18/4/49	28	21
18/8/47	50	3	21/6/48	5	76	25/4/49	37	26
25/8/47	58	7	28/6/48	1	79	2/5/49	45	31
1/9/47	67	12	5/7/48	87	83	9/5/49	54	37
8/9/47	76	16	12/7/48	85	87	16/5/49	62	42
15/9/47	84	20	19/7/48	85	1	23/5/49	71	47
22/9/47	3	25	26/7/48	86	5	30/5/49	80	52
29/9/47	12	29	2/8/48	89	9	6/6/49	88	57
6/10/47	21	33	9/8/48	4	14	13/6/49	7	62
13/10/47	29	37	16/8/48	9	18	20/6/49	15	67
20/10/47	38	41	23/8/48	14	22	27/6/49	24	72
27/10/47	47	44	30/8/48	21	27	4/7/49	32	77
3/11/47	56	48	6/9/48	27	32	11/7/49	41	82
10/11/47	64	51	13/9/48	35	36	18/7/49	50	86
17/11/47	73	54	20/9/48	42	41	25/7/49	58	1
24/11/47	82	57	27/9/48	49	46	1/8/49	66	6
1/12/47	90	60	4/10/48	57	51	8/8/49	75	11
8/12/47	9	62	11/10/48	65	56	15/8/49	83	15
15/12/47	18	64	18/10/48	73	61	22/8/49	2	20
22/12/47	27	66	25/10/48	81	66	29/8/49	10	24
29/12/47	35	67	1/11/48	90	71	5/9/49	19	29
5/1/48	44	68	8/11/48	8	76	12/9/49	27	33
12/1/48	53	68	15/11/48	17	81	19/9/49	35	37
19/1/48	61	67	22/11/48	25	86	26/9/49	43	42
26/1/48	70	66	29/11/48	34	2	3/10/49	51	46
2/2/48	78	64	6/12/48	42	7	10/10/49	60	50
9/2/48	87	61	13/12/48	51	12	17/10/49	68	54
16/2/48	5	59	20/12/48	60	18	24/10/49	75	58
23/2/48	13	56	27/12/48	68	23	31/10/49	83	62
1/3/48	22	53	3/1/49	77	29	7/11/49	1	66
8/3/48	30	51	10/1/49	86	34	14/11/49	8	70
15/3/48	38	49	17/1/49	5	40	21/11/49	16	74
22/3/48	45	48	24/1/49	13	45	28/11/49	22	77
29/3/48	53	48	31/1/49	22	51	5/12/49	29	81

Table 3   **193**

Dates in this table appear day/month/year

Date	Ven.	Mars	Date	Ven.	Mars	Date	Ven.	Mars
12/12/49	35	84	16/10/50	15	74	20/8/51	77	31
19/12/49	40	87	23/10/50	23	79	27/8/51	75	36
26/12/49	44	90	30/10/50	32	85	3/9/51	71	40
2/1/50	47	3	6/11/50	41	90	10/9/51	67	44
9/1/50	49	5	13/11/50	50	5	17/9/51	63	49
16/1/50	48	7	20/11/50	59	10	24/9/51	62	53
23/1/50	46	9	27/11/50	67	16	1/10/51	63	58
30/1/50	42	10	4/12/50	76	21	8/10/51	65	62
6/2/50	37	11	11/12/50	85	27	15/10/51	69	66
13/2/50	34	11	18/12/50	4	32	22/10/51	74	70
20/2/50	33	11	25/12/50	13	38	29/10/51	79	75
27/2/50	34	10	1/1/51	21	43	5/11/51	85	79
6/3/50	36	8	8/1/51	30	49	12/11/51	2	83
13/3/50	40	6	15/1/51	39	54	19/11/51	9	87
20/3/50	45	3	22/1/51	48	60	26/11/51	17	1
27/3/50	50	1	29/1/51	56	65	3/12/51	24	5
3/4/50	57	88	5/2/51	65	71	10/12/51	32	9
10/4/50	63	86	12/2/51	74	76	17/12/51	40	13
17/4/50	70	84	19/2/51	83	82	24/12/51	48	16
24/4/50	77	83	26/2/51	1	87	31/12/51	57	20
1/5/50	85	82	5/3/51	10	2	7/1/52	65	24
8/5/50	2	82	12/3/51	19	8	14/1/52	73	27
15/5/50	10	83	19/3/51	27	13	21/1/52	82	30
22/5/50	18	84	26/3/51	36	18	28/1/52	90	34
29/5/50	26	86	2/4/51	44	24	4/2/52	9	37
5/6/50	34	88	9/4/51	52	29	11/2/52	18	39
12/6/50	42	90	16/4/51	61	34	18/2/52	26	42
19/6/50	50	3	23/4/51	69	39	25/2/52	35	44
26/6/50	58	6	30/4/51	77	44	3/3/52	43	46
3/7/50	67	9	7/5/51	85	50	10/3/52	52	47
10/7/50	75	12	14/5/51	3	55	17/3/52	61	48
17/7/50	83	16	21/5/51	11	60	24/3/52	69	48
24/7/50	2	20	28/5/51	19	65	31/3/52	78	48
31/7/50	10	24	4/6/51	27	69	7/4/52	86	47
7/8/50	18	28	11/6/51	34	74	14/4/52	5	46
14/8/50	27	32	18/6/51	41	79	21/4/52	14	44
21/8/50	35	36	25/6/51	48	84	28/4/52	22	42
28/8/50	44	41	2/7/51	55	89	5/5/52	31	39
4/9/50	53	45	9/7/51	61	3	12/5/52	39	37
11/9/50	61	50	16/7/51	66	8	19/5/52	48	34
18/9/50	70	55	23/7/51	71	13	26/5/52	57	33
25/9/50	79	59	30/7/51	75	17	2/6/52	65	32
2/10/50	87	64	6/8/51	77	22	9/6/52	74	31
9/10/50	6	69	13/8/51	78	26	16/6/52	82	31

Dates in this table appear day/month/year

Date	Ven.	Mars	Date	Ven.	Mars	Date	Ven.	Mars
23/6/52	1	32	27/4/53	16	57	1/3/54	77	70
30/6/52	10	34	4/5/53	15	62	8/3/54	86	74
7/7/52	18	35	11/5/53	16	67	15/3/54	5	77
14/7/52	27	38	18/5/53	18	72	22/3/54	13	81
21/7/52	35	41	25/5/53	22	76	29/3/54	22	84
28/7/52	44	44	1/6/53	27	81	5/4/54	31	87
4/8/52	53	47	8/6/53	32	86	12/4/54	39	90
11/8/52	61	51	15/6/53	38	1	19/4/54	48	2
18/8/52	70	54	22/6/53	45	5	26/4/54	56	4
25/8/52	79	58	29/6/53	51	10	3/5/54	65	6
1/9/52	87	63	6/7/53	59	14	10/5/54	74	7
8/9/52	6	67	13/7/53	66	19	17/5/54	82	8
15/9/52	14	71	20/7/53	73	24	24/5/54	90	8
22/9/52	23	76	27/7/53	81	28	31/5/54	9	8
29/9/52	32	81	3/8/53	89	33	7/6/54	17	7
6/10/52	40	86	10/8/53	7	37	14/6/54	26	6
13/10/52	49	1	17/8/53	15	42	21/6/54	34	4
20/10/52	57	6	24/8/53	23	46	28/6/54	42	2
27/10/52	66	11	31/8/53	31	51	5/7/54	50	89
3/11/52	74	16	7/9/53	39	55	12/7/54	58	88
10/11/52	83	21	14/9/53	48	60	19/7/54	66	86
17/11/52	1	26	21/9/53	56	64	26/7/54	74	86
24/11/52	10	32	28/9/53	65	68	2/8/54	82	86
1/12/52	18	37	5/10/53	73	73	9/8/54	90	86
8/12/52	27	42	12/10/53	82	77	16/8/54	8	88
15/12/52	35	48	19/10/53	90	82	23/8/54	15	89
22/12/52	43	53	26/10/53	9	86	30/8/54	22	2
29/12/52	51	59	2/11/53	18	90	6/9/54	29	5
5/1/53	59	64	9/11/53	27	5	13/9/54	36	8
12/1/53	67	69	16/11/53	35	9	20/9/54	42	11
19/1/53	75	75	23/11/53	44	13	27/9/54	47	15
26/1/53	83	80	30/11/53	53	18	4/10/54	52	19
2/2/53	90	85	7/12/53	62	22	11/10/54	56	23
9/2/53	7	1	14/12/53	70	26	18/10/54	59	28
16/2/53	13	6	21/12/53	79	30	25/10/54	60	32
23/2/53	19	11	28/12/53	88	35	1/11/54	59	37
2/3/53	24	17	4/1/54	7	39	8/11/54	57	42
9/3/53	28	22	11/1/54	16	43	15/11/54	53	46
16/3/53	30	27	18/1/54	25	47	22/11/54	49	51
23/3/53	31	32	25/1/54	33	51	29/11/54	46	56
30/3/53	30	37	1/2/54	42	55	6/12/54	45	61
6/4/53	27	42	8/2/54	51	59	13/12/54	46	66
13/4/53	23	47	15/2/54	60	63	20/12/54	48	71
20/4/53	19	52	22/2/54	68	67	27/12/54	52	76

Table 3   195

Dates in this table appear day/month/year

Date	Ven.	Mars	Date	Ven.	Mars	Date	Ven.	Mars
3/1/55	57	81	7/11/55	61	16	10/9/56	32	78
10/1/55	63	86	14/11/55	70	20	17/9/56	39	77
17/1/55	70	1	21/11/55	79	25	24/9/56	46	75
24/1/55	76	6	28/11/55	87	29	1/10/56	54	74
31/1/55	84	11	5/12/55	6	34	8/10/56	62	73
7/2/55	1	16	12/12/55	15	38	15/10/56	70	73
14/2/55	9	21	19/12/55	23	43	22/10/56	78	74
21/2/55	17	26	26/12/55	32	48	29/10/56	87	75
28/2/55	24	31	2/1/56	41	52	5/11/56	5	77
7/3/55	32	36	9/1/56	49	57	12/11/56	13	79
14/3/55	41	41	16/1/56	58	61	19/11/56	22	82
21/3/55	49	46	23/1/56	67	66	26/11/56	31	85
28/3/55	57	50	30/1/56	75	70	3/12/56	39	88
4/4/55	65	55	6/2/56	84	75	10/12/56	48	2
11/4/55	74	60	13/2/56	2	80	17/12/56	57	5
18/4/55	82	65	20/2/56	10	84	24/12/56	65	9
25/4/55	90	69	27/2/56	19	89	31/12/56	74	13
2/5/55	9	74	5/3/56	27	3	7/1/57	83	17
9/5/55	17	79	12/3/56	35	8	14/1/57	1	21
16/5/55	26	83	19/3/56	43	13	21/1/57	10	25
23/5/55	34	88	26/3/56	50	17	28/1/57	19	30
30/5/55	43	3	2/4/56	58	22	4/2/57	28	34
6/6/55	51	7	9/4/56	65	26	11/2/57	36	38
13/6/55	60	12	16/4/56	72	31	18/2/57	45	43
20/6/55	68	16	23/4/56	78	35	25/2/57	54	47
27/6/55	77	21	30/4/56	84	40	4/3/57	63	51
4/7/55	85	25	7/5/56	89	44	11/3/57	71	56
11/7/55	4	30	14/5/56	4	48	18/3/57	80	60
18/7/55	12	34	21/5/56	7	52	25/3/57	89	64
25/7/55	21	39	28/5/56	9	56	1/4/57	8	69
1/8/55	29	43	4/6/56	9	60	8/4/57	16	73
8/8/55	38	48	11/6/56	7	64	15/4/57	25	78
15/8/55	47	52	18/6/56	3	68	22/4/57	34	82
22/8/55	55	57	25/6/56	89	71	29/4/57	42	86
29/8/55	64	61	2/7/56	85	74	6/5/57	51	1
5/9/55	73	65	9/7/56	83	77	13/5/57	59	5
12/9/55	81	70	16/7/56	83	79	20/5/57	68	10
19/9/55	90	74	23/7/56	84	81	27/5/57	77	14
26/9/55	9	79	30/7/56	87	83	3/6/57	85	18
3/10/55	18	83	6/8/56	1	84	10/6/57	4	23
10/10/55	26	88	13/8/56	6	84	17/6/57	12	27
17/10/55	35	2	20/8/56	12	83	24/6/57	21	32
24/10/55	44	7	27/8/56	18	82	1/7/57	29	36
31/10/55	52	11	3/9/56	25	80	8/7/57	38	40

Dates in this table appear day/month/year

Date	Ven.	Mars	Date	Ven.	Mars	Date	Ven.	Mars
15/7/57	47	45	19/5/58	15	76	23/3/59	33	80
22/7/57	55	49	26/5/58	23	81	30/3/59	41	84
29/7/57	63	54	2/6/58	31	86	6/4/59	49	88
5/8/57	72	58	9/6/58	39	1	13/4/59	58	1
12/8/57	80	62	16/6/58	47	6	20/4/59	66	5
19/8/57	89	67	23/6/58	55	11	27/4/59	74	9
26/8/57	7	71	30/6/58	64	16	4/5/59	82	13
2/9/57	15	76	7/7/58	72	21	11/5/59	90	18
9/9/57	24	80	14/7/58	80	25	18/5/59	8	22
16/9/57	32	85	21/7/58	89	30	25/5/59	16	26
23/9/57	40	89	28/7/58	7	34	1/6/59	24	30
30/9/57	48	4	4/8/58	15	38	8/6/59	31	34
7/10/57	57	8	11/8/58	24	42	15/6/59	38	38
14/10/57	65	13	18/8/58	32	46	22/6/59	45	43
21/10/57	72	18	25/8/58	41	50	29/6/59	52	47
28/10/57	80	22	1/9/58	50	53	6/7/59	58	51
4/11/57	88	27	8/9/58	58	56	13/7/59	64	55
11/11/57	5	31	15/9/58	67	58	20/7/59	68	60
18/11/57	13	36	22/9/58	75	60	27/7/59	72	64
25/11/57	19	41	29/9/58	84	62	3/8/59	75	68
2/12/57	26	46	6/10/58	3	62	10/8/59	76	73
9/12/57	32	50	13/10/58	12	63	17/8/59	75	77
16/12/57	37	55	20/10/58	20	62	24/8/59	73	82
23/12/57	42	60	27/10/58	29	61	31/8/59	69	86
30/12/57	45	65	3/11/58	38	59	7/9/59	65	1
6/1/58	46	70	10/11/58	47	56	14/9/59	61	5
13/1/58	46	75	17/11/58	56	54	21/9/59	60	10
20/1/58	43	80	24/11/58	64	51	28/9/59	60	14
27/1/58	40	84	1/12/58	73	49	5/10/59	63	19
3/2/58	35	89	8/12/58	82	48	12/10/59	66	24
10/2/58	32	4	15/12/58	1	47	19/10/59	71	28
17/2/58	31	9	22/12/58	10	47	26/10/59	76	33
24/2/58	31	15	29/12/58	18	47	2/11/59	83	38
3/3/58	34	20	5/1/59	27	48	9/11/59	89	43
10/3/58	37	25	12/1/59	36	50	16/11/59	6	48
17/3/58	42	30	19/1/59	45	52	23/11/59	14	52
24/3/58	48	35	26/1/59	53	54	30/11/59	21	57
31/3/58	54	40	2/2/59	62	56	7/12/59	29	62
7/4/58	60	45	9/2/59	71	59	14/12/59	37	67
14/4/58	67	50	16/2/59	80	62	21/12/59	45	72
21/4/58	74	56	23/2/59	88	66	28/12/59	54	77
28/4/58	82	61	2/3/59	7	69	4/1/60	62	83
5/5/58	89	66	9/3/59	15	73	11/1/60	70	88
12/5/58	7	71	16/3/59	24	76	18/1/60	79	3

Table 3   197

Dates in this table appear day/month/year

Date	Ven.	Mars	Date	Ven.	Mars	Date	Ven.	Mars
25/1/60	87	8	28/11/60	15	18	2/10/61	70	30
1/2/60	6	13	5/12/60	24	17	9/10/61	79	35
8/2/60	14	19	12/12/60	32	15	16/10/61	87	40
15/2/60	23	24	19/12/60	40	13	23/10/61	6	45
22/2/60	32	29	26/12/60	48	11	30/10/61	15	49
29/2/60	40	34	2/1/61	56	8	6/11/61	23	54
7/3/60	49	40	9/1/61	64	5	13/11/61	32	59
14/3/60	57	45	16/1/61	72	3	20/11/61	41	64
21/3/60	66	51	23/1/61	80	1	27/11/61	50	69
28/3/60	75	56	30/1/61	87	90	4/12/61	59	75
4/4/60	83	61	6/2/61	4	90	11/12/61	67	80
11/4/60	2	67	13/2/61	10	90	18/12/61	76	85
18/4/60	11	72	20/2/61	16	1	25/12/61	85	90
25/4/60	19	78	27/2/61	21	2	1/1/62	4	6
2/5/60	28	83	6/3/61	25	4	8/1/62	13	11
9/5/60	36	88	13/3/61	28	6	15/1/62	21	16
16/5/60	45	4	20/3/61	29	9	22/1/62	30	22
23/5/60	54	9	27/3/61	28	11	29/1/62	39	27
30/5/60	62	14	3/4/61	26	14	5/2/62	48	32
6/6/60	71	19	10/4/61	22	17	12/2/62	57	38
13/6/60	79	25	17/4/61	17	21	19/2/62	65	43
20/6/60	88	30	24/4/61	14	24	26/2/62	74	49
27/6/60	7	35	1/5/61	13	27	5/3/62	83	54
4/7/60	15	40	8/5/61	13	31	12/3/62	2	60
11/7/60	24	45	15/5/61	16	35	19/3/62	10	65
18/7/60	32	50	22/5/61	19	38	26/3/62	19	71
25/7/60	41	55	29/5/61	24	42	2/4/62	28	76
1/8/60	50	59	5/6/61	29	46	9/4/62	36	82
8/8/60	58	64	12/6/61	35	50	16/4/62	45	87
15/8/60	67	68	19/6/61	42	54	23/4/62	53	3
22/8/60	75	73	26/6/61	49	58	30/4/62	62	8
29/8/60	84	77	3/7/61	56	62	7/5/62	71	13
5/9/60	3	81	10/7/61	63	67	14/5/62	79	19
12/9/60	11	85	17/7/61	70	71	21/5/62	87	24
19/9/60	20	89	24/7/61	78	75	28/5/62	6	29
26/9/60	29	2	31/7/61	86	79	4/6/62	14	35
3/10/60	37	6	7/8/61	4	84	11/6/62	23	40
10/10/60	46	9	14/8/61	12	88	18/6/62	31	45
17/10/60	54	12	21/8/61	20	3	25/6/62	39	50
24/10/60	63	14	28/8/61	28	7	2/7/62	47	55
31/10/60	71	16	4/9/61	36	12	9/7/62	55	60
7/11/60	80	17	11/9/61	45	16	16/7/62	64	65
14/11/60	88	18	18/9/61	53	21	23/7/62	71	70
21/11/60	7	19	25/9/61	62	25	30/7/62	79	74

Dates in this table appear day/month/year

Date	Ven.	Mars	Date	Ven.	Mars	Date	Ven.	Mars
6/8/62	87	79	10/6/63	57	63	13/4/64	69	11
13/8/62	5	84	17/6/63	65	67	20/4/64	75	17
20/8/62	12	88	24/6/63	74	71	27/4/64	81	22
27/8/62	19	3	1/7/63	82	75	4/5/64	87	27
3/9/62	26	7	8/7/63	1	79	11/5/64	1	33
10/9/62	33	12	15/7/63	9	83	18/5/64	5	38
17/9/62	39	16	22/7/63	18	87	25/5/64	6	43
24/9/62	45	20	29/7/63	26	1	1/6/64	7	48
1/10/62	50	24	5/8/63	35	5	8/6/64	5	53
8/10/62	54	28	12/8/63	44	10	15/6/64	2	58
15/10/62	56	32	19/8/63	52	14	22/6/64	87	63
22/10/62	58	35	26/8/63	61	19	29/6/64	83	68
29/10/62	57	39	2/9/63	70	23	6/7/64	81	73
5/11/62	54	42	9/9/63	78	28	13/7/64	80	78
12/11/62	50	45	16/9/63	87	32	20/7/64	82	83
19/11/62	46	47	23/9/63	6	37	27/7/64	84	87
26/11/62	43	50	30/9/63	14	42	3/8/64	88	2
3/12/62	42	52	7/10/63	23	47	10/8/64	3	7
10/12/62	43	53	14/10/63	32	52	17/8/64	9	11
17/12/62	46	54	21/10/63	41	57	24/8/64	15	16
24/12/62	50	55	28/10/63	49	62	31/8/64	22	20
31/12/62	54	55	4/11/63	58	67	7/9/64	29	25
7/1/63	60	54	11/11/63	67	72	14/9/64	36	29
14/1/63	67	52	18/11/63	76	77	21/9/64	44	34
21/1/63	73	50	25/11/63	84	82	28/9/64	51	38
28/1/63	81	48	2/12/63	3	87	5/10/64	59	42
4/2/63	88	45	9/12/63	12	3	12/10/64	67	46
11/2/63	6	42	16/12/63	20	8	19/10/64	75	50
18/2/63	13	40	23/12/63	29	13	26/10/64	84	54
25/2/63	21	38	30/12/63	38	19	2/11/64	2	58
4/3/63	29	36	6/1/64	46	24	9/11/64	10	62
11/3/63	38	36	13/1/64	55	30	16/11/64	19	65
18/3/63	46	35	20/1/64	64	35	23/11/64	27	69
25/3/63	54	36	27/1/64	72	41	30/11/64	36	72
1/4/63	62	37	3/2/64	81	46	7/12/64	45	75
8/4/63	71	38	10/2/64	89	52	14/12/64	53	78
15/4/63	79	40	17/2/64	7	57	21/12/64	62	80
22/4/63	87	42	24/2/64	16	63	28/12/64	71	83
29/4/63	6	44	2/3/64	24	68	4/1/65	80	85
6/5/63	14	47	9/3/64	32	74	11/1/65	88	86
13/5/63	23	50	16/3/64	40	79	18/1/65	7	87
20/5/63	31	53	23/3/64	47	85	25/1/65	16	88
27/5/63	40	56	30/3/64	55	90	1/2/65	25	88
3/6/63	48	60	6/4/64	62	6	8/2/65	33	87

Table 3   199

Dates in this table appear day/month/year

Date	Ven.	Mars	Date	Ven.	Mars	Date	Ven.	Mars
15/2/65	42	86	20/12/65	39	27	24/10/66	26	67
22/2/65	51	84	27/12/65	42	33	31/10/66	35	71
1/3/65	60	82	3/1/66	44	38	7/11/66	44	75
8/3/65	68	79	10/1/66	43	44	14/11/66	52	79
15/3/65	77	77	17/1/66	41	50	21/11/66	61	83
22/3/65	86	74	24/1/66	37	55	28/11/66	70	87
29/3/65	4	72	31/1/66	33	61	5/12/66	79	1
5/4/65	13	70	7/2/66	30	66	12/12/66	88	4
12/4/65	22	69	14/2/66	28	72	19/12/66	6	8
19/4/65	31	69	21/2/66	29	77	26/12/66	15	11
26/4/65	39	69	28/2/66	31	83	2/1/67	24	15
3/5/65	48	70	7/3/66	35	88	9/1/67	33	18
10/5/65	56	71	14/3/66	39	3	16/1/67	42	21
17/5/65	65	73	21/3/66	45	9	23/1/67	50	24
24/5/65	74	75	28/3/66	51 1	4	30/1/67	59	26
31/5/65	82	77	4/4/66	57	20	6/2/67	68	28
7/6/65	1	80	11/4/66	64	25	13/2/67	76	30
14/6/65	9	83	18/4/66	72	30	20/2/67	85	32
21/6/65	18	86	25/4/66	79 3	5	27/2/67	4	33
28/6/65	26	89	2/5/66	87	41	6/3/67	12	33
5/7/65	35	3	9/5/66	4	46	13/3/67	21	33
12/7/65	44	7	16/5/66	12	51	20/3/67	30	32
19/7/65	52	11	23/5/66	20	56	27/3/67	38	31
26/7/65	60	15	30/5/66	28	61	3/4/67	46	29
2/8/65	69	19	6/6/66	36	66	10/4/67	55	27
9/8/65	77	23	13/6/66	44	71	17/4/67	63	24
16/8/65	86	27	20/6/66	52	76	24/4/67	71	22
23/8/65	4	32	27/6/66	61	80	1/5/67	79	19
30/8/65	12	36	4/7/66	69	85	8/5/67	87	17
6/9/65	21	41	11/7/66	77	90	15/5/67	5	16
13/9/65	29	45	18/7/66	86	5	22/5/67	13	15
20/9/65	37	50	25/7/66	4	9	29/5/67	21	15
27/9/65	45	55	1/8/66	12	14	5/6/67	28	16
4/10/65	53	60	8/8/66	21	19	12/6/67	35	17
11/10/65	61	65	15/8/66	29	23	19/6/67	42	18
18/10/65	69	70	22/8/66	38	28	26/6/67	49	20
25/10/65	77	75	29/8/66	46	32	3/7/67	55	23
1/11/65	85	80	5/9/66	55	37	10/7/67	61	26
8/11/65	2	85	12/9/66	64	41	17/7/67	66	29
15/11/65	10	1	19/9/66	72	45	24/7/67	70	32
22/11/65	16	6	26/9/66	81	50	31/7/67	73	36
29/11/65	23	11	3/10/66	90	54	7/8/67	74	39
6/12/65	29	17	10/10/66	9	58	14/8/67	73	43
13/12/65	34	22	17/10/66	17	63	21/8/67	71	47

Dates in this table appear day/month/year

Date	Ven.	Mars	Date	Ven.	Mars	Date	Ven.	Mars
28/8/67	67	52	1/7/68	12	7	5/5/69	11	76
4/9/67	63	56	8/7/68	21	11	12/5/69	13	75
11/9/67	59	61	15/7/68	29	16	19/5/69	17	74
18/9/67	58	65	22/7/68	38	20	26/5/69	21	72
25/9/67	58	70	29/7/68	47	25	2/6/69	27	70
2/10/67	60	75	5/8/68	55	30	9/6/69	33	67
9/10/67	64	80	12/8/68	64	34	16/6/69	39	65
16/10/67	68	85	19/8/68	72	39	23/6/69	46	63
23/10/67	74	90	26/8/68	81	43	30/6/69	53	62
30/10/67	80	5	2/9/68	90	48	7/7/69	60	62
6/11/67	86	10	9/9/68	8	52	14/7/69	68	62
13/11/67	3	16	16/9/68	17	56	21/7/69	75	63
20/11/67	11	21	23/9/68	25	61	28/7/69	83	64
27/11/67	18	26	30/9/68	34	65	4/8/69	1	66
4/12/67	26	32	7/10/68	43	70	11/8/69	9	69
11/12/67	34	37	14/10/68	51	74	18/8/69	17	72
18/12/67	42	43	21/10/68	60	78	25/8/69	25	75
25/12/67	51	48	28/10/68	68	83	1/9/69	33	78
1/1/68	59	53	4/11/68	77	87	8/9/69	42	82
8/1/68	67	59	11/11/68	85	1	15/9/69	50	86
15/1/68	76	64	18/11/68	4	5	22/9/69	59	90
22/1/68	84	70	25/11/68	12	10	29/9/69	67	5
29/1/68	3	75	2/12/68	21	14	6/10/69	76	9
5/2/68	11	81	9/12/68	29	18	13/10/69	84	14
12/2/68	20	86	16/12/68	37	22	20/10/69	3	19
19/2/68	29	1	23/12/68	45	26	27/10/69	12	24
26/2/68	37	7	30/12/68	53	30	3/11/69	20	29
4/3/68	46	12	6/1/69	61	34	10/11/69	29	34
11/3/68	54	17	13/1/69	69	38	17/11/69	38	39
18/3/68	63	23	20/1/69	77	42	24/11/69	47	44
25/3/68	72	28	27/1/69	84	46	1/12/69	55	49
1/4/68	80	33	3/2/69	1	49	8/12/69	64	54
8/4/68	89	38	10/2/69	7	53	15/12/69	73	60
15/4/68	8	43	17/2/69	13	56	22/12/69	82	65
22/4/68	16	48	24/2/69	18	59	29/12/69	1	70
29/4/68	25	53	3/3/69	23	63	5/1/70	10	75
6/5/68	33	58	10/3/69	25	65	12/1/70	18	80
13/5/68	42	63	17/3/69	27	68	19/1/70	27	86
20/5/68	51	68	24/3/69	26	71	26/1/70	36	1
27/5/68	59	73	31/3/69	24	73	2/2/70	45	6
3/6/68	68	78	7/4/69	20	74	9/2/70	53	11
10/6/68	76	82	14/4/69	15	76	16/2/70	62	16
17/6/68	85	87	21/4/69	12	77	23/2/70	71	21
24/6/68	4	2	28/4/69	11	77	2/3/70	80	26

Table 3　　201

Dates in this table appear day/month/year

Date	Ven.	Mars	Date	Ven.	Mars	Date	Ven.	Mars
9/3/70	88	31	11/1/71	64	52	15/11/71	72	65
16/3/70	7	36	18/1/71	70	57	22/11/71	81	69
23/3/70	16	41	25/1/71	78	61	29/11/71	90	73
30/3/70	25	46	1/2/71	85	66	6/12/71	9	77
6/4/70	33	51	8/2/71	3	70	13/12/71	17	81
13/4/70	42	56	15/2/71	10	74	20/12/71	26	86
20/4/70	50	61	22/2/71	18	79	27/12/71	35	90
27/4/70	59	66	1/3/71	26	83	3/1/72	43	5
4/5/70	68	70	8/3/71	35	87	10/1/72	52	9
11/5/70	76	75	15/3/71	43	2	17/1/72	60	14
18/5/70	84	80	22/3/71	51	6	24/1/72	69	18
25/5/70	3	85	29/3/71	59	10	31/1/72	77	23
1/6/70	11	89	5/4/71	68	14	7/2/72	86	28
8/6/70	20	4	12/4/71	76	18	14/2/72	4	32
15/6/70	28	8	19/4/71	84	22	21/2/72	13	37
22/6/70	36	13	26/4/71	3	26	28/2/72	21	42
29/6/70	44	18	3/5/71	11	30	6/3/72	29	46
6/7/70	53	22	10/5/71	20	33	13/3/72	37	51
13/7/70	61	27	17/5/71	28	37	20/3/72	44	55
20/7/70	69	31	24/5/71	37	40	27/3/72	52	60
27/7/70	76	36	31/5/71	45	43	3/4/72	59	64
3/8/70	84	40	7/6/71	54	45	10/4/72	66	69
10/8/70	2	45	14/6/71	62	48	17/4/72	73	74
17/8/70	9	49	21/6/71	71	49	24/4/72	79	78
24/8/70	16	54	28/6/71	79	51	1/5/72	84	83
31/8/70	23	58	5/7/71	88	52	8/5/72	89	87
7/9/70	30	62	12/7/71	6	52	15/5/72	2	2
14/9/70	36	67	19/7/71	15	52	22/5/72	4	6
21/9/70	42	71	26/7/71	23	51	29/5/72	5	11
28/9/70	47	76	2/8/71	32	49	5/6/72	3	15
5/10/70	51	80	9/8/71	41	47	12/6/72	90	19
12/10/70	54	85	16/8/71	49	46	19/6/72	86	24
19/10/70	55	89	23/8/71	58	44	26/6/72	82	28
26/10/70	55	4	30/8/71	67	43	3/7/72	79	33
2/11/70	52	8	6/9/71	75	42	10/7/72	78	37
9/11/70	48	12	13/9/71	84	42	17/7/72	79	42
16/11/70	44	17	20/9/71	3	43	24/7/72	82	46
23/11/70	41	21	27/9/71	11	44	31/7/72	86	50
30/11/70	40	26	4/10/71	20	46	7/8/72	1	55
7/12/70	40	30	11/10/71	29	48	14/8/72	6	59
14/12/70	43	35	18/10/71	38	51	21/8/72	12	64
21/12/70	47	39	25/10/71	46	54	28/8/72	19	68
28/12/70	52	44	1/11/71	55	57	4/9/72	26	73
4/1/71	57	48	8/11/71	64	61	11/9/72	33	77

Dates in this table appear day/month/year

Date	Ven.	Mars	Date	Ven.	Mars	Date	Ven.	Mars
18/9/72	41	82	23/7/73	57	20	27/5/74	25	22
25/9/72	48	86	30/7/73	66	23	3/6/74	33	26
2/10/72	56	1	6/8/73	74	27	10/6/74	41	31
9/10/72	64	5	13/8/73	83	30	17/6/74	49	35
16/10/72	72	10	20/8/73	1	33	24/6/74	58	39
23/10/72	81	14	27/8/73	9	35	1/7/74	66	43
30/10/72	89	19	3/9/73	18	37	8/7/74	74	48
6/11/72	7	23	10/9/73	26	39	15/7/74	83	52
13/11/72	16	28	17/9/73	34	39	22/7/74	1	57
20/11/72	24	33	24/9/73	42	39	29/7/74	9	61
27/11/72	33	37	1/10/73	50	38	5/8/74	18	65
4/12/72	42	42	8/10/73	58	37	12/8/74	26	70
11/12/72	50	47	15/10/73	66	35	19/8/74	35	74
18/12/72	59	51	22/10/73	74	33	26/8/74	43	79
25/12/72	68	56	29/10/73	82	30	2/9/74	52	83
1/1/73	77	61	5/11/73	89	28	9/9/74	61	88
8/1/73	85	66	12/11/73	7	27	16/9/74	69	2
15/1/73	4	70	19/11/73	14	26	23/9/74	78	7
22/1/73	13	75	26/11/73	20	25	30/9/74	87	11
29/1/73	22	80	3/12/73	26	26	7/10/74	6	16
5/2/73	30	85	10/12/73	32	27	14/10/74	14	20
12/2/73	39	90	17/12/73	36	28	21/10/74	23	25
19/2/73	48	5	24/12/73	39	30	28/10/74	32	30
26/2/73	57	10	31/12/73	41	32	4/11/74	41	35
5/3/73	65	15	7/1/74	41	35	11/11/74	49	39
12/3/73	74	19	14/1/74	39	38	18/11/74	58	44
19/3/73	83	24	21/1/74	35	41	25/11/74	67	49
26/3/73	1	29	28/1/74	31	44	2/12/74	76	54
2/4/73	10	34	4/2/74	28	48	9/12/74	85	59
9/4/73	19	39	11/2/74	26	51	16/12/74	3	64
16/4/73	27	44	18/2/74	26	55	23/12/74	12	69
23/4/73	36	49	25/2/74	28	59	30/12/74	21	74
30/4/73	45	54	4/3/74	32	63	6/1/75	30	79
7/5/73	53	59	11/3/74	36	66	13/1/75	38	84
14/5/73	62	64	18/3/74	42	70	20/1/75	47	89
21/5/73	71	69	25/3/74	48	75	27/1/75	56	4
28/5/73	79	74	1/4/74	55	79	3/2/75	65	9
4/6/73	88	79	8/4/74	61	83	10/2/75	73	14
11/6/73	6	83	15/4/74	69	87	17/2/75	82	19
18/6/73	15	88	22/4/74	76	1	24/2/75	1	25
25/6/73	23	3	29/4/74	84	5	3/3/75	9	30
2/7/73	32	7	6/5/74	1	9	10/3/75	18	35
9/7/73	41	12	13/5/74	9	14	17/3/75	26	40
16/7/73	49	16	20/5/74	17	18	24/3/75	35	46

Table 3   203

Dates in this table appear day/month/year

Date	Ven.	Mars	Date	Ven.	Mars	Date	Ven.	Mars
31/3/75	43	51	2/2/76	8	76	6/12/76	26	71
7/4/75	52	56	9/2/76	17	77	13/12/76	34	76
14/4/75	60	62	16/2/76	25	79	20/12/76	42	81
21/4/75	68	67	23/2/76	34	81	27/12/76	50	86
28/4/75	76	72	1/3/76	43	83	3/1/77	58	1
5/5/75	85	78	8/3/76	51	86	10/1/77	66	7
12/5/75	2	83	15/3/76	60	88	17/1/77	74	12
19/5/75	10	88	22/3/76	69	2	24/1/77	81	17
26/5/75	18	4	29/3/76	77	5	31/1/77	88	23
2/6/75	25	9	5/4/76	86	8	7/2/77	4	28
9/6/75	33	14	12/4/76	4	12	14/2/77	10	33
16/6/75	40	19	19/4/76	13	15	21/2/77	16	39
23/6/75	46	24	26/4/76	22	19	28/2/77	20	44
30/6/75	52	29	3/5/76	30	23	7/3/77	23	50
7/7/75	58	34	10/5/76	39	26	14/3/77	24	55
14/7/75	63	39	17/5/76	48	30	21/3/77	24	61
21/7/75	67	44	24/5/76	56	34	28/3/77	22	66
28/7/75	70	49	31/5/76	65	38	4/4/77	18	72
4/8/75	72	53	7/6/76	73	42	11/4/77	13	77
11/8/75	71	58	14/6/76	82	46	18/4/77	10	83
18/8/75	69	62	21/6/76	1	50	25/4/77	8	88
25/8/75	65	66	28/6/76	9	55	2/5/77	9	3
1/9/75	61	70	5/7/76	18	59	9/5/77	11	9
8/9/75	57	74	12/7/76	26	63	16/5/77	14	14
15/9/75	56	78	19/7/76	35	67	23/5/77	19	19
22/9/75	56	81	26/7/76	44	72	30/5/77	24	25
29/9/75	58	84	2/8/76	52	76	6/6/77	30	30
6/10/75	61	87	9/8/76	61	80	13/6/77	36	35
13/10/75	65	89	16/8/76	69	85	20/6/77	43	40
20/10/75	71	1	23/8/76	78	89	27/6/77	50	45
27/10/75	77	2	30/8/76	87	4	4/7/77	57	50
3/11/75	83	3	6/9/76	5	8	11/7/77	65	55
10/11/75	90	3	13/9/76	14	13	18/7/77	72	60
17/11/75	8	2	20/9/76	22	17	25/7/77	80	65
24/11/75	15	90	27/9/76	31	22	1/8/77	88	70
1/12/75	23	88	4/10/76	40	27	8/8/77	6	75
8/12/75	31	86	11/10/76	48	31	15/8/77	14	79
15/12/75	39	83	18/10/76	57	36	22/8/77	22	84
22/12/75	47	81	25/10/76	65	41	29/8/77	30	88
29/12/75	56	78	1/11/76	74	46	5/9/77	39	2
5/1/76	64	76	8/11/76	82	51	12/9/77	47	7
12/1/76	73	75	15/11/76	1	56	19/9/77	56	11
19/1/76	81	75	22/11/76	9	61	26/9/77	64	15
26/1/76	90	75	29/11/76	17	66	3/10/77	73	19

Dates in this table appear day/month/year

Date	Ven.	Mars	Date	Ven.	Mars	Date	Ven.	Mars
10/10/77	81	22	14/8/78	6	6	18/6/79	68	54
17/10/77	90	26	21/8/78	13	10	25/6/79	76	59
24/10/77	9	29	28/8/78	20	15	2/7/79	85	64
31/10/77	17	32	4/9/78	27	20	9/7/79	3	69
7/11/77	26	34	11/9/78	33	24	16/7/79	12	74
14/11/77	35	37	18/9/78	39	29	23/7/79	20	79
21/11/77	44	39	25/9/78	44	33	30/7/79	29	84
28/11/77	52	40	2/10/78	48	38	6/8/79	38	88
5/12/77	61	41	9/10/78	51	43	13/8/79	46	3
12/12/77	70	42	16/10/78	53	48	20/8/79	55	8
19/12/77	79	41	23/10/78	52	53	27/8/79	64	12
26/12/77	88	40	30/10/78	50	58	3/9/79	72	17
2/1/78	6	39	6/11/78	46	63	10/9/79	81	21
9/1/78	15	37	13/11/78	42	68	17/9/79	90	25
16/1/78	24	34	20/11/78	39	73	24/9/79	8	29
23/1/78	33	31	27/11/78	37	78	1/10/79	17	34
30/1/78	42	29	4/12/78	38	83	8/10/79	26	38
6/2/78	50	26	11/12/78	40	89	15/10/79	35	42
13/2/78	59	24	18/12/78	44	4	22/10/79	43	46
20/2/78	68	23	25/12/78	49	9	29/10/79	52	49
27/2/78	77	22	1/1/79	54	15	5/11/79	61	53
6/3/78	85	22	8/1/79	61	20	12/11/79	69	56
13/3/78	4	23	15/1/79	67	26	19/11/79	78	60
20/3/78	13	24	22/1/79	75	31	26/11/79	87	63
27/3/78	22	26	29/1/79	82	37	3/12/79	5	66
3/4/78	30	28	5/2/79	90	42	10/12/79	14	68
10/4/78	39	30	12/2/79	7	48	17/12/79	23	70
17/4/78	47	32	19/2/79	15	53	24/12/79	32	72
24/4/78	56	35	26/2/79	23	59	31/12/79	40	74
1/5/78	64	38	5/3/79	32	64	7/1/80	49	75
8/5/78	73	41	12/3/79	40	70	14/1/80	57	75
15/5/78	81	44	19/3/79	48	75	21/1/80	66	75
22/5/78	90	48	26/3/79	56	81	28/1/80	74	74
29/5/78	8	51	2/4/79	65	86	4/2/80	83	73
5/6/78	17	55	9/4/79	73	2	11/2/80	1	71
12/6/78	25	59	16/4/79	81	7	18/2/80	9	69
19/6/78	33	63	23/4/79	90	12	25/2/80	18	66
26/6/78	41	67	30/4/79	8	18	3/3/80	26	63
3/7/78	50	71	7/5/79	17	23	10/3/80	34	61
10/7/78	58	75	14/5/79	25	28	17/3/80	41	59
17/7/78	66	79	21/5/79	34	34	24/3/80	49	57
24/7/78	73	83	28/5/79	42	39	31/3/80	56	56
31/7/78	81	87	4/6/79	51	44	7/4/80	63	56
7/8/78	89	2	11/6/79	59	49	14/4/80	70	56

Table 3   205

Dates in this table appear day/month/year

Date	Ven.	Mars	Date	Ven.	Mars	Date	Ven.	Mars
21/4/80	76	57	23/2/81	53	73	28/12/81	39	5
28/4/80	81	58	2/3/81	62	78	4/1/82	39	8
5/5/80	86	60	9/3/81	71	84	11/1/82	37	11
12/5/80	90	62	16/3/81	80	89	18/1/82	33	13
19/5/80	2	65	23/3/81	88	5	25/1/82	29	15
26/5/80	3	68	30/3/81	7	10	1/2/82	25	17
2/6/80	1	71	6/4/81	16	15	8/2/82	24	18
9/6/80	88	74	13/4/81	24	21	15/2/82	24	19
16/6/80	84	77	20/4/81	33	26	22/2/82	26	19
23/6/80	80	81	27/4/81	42	31	1/3/82	29	19
30/6/80	77	84	4/5/81	50	37	8/3/82	34	18
7/7/80	76	88	11/5/81	59	42	15/3/82	39	16
14/7/80	77	2	18/5/81	68	47	22/3/82	45	14
21/7/80	80	6	25/5/81	76	52	29/3/82	52	11
28/7/80	83	10	1/6/81	85	57	5/4/82	58	9
4/8/80	88	14	8/6/81	3	62	12/4/82	66	6
11/8/80	4	18	15/6/81	12	67	19/4/82	73	4
18/8/80	10	23	22/6/81	20	72	26/4/82	81	2
25/8/80	16	27	29/6/81	29	77	3/5/82	88	1
1/9/80	23	32	6/7/81	38	82	10/5/82	6	90
8/9/80	30	36	13/7/81	46	86	17/5/82	14	1
15/9/80	38	41	20/7/81	54	1	24/5/82	22	1
22/9/80	45	46	27/7/81	63	6	31/5/82	30	3
29/9/80	53	51	3/8/81	71	10	7/6/82	38	4
6/10/80	61	56	10/8/81	80	15	14/6/82	46	6
13/10/80	69	61	17/8/81	88	20	21/6/82	55	9
20/10/80	78	66	24/8/81	6	24	28/6/82	63	12
27/10/80	86	71	31/8/81	15	29	5/7/82	71	15
3/11/80	4	76	7/9/81	23	33	12/7/82	80	18
10/11/80	13	81	14/9/81	31	38	19/7/82	88	22
17/11/80	21	86	21/9/81	39	42	26/7/82	6	25
24/11/80	30	1	28/9/81	47	46	2/8/82	15	29
1/12/80	39	7	5/10/81	55	50	9/8/82	23	33
8/12/80	47	12	12/10/81	63	55	16/8/82	32	37
15/12/80	56	18	19/10/81	71	59	23/8/82	40	42
22/12/80	65	23	26/10/81	79	63	30/8/82	49	46
29/12/80	73	29	2/11/81	86	67	6/9/82	58	51
5/1/81	82	34	9/11/81	4	71	13/9/82	66	55
12/1/81	1	40	16/11/81	11	75	20/9/82	75	60
19/1/81	10	45	23/11/81	17	78	27/9/82	84	65
26/1/81	18	51	30/11/81	23	82	4/10/82	2	70
2/2/81	27	56	7/12/81	29	86	11/10/82	11	75
9/2/81	36	62	14/12/81	33	89	18/10/82	20	80
16/2/81	45	67	21/12/81	37	2	25/10/82	29	85

Dates in this table appear day/month/year

Date	Ven.	Mars	Date	Ven.	Mars	Date	Ven.	Mars
1/11/82	37	90	5/9/83	55	44	9/7/84	23	44
8/11/82	46	5	12/9/83	53	49	16/7/84	32	46
15/11/82	55	11	19/9/83	53	53	23/7/84	41	48
22/11/82	64	16	26/9/83	55	58	30/7/84	49	51
29/11/82	73	21	3/10/83	58	62	6/8/84	58	54
6/12/82	81	27	10/10/83	63	66	13/8/84	66	58
13/12/82	90	32	17/10/83	68	71	20/8/84	75	61
20/12/82	9	38	24/10/83	74	75	27/8/84	84	65
27/12/82	18	43	31/10/83	81	79	3/9/84	2	69
3/1/83	27	49	7/11/83	87	83	10/9/84	11	73
10/1/83	35	54	14/11/83	5	87	17/9/84	19	78
17/1/83	44	60	21/11/83	12	2	24/9/84	28	82
24/1/83	53	65	28/11/83	20	6	1/10/84	37	87
31/1/83	62	71	5/12/83	28	10	8/10/84	45	2
7/2/83	70	76	12/12/83	36	14	15/10/84	54	7
14/2/83	79	82	19/12/83	44	18	22/10/84	62	12
21/2/83	88	87	26/12/83	53	21	29/10/84	71	17
28/2/83	6	2	2/1/84	61	25	5/11/84	79	22
7/3/83	15	8	9/1/84	70	29	12/11/84	88	27
14/3/83	23	13	16/1/84	78	32	19/11/84	6	32
21/3/83	32	18	23/1/84	87	36	26/11/84	14	38
28/3/83	40	24	30/1/84	5	39	3/12/84	23	43
4/4/83	49	29	6/2/84	14	42	10/12/84	31	48
11/4/83	57	34	13/2/84	22	46	17/12/84	39	54
18/4/83	65	39	20/2/84	31	48	24/12/84	47	59
25/4/83	73	44	27/2/84	40	51	31/12/84	55	64
2/5/83	82	49	5/3/84	48	53	7/1/85	63	70
9/5/83	90	54	12/3/84	57	55	14/1/85	71	75
16/5/83	7	59	19/3/84	66	57	21/1/85	78	80
23/5/83	15	64	26/3/84	74	58	28/1/85	85	86
30/5/83	22	69	2/4/84	83	58	4/2/85	2	1
6/6/83	30	74	9/4/84	1	58	11/2/85	8	6
13/6/83	37	79	16/4/84	10	58	18/2/85	13	11
20/6/83	43	84	23/4/84	19	56	25/2/85	17	17
27/6/83	50	88	30/4/84	27	55	4/3/85	20	22
4/7/83	55	3	7/5/84	36	52	11/3/85	22	27
11/7/83	61	8	14/5/84	45	50	18/3/85	22	32
18/7/83	65	13	21/5/84	53	47	25/3/85	20	37
25/7/83	68	17	28/5/84	62	45	1/4/85	16	42
1/8/83	69	22	4/6/84	70	43	8/4/85	12	47
8/8/83	69	26	11/6/84	79	42	15/4/85	8	52
15/8/83	67	31	18/6/84	88	42	22/4/85	6	57
22/8/83	63	35	25/6/84	6	42	29/4/85	6	62
29/8/83	59	40	2/7/84	15	43	6/5/85	8	67

Table 3   207

Dates in this table appear day/month/year

Date	Ven.	Mars	Date	Ven.	Mars	Date	Ven.	Mars
13/5/85	12	71	17/3/86	10	84	19/1/87	72	7
20/5/85	16	76	24/3/86	18	88	26/1/87	79	12
27/5/85	21	81	31/3/86	27	1	2/2/87	87	17
3/6/85	27	86	7/4/86	36	5	9/2/87	4	22
10/6/85	33	90	14/4/86	44	8	16/2/87	12	27
17/6/85	40	5	21/4/86	53	11	23/2/87	20	32
24/6/85	47	10	28/4/86	61	14	2/3/87	28	36
1/7/85	54	14	5/5/86	70	17	9/3/87	37	41
8/7/85	62	19	12/5/86	78	19	16/3/87	45	46
15/7/85	69	23	19/5/86	87	21	23/3/87	53	51
22/7/85	77	28	26/5/86	5	22	30/3/87	62	56
29/7/85	85	32	2/6/86	14	23	6/4/87	70	60
5/8/85	3	37	9/6/86	22	23	13/4/87	78	65
12/8/85	11	42	16/6/86	30	23	20/4/87	87	70
19/8/85	19	46	23/6/86	38	22	27/4/87	5	74
26/8/85	27	50	30/6/86	47	20	4/5/87	14	79
2/9/85	36	55	7/7/86	55	19	11/5/87	22	83
9/9/85	44	59	14/7/86	63	17	18/5/87	31	88
16/9/85	53	64	21/7/86	71	15	25/5/87	39	3
23/9/85	61	68	28/7/86	78	13	1/6/87	48	7
30/9/85	70	73	4/8/86	86	12	8/6/87	56	12
7/10/85	78	77	11/8/86	3	11	15/6/87	65	16
14/10/85	87	81	18/8/86	11	12	22/6/87	73	21
21/10/85	6	86	25/8/86	18	13	29/6/87	82	25
28/10/85	14	90	1/9/86	24	14	6/7/87	90	30
4/11/85	23	5	8/9/86	31	16	13/7/87	9	34
11/11/85	32	9	15/9/86	36	19	20/7/87	17	39
18/11/85	41	13	22/9/86	41	22	27/7/87	26	43
25/11/85	49	18	29/9/86	46	25	3/8/87	35	47
2/12/85	58	22	6/10/86	49	28	10/8/87	43	52
9/12/85	67	26	13/10/86	50	32	17/8/87	52	56
16/12/85	76	31	20/10/86	50	36	24/8/87	61	61
23/12/85	85	35	27/10/86	48	40	31/8/87	69	65
30/12/85	3	39	3/11/86	44	45	7/9/87	78	70
6/1/86	12	44	10/11/86	40	49	14/9/87	87	74
13/1/86	21	48	17/11/86	37	54	21/9/87	5	79
20/1/86	30	52	24/11/86	35	59	28/9/87	14	83
27/1/86	39	56	1/12/86	35	63	5/10/87	23	88
3/2/86	47	60	8/12/86	38	68	12/10/87	31	2
10/2/86	56	65	15/12/86	41	73	19/10/87	40	7
17/2/86	65	69	22/12/86	46	78	26/10/87	49	11
24/2/86	74	73	29/12/86	51	83	2/11/87	58	16
3/3/86	82	77	5/1/87	58	88	9/11/87	66	20
10/3/86	1	80	12/1/87	64	2	16/11/87	75	25

Dates in this table appear day/month/year

Date	Ven.	Mars	Date	Ven.	Mars	Date	Ven.	Mars
23/11/87	84	29	8/8/88	1	9	24/4/89	39	87
30/11/87	2	34	15/8/88	7	11	1/5/89	47	1
7/12/87	11	38	22/8/88	13	11	8/5/89	56	5
14/12/87	20	43	29/8/88	20	11	15/5/89	65	10
21/12/87	28	48	5/9/88	27	11	22/5/89	73	14
28/12/87	37	52	12/9/88	35	10	29/5/89	82	18
4/1/88	46	57	19/9/88	42	8	5/6/89	90	23
11/1/88	54	62	26/9/88	50	6	12/6/89	9	27
18/1/88	63	66	3/10/88	58	4	19/6/89	17	32
25/1/88	71	71	10/10/88	66	2	26/6/89	26	36
1/2/88	80	76	17/10/88	75	1	3/7/89	35	40
8/2/88	88	80	24/10/88	83	90	10/7/89	43	45
15/2/88	6	85	31/10/88	1	90	17/7/89	51	49
22/2/88	15	90	7/11/88	10	1	24/7/89	60	53
29/2/88	23	4	14/11/88	18	2	31/7/89	68	58
7/3/88	31	9	21/11/88	27	3	7/8/89	77	62
14/3/88	38	14	28/11/88	35	5	14/8/89	85	67
21/3/88	46	19	5/12/88	44	8	21/8/89	3	71
28/3/88	53	23	12/12/88	53	11	28/8/89	12	76
4/4/88	60	28	19/12/88	62	14	4/9/89	20	80
11/4/88	67	33	26/12/88	70	17	11/9/89	28	84
18/4/88	73	37	2/1/89	79	21	18/9/89	36	89
25/4/88	79	42	9/1/89	88	24	25/9/89	44	4
2/5/88	83	47	16/1/89	7	28	2/10/89	52	8
9/5/88	87	51	23/1/89	15	32	9/10/89	60	13
16/5/88	90	56	30/1/89	24	36	16/10/89	68	17
23/5/88	90	60	6/2/89	33	40	23/10/89	76	22
30/5/88	89	65	13/2/89	42	44	30/10/89	83	27
6/6/88	86	69	20/2/89	50	48	6/11/89	1	31
13/6/88	82	73	27/2/89	59	53	13/11/89	8	36
20/6/88	78	78	6/3/89	68	57	20/11/89	14	41
27/6/88	75	81	13/3/89	77	61	27/11/89	20	45
4/7/88	74	85	20/3/89	85	65	4/12/89	26	50
11/7/88	75	89	27/3/89	4	70	11/12/89	30	55
18/7/88	77	2	3/4/89	13	74	18/12/89	34	60
25/7/88	81	5	10/4/89	21	78	25/12/89	36	65
1/8/88	85	7	17/4/89	30	82			

Table 4: Mercury Retrograde Periods

Year	From	To	From	To	From	To	From	To
2001	4 Feb	25 Feb	4 Jun	28 Jun	1 Oct	23 Oct		
2002	18 Jan	8 Feb	15 May	8 Jun	14 Sep	6 Oct		
2003	2 Jan	23 Jan	26 Apr	20 May	28 Aug	20 Sep	17 Dec	6 Jan 2004
2004	6 Apr	30 Apr	10 Aug	2 Sep	30 Nov	20 Dec		
2005	20 Mar	12 Apr	23 Jul	16 Aug	14 Nov	14 Dec		
2006	2 Mar	25 Mar	4 Jul	29 Jul	28 Oct	18 Nov		
2007	14 Feb	8 Mar	15 Jun	10 Jul	12 Oct	1 Nov		
2008	28 Jan	19 Feb	26 May	19 Jun	24 Sep	15 Oct		
2009	11 Jan	1 Feb	7 May	31 May	7 Sep	29 Sep	26 Dec	15 Jan 2010
2010	18 Apr	11 May	20 Aug	12 Sep	10 Dec	30 Dec		
2011	30 Mar	23 Apr	3 Aug	26 Aug	24 Nov	14 Dec		
2012	12 Mar	4 Apr	15 Jul	8 Aug	6 Nov	26 Nov		
2013	23 Feb	17 Mar	26 Jun	20 Jul	21 Oct	10 Nov		
2014	6 Feb	28 Feb	7 Jun	1 Jul	4 Oct	25 Oct		
2015	21 Jan	11 Feb	19 May	11 Jun	17 Sep	9 Oct		
2016	5 Jan	25 Jan	28 Apr	22 May	30 Aug	22 Sep	19 Dec	8 Jan 2017
2017	9 Apr	3 May	13 Aug	5 Sep	3 Dec	23 Dec		
2018	23 Mar	15 Apr	26 Jul	19 Aug	17 Nov	6 Dec		
2019	5 Mar	28 Mar	7 Jul	1 Aug	31 Oct	20 Nov		
2020	17 Feb	10 Mar	18 Jun	12 Jul	14 Oct	3 Nov		

Table 5: The 12 Life Areas for Saturn Return and Pluto Power Crisis

In the same way we can identify each of the twelve numbers around the dial of the clock, we can identify each of the twelve stages along the cycle of the rotating planets.

You will usually find that the Saturn return involves one of the twelve issues listed here, while the major Pluto crisis involves two of them (although some people will find more of these issues creeping in). Put very simply, the areas of life from which these may come are:

- The identity, appearance, and appearance in others' eyes
- Resources, money, self-esteem
- Information, communication, travel, siblings and neighbors
- Home, domestic life, family, parents, roots
- Children, creative life, romance, who and what you love
- Work and health
- Relationships and partnerships
- Sex, resources that come from or through others, shared things, death
- Education, foreign things and foreign places
- Goals, profession, standing in the world, public life
- Ideals, friendship, view of the future, esteem by others
- Spiritual life, secrets, hidden health issues, sacrifices

These twelve stages are the twelve "seasons" expressed as areas of human activity and are known as the twelve houses of astrology.

Table 6: Mars Numbers 1990-2020

Dates in this table appear day/month/year

Date	Mars	Date	Mars	Date	Mars
1/1/1990	70	8/10/1990	73	15/7/1991	60
8/1/1990	75	15/10/1990	74	22/7/1991	64
15/1/1990	80	22/10/1990	75	29/7/1991	68
22/1/1990	85	29/10/1990	74	5/8/1991	73
29/1/1990	90	5/11/1990	73	12/8/1991	77
5/2/1990	5	12/11/1990	71	19/8/1991	82
12/2/1990	10	19/11/1990	69	26/8/1991	86
19/2/1990	15	26/11/1990	66	2/9/1991	90
26/2/1990	20	3/12/1990	63	9/9/1991	5
5/3/1990	25	10/12/1990	61	16/9/1991	10
12/3/1990	30	17/12/1990	59	23/9/1991	14
19/3/1990	35	24/12/1990	58	30/9/1991	19
26/3/1990	41	31/12/1990	58	7/10/1991	23
2/4/1990	46	7/1/1991	58	14/10/1991	28
9/4/1990	51	14/1/1991	59	21/10/1991	33
16/4/1990	56	21/1/1991	60	28/10/1991	38
23/4/1990	62	28/1/1991	62	4/11/1991	42
30/4/1990	67	4/2/1991	64	11/11/1991	47
7/5/1990	72	11/2/1991	66	18/11/1991	52
14/5/1990	77	18/2/1991	69	25/11/1991	57
21/5/1990	82	25/2/1991	72	2/12/1991	62
28/5/1990	88	4/3/1991	75	9/12/1991	67
4/6/1990	3	11/3/1991	78	16/12/1991	72
11/6/1990	8	18/3/1991	82	23/12/1991	77
18/6/1990	13	25/3/1991	85	30/12/1991	82
25/6/1990	18	1/4/1991	89	6/1/1992	88
2/7/1990	23	8/4/1991	3	13/1/1992	3
9/7/1990	28	15/4/1991	6	20/1/1992	8
16/7/1990	32	22/4/1991	10	27/1/1992	13
23/7/1990	37	29/4/1991	14	3/2/1992	18
30/7/1990	41	6/5/1991	18	10/2/1992	24
6/8/1990	46	13/5/1991	22	17/2/1992	29
13/8/1990	50	20/5/1991	26	24/2/1992	34
20/8/1990	54	27/5/1991	30	2/3/1992	40
27/8/1990	58	3/6/1991	34	9/3/1992	45
3/9/1990	61	10/6/1991	39	16/3/1992	51
10/9/1990	64	17/6/1991	43	23/3/1992	56
17/9/1990	67	24/6/1991	47	30/3/1992	62
24/9/1990	70	1/7/1991	51	6/4/1992	67
1/10/1990	72	8/7/1991	55	13/4/1992	72

Dates in this table appear day/month/year

Date	Mars	Date	Mars	Date	Mars
20/4/1992	78	15/2/1993	9	13/12/1993	85
27/4/1992	83	22/2/1993	9	20/12/1993	90
4/5/1992	89	1/3/1993	10	27/12/1993	5
11/5/1992	4	8/3/1993	11	3/1/1994	11
18/5/1992	9	15/3/1993	13	10/1/1994	16
25/5/1992	15	22/3/1993	15	17/1/1994	21
1/6/1992	20	29/3/1993	17	24/1/1994	27
8/6/1992	25	5/4/1993	20	31/1/1994	32
15/6/1992	30	12/4/1993	23	7/2/1994	38
22/6/1992	35	19/4/1993	26	14/2/1994	43
29/6/1992	40	26/4/1993	29	21/2/1994	49
6/7/1992	45	3/5/1993	32	28/2/1994	54
13/7/1992	50	10/5/1993	36	7/3/1994	60
20/7/1992	55	17/5/1993	39	14/3/1994	65
27/7/1992	60	24/5/1993	43	21/3/1994	71
3/8/1992	65	31/5/1993	47	28/3/1994	76
10/8/1992	70	7/6/1993	51	4/4/1994	82
17/8/1992	74	14/6/1993	55	11/4/1994	87
24/8/1992	78	21/6/1993	59	18/4/1994	3
31/8/1992	83	28/6/1993	63	25/4/1994	8
7/9/1992	87	5/7/1993	67	2/5/1994	13
14/9/1992	1	12/7/1993	71	9/5/1994	19
21/9/1992	5	19/7/1993	75	16/5/1994	24
28/9/1992	9	26/7/1993	79	23/5/1994	29
5/10/1992	12	2/8/1993	84	30/5/1994	35
12/10/1992	15	9/8/1993	88	6/6/1994	40
19/10/1992	18	16/8/1993	3	13/6/1994	45
26/10/1992	21	23/8/1993	7	20/6/1994	50
2/11/1992	23	30/8/1993	11	27/6/1994	55
9/11/1992	25	6/9/1993	16	4/7/1994	60
16/11/1992	27	13/9/1993	21	11/7/1994	65
23/11/1992	27	20/9/1993	25	18/7/1994	70
30/11/1992	28	27/9/1993	30	25/7/1994	75
7/12/1992	27	4/10/1993	35	1/8/1994	79
14/12/1992	26	11/10/1993	39	8/8/1994	84
21/12/1992	24	18/10/1993	44	15/8/1994	89
28/12/1992	22	25/10/1993	49	22/8/1994	3
4/1/1993	19	1/11/1993	54	29/8/1994	8
11/1/1993	16	8/11/1993	59	5/9/1994	12
18/1/1993	14	15/11/1993	64	12/9/1994	17
25/1/1993	12	22/11/1993	69	19/9/1994	21
1/2/1993	10	29/11/1993	74	26/9/1994	25
8/2/1993	9	6/12/1993	80	3/10/1994	29

Table 6   *215*

Dates in this table appear day/month/year

Date	Mars	Date	Mars	Date	Mars
10/10/1994	33	7/8/1995	10	3/6/1996	53
17/10/1994	37	14/8/1995	14	10/6/1996	58
24/10/1994	40	21/8/1995	19	17/6/1996	63
31/10/1994	44	28/8/1995	23	24/6/1996	68
7/11/1994	47	4/9/1995	28	1/7/1996	73
14/11/1994	50	11/9/1995	32	8/7/1996	78
21/11/1994	53	18/9/1995	37	15/7/1996	83
28/11/1994	56	25/9/1995	42	22/7/1996	87
5/12/1994	58	2/10/1995	47	29/7/1996	2
12/12/1994	60	9/10/1995	52	5/8/1996	7
19/12/1994	61	16/10/1995	57	12/8/1996	11
26/12/1994	62	23/10/1995	62	19/8/1996	16
2/1/1995	63	30/10/1995	67	26/8/1996	21
9/1/1995	62	6/11/1995	72	2/9/1996	25
16/1/1995	62	13/11/1995	77	9/9/1996	29
23/1/1995	60	20/11/1995	82	16/9/1996	34
30/1/1995	58	27/11/1995	87	23/9/1996	38
6/2/1995	55	4/12/1995	3	30/9/1996	42
13/2/1995	53	11/12/1995	8	7/10/1996	47
20/2/1995	50	18/12/1995	13	14/10/1996	51
27/2/1995	47	25/12/1995	19	21/10/1996	55
6/3/1995	45	1/1/1996	24	28/10/1996	59
13/3/1995	44	8/1/1996	30	4/11/1996	63
20/3/1995	43	15/1/1996	35	11/11/1996	66
27/3/1995	43	22/1/1996	41	18/11/1996	70
3/4/1995	44	29/1/1996	46	25/11/1996	74
10/4/1995	45	5/2/1996	52	2/12/1996	77
17/4/1995	46	12/2/1996	57	9/12/1996	80
24/4/1995	48	19/2/1996	63	16/12/1996	83
1/5/1995	50	26/2/1996	68	23/12/1996	86
8/5/1995	53	4/3/1996	74	30/12/1996	89
15/5/1995	55	11/3/1996	79	6/1/1997	1
22/5/1995	58	18/3/1996	85	13/1/1997	3
29/5/1995	62	25/3/1996	90	20/1/1997	4
5/6/1995	65	1/4/1996	6	27/1/1997	5
12/6/1995	68	8/4/1996	11	3/2/1997	6
19/6/1995	72	15/4/1996	17	10/2/1997	6
26/6/1995	76	22/4/1996	22	17/2/1997	5
3/7/1995	79	29/4/1996	27	24/2/1997	4
10/7/1995	83	6/5/1996	32	3/3/1997	2
17/7/1995	87	13/5/1996	38	10/3/1997	90
24/7/1995	2	20/5/1996	43	17/3/1997	87
31/7/1995	6	27/5/1996	48	24/3/1997	84

Dates in this table appear day/month/year

Date	Mars	Date	Mars	Date	Mars
31/3/1997	82	26/1/1998	60	23/11/1998	88
7/4/1997	80	2/2/1998	66	30/11/1998	1
14/4/1997	78	9/2/1998	72	7/12/1998	5
21/4/1997	77	16/2/1998	77	14/12/1998	9
28/4/1997	77	23/2/1998	82	21/12/1998	13
5/5/1997	77	2/3/1998	88	28/12/1998	16
12/5/1997	78	9/3/1998	3	4/1/1999	20
19/5/1997	79	16/3/1998	9	11/1/1999	23
26/5/1997	81	23/3/1998	14	18/1/1999	26
2/6/1997	83	30/3/1998	19	25/1/1999	29
9/6/1997	86	6/4/1998	25	1/2/1999	32
16/6/1997	89	13/4/1998	30	8/2/1999	35
23/6/1997	2	20/4/1998	35	15/2/1999	37
30/6/1997	5	27/4/1998	40	22/2/1999	39
7/7/1997	8	4/5/1998	45	1/3/1999	40
14/7/1997	12	11/5/1998	51	8/3/1999	42
21/7/1997	16	18/5/1998	56	15/3/1999	42
28/7/1997	20	25/5/1998	61	22/3/1999	42
4/8/1997	24	1/6/1998	66	29/3/1999	41
11/8/1997	28	8/6/1998	70	5/4/1999	40
18/8/1997	32	15/6/1998	75	12/4/1999	38
25/8/1997	37	22/6/1998	80	19/4/1999	36
1/9/1997	41	29/6/1998	85	26/4/1999	34
8/9/1997	46	6/7/1998	90	3/5/1999	31
15/9/1997	50	13/7/1998	4	10/5/1999	29
22/9/1997	55	20/7/1998	9	17/5/1999	27
29/9/1997	60	27/7/1998	14	24/5/1999	25
6/10/1997	65	3/8/1998	18	31/5/1999	25
13/10/1997	70	10/8/1998	23	7/6/1999	24
20/10/1997	75	17/8/1998	28	14/6/1999	25
27/10/1997	80	24/8/1998	32	21/6/1999	26
3/11/1997	85	31/8/1998	37	28/6/1999	28
10/11/1997	1	7/9/1998	41	5/7/1999	30
17/11/1997	6	14/9/1998	45	12/7/1999	32
24/11/1997	11	21/9/1998	50	19/7/1999	35
1/12/1997	17	28/9/1998	54	26/7/1999	38
8/12/1997	22	5/10/1998	58	2/8/1999	42
15/12/1997	27	12/10/1998	63	9/8/1999	46
22/12/1997	33	19/10/1998	67	16/8/1999	49
29/12/1997	38	26/10/1998	71	23/8/1999	53
5/1/1998	44	2/11/1998	75	30/8/1999	58
12/1/1998	49	9/11/1998	79	6/9/1999	62
19/1/1998	55	16/11/1998	84	13/9/1999	67

Table 6   217

Dates in this table appear day/month/year

Date	Mars	Date	Mars	Date	Mars
20/9/1999	71	17/7/2000	20	14/5/2001	89
27/9/1999	76	24/7/2000	25	21/5/2001	88
4/10/1999	81	31/7/2000	29	28/5/2001	87
11/10/1999	86	7/8/2000	34	4/6/2001	86
18/10/1999	1	14/8/2000	38	11/6/2001	84
25/10/1999	6	21/8/2000	43	18/6/2001	81
1/11/1999	11	28/8/2000	47	25/6/2001	79
8/11/1999	16	4/9/2000	52	2/7/2001	77
15/11/1999	21	11/9/2000	56	9/7/2001	76
22/11/1999	27	18/9/2000	61	16/7/2001	75
29/11/1999	32	25/9/2000	65	23/7/2001	75
6/12/1999	37	2/10/2000	69	30/7/2001	76
13/12/1999	43	9/10/2000	74	6/8/2001	77
20/12/1999	48	16/10/2000	78	13/8/2001	79
27/12/1999	54	23/10/2000	83	20/8/2001	81
3/1/2000	59	30/10/2000	87	27/8/2001	84
10/1/2000	65	6/11/2000	1	3/9/2001	87
17/1/2000	70	13/11/2000	6	10/9/2001	1
24/1/2000	75	20/11/2000	10	17/9/2001	4
31/1/2000	81	27/11/2000	14	24/9/2001	8
7/2/2000	86	4/12/2000	18	1/10/2001	13
14/2/2000	2	11/12/2000	23	8/10/2001	17
21/2/2000	7	18/12/2000	27	15/10/2001	21
28/2/2000	12	25/12/2000	31	22/10/2001	26
6/3/2000	17	1/1/2001	35	29/10/2001	31
13/3/2000	23	8/1/2001	39	5/11/2001	36
20/3/2000	28	15/1/2001	43	12/11/2001	41
27/3/2000	33	22/1/2001	47	19/11/2001	46
3/4/2000	38	29/1/2001	51	26/11/2001	51
10/4/2000	43	5/2/2001	55	3/12/2001	56
17/4/2000	48	12/2/2001	59	10/12/2001	61
24/4/2000	53	19/2/2001	62	17/12/2001	66
1/5/2000	58	26/2/2001	66	24/12/2001	71
8/5/2000	63	5/3/2001	69	31/12/2001	76
15/5/2000	68	12/3/2001	72	7/1/2002	81
22/5/2000	73	19/3/2001	75	14/1/2002	86
29/5/2000	77	26/3/2001	78	21/1/2002	1
5/6/2000	82	2/4/2001	81	28/1/2002	7
12/6/2000	87	9/4/2001	83	4/2/2002	12
19/6/2000	2	16/4/2001	85	11/2/2002	17
26/6/2000	6	23/4/2001	87	18/2/2002	22
3/7/2000	11	30/4/2001	88	25/2/2002	27
10/7/2000	16	7/5/2001	89	4/3/2002	32

Table 6

Dates in this table appear day/month/year

Date	Mars	Date	Mars	Date	Mars
11/3/2002	37	6/1/2003	53	3/11/2003	68
18/3/2002	42	13/1/2003	57	10/11/2003	71
25/3/2002	46	20/1/2003	62	17/11/2003	74
1/4/2002	51	27/1/2003	66	24/11/2003	78
8/4/2002	56	3/2/2003	71	1/12/2003	81
15/4/2002	61	10/2/2003	75	8/12/2003	85
22/4/2002	66	17/2/2003	80	15/12/2003	89
29/4/2002	70	24/2/2003	84	22/12/2003	3
6/5/2002	75	3/3/2003	89	29/12/2003	7
13/5/2002	80	10/3/2003	3	5/1/2004	12
20/5/2002	84	17/3/2003	8	12/1/2004	16
27/5/2002	89	24/3/2003	12	19/1/2004	20
3/6/2002	4	31/3/2003	17	26/1/2004	25
10/6/2002	8	7/4/2003	21	2/2/2004	29
17/6/2002	13	14/4/2003	25	9/2/2004	34
24/6/2002	17	21/4/2003	29	16/2/2004	38
1/7/2002	22	28/4/2003	34	23/2/2004	42
8/7/2002	26	5/5/2003	38	1/3/2004	47
15/7/2002	31	12/5/2003	42	8/3/2004	51
22/7/2002	35	19/5/2003	46	15/3/2004	56
29/7/2002	40	26/5/2003	49	22/3/2004	60
5/8/2002	44	2/6/2003	53	29/3/2004	65
12/8/2002	49	9/6/2003	56	5/4/2004	69
19/8/2002	53	16/6/2003	60	12/4/2004	74
26/8/2002	58	23/6/2003	62	19/4/2004	78
2/9/2002	62	30/6/2003	65	26/4/2004	83
9/9/2002	67	7/7/2003	67	3/5/2004	87
16/9/2002	71	14/7/2003	69	10/5/2004	2
23/9/2002	76	21/7/2003	70	17/5/2004	6
30/9/2002	80	28/7/2003	70	24/5/2004	11
7/10/2002	84	4/8/2003	70	31/5/2004	15
14/10/2002	89	11/8/2003	69	7/6/2004	19
21/10/2002	3	18/8/2003	68	14/6/2004	24
28/10/2002	8	25/8/2003	66	21/6/2004	28
4/11/2002	12	1/9/2003	64	28/6/2004	33
11/11/2002	17	8/9/2003	62	5/7/2004	37
18/11/2002	21	15/9/2003	61	12/7/2004	41
25/11/2002	26	22/9/2003	60	19/7/2004	46
2/12/2002	30	29/9/2003	60	26/7/2004	50
9/12/2002	35	6/10/2003	61	2/8/2004	55
16/12/2002	39	13/10/2003	62	9/8/2004	59
23/12/2002	44	20/10/2003	63	16/8/2004	64
30/12/2002	48	27/10/2003	66	23/8/2004	68

Table 6   *219*

Dates in this table appear day/month/year

Date	Mars	Date	Mars	Date	Mars
30/8/2004	72	27/6/2005	10	24/4/2006	6
6/9/2004	77	4/7/2005	15	1/5/2006	10
13/9/2004	81	11/7/2005	19	8/5/2006	14
20/9/2004	86	18/7/2005	24	15/5/2006	18
27/9/2004	90	25/7/2005	28	22/5/2006	22
4/10/2004	5	1/8/2005	32	29/5/2006	27
11/10/2004	9	8/8/2005	36	5/6/2006	31
18/10/2004	14	15/8/2005	40	12/6/2006	35
25/10/2004	19	22/8/2005	43	19/6/2006	39
1/11/2004	23	29/8/2005	46	26/6/2006	44
8/11/2004	28	5/9/2005	49	3/7/2006	48
15/11/2004	33	12/9/2005	51	10/7/2006	52
22/11/2004	37	19/9/2005	52	17/7/2006	56
29/11/2004	42	26/9/2005	53	24/7/2006	61
6/12/2004	47	3/10/2005	53	31/7/2006	65
13/12/2004	51	10/10/2005	53	7/8/2006	70
20/12/2004	56	17/10/2005	52	14/8/2006	74
27/12/2004	61	24/10/2005	50	21/8/2006	78
3/1/2005	66	31/10/2005	48	28/8/2006	83
10/1/2005	71	7/11/2005	45	4/9/2006	87
17/1/2005	75	14/11/2005	43	11/9/2006	2
24/1/2005	80	21/11/2005	41	18/9/2006	6
31/1/2005	85	28/11/2005	39	25/9/2006	11
7/2/2005	90	5/12/2005	38	2/10/2006	16
14/2/2005	5	12/12/2005	38	9/10/2006	20
21/2/2005	10	19/12/2005	39	16/10/2006	25
28/2/2005	15	26/12/2005	40	23/10/2006	30
7/3/2005	20	2/1/2006	41	30/10/2006	34
14/3/2005	25	9/1/2006	43	6/11/2006	39
21/3/2005	30	16/1/2006	46	13/11/2006	44
28/3/2005	35	23/1/2006	48	20/11/2006	49
4/4/2005	40	30/1/2006	51	27/11/2006	54
11/4/2005	45	6/2/2006	54	4/12/2006	58
18/4/2005	51	13/2/2006	58	11/12/2006	63
25/4/2005	56	20/2/2006	61	18/12/2006	68
2/5/2005	61	27/2/2006	65	25/12/2006	73
9/5/2005	66	6/3/2006	68	1/1/2007	78
16/5/2005	71	13/3/2006	72	8/1/2007	84
23/5/2005	76	20/3/2006	76	15/1/2007	89
30/5/2005	81	27/3/2006	80	22/1/2007	4
6/6/2005	86	3/4/2006	84	29/1/2007	9
13/6/2005	1	10/4/2006	88	5/2/2007	14
20/6/2005	5	17/4/2006	2	12/2/2007	19

Dates in this table appear day/month/year

Date	Mars	Date	Mars	Date	Mars
19/2/2007	25	17/12/2007	6	13/10/2008	36
26/2/2007	30	24/12/2007	3	20/10/2008	41
5/3/2007	35	31/12/2007	90	27/10/2008	46
12/3/2007	41	7/1/2008	88	3/11/2008	51
19/3/2007	46	14/1/2008	86	10/11/2008	56
26/3/2007	51	21/1/2008	85	17/11/2008	60
2/4/2007	57	28/1/2008	84	24/11/2008	66
9/4/2007	62	4/2/2008	84	1/12/2008	71
16/4/2007	67	11/2/2008	85	8/12/2008	76
23/4/2007	73	18/2/2008	86	15/12/2008	81
30/4/2007	78	25/2/2008	88	22/12/2008	86
7/5/2007	83	3/3/2008	90	29/12/2008	1
14/5/2007	89	10/3/2008	2	5/1/2009	7
21/5/2007	4	17/3/2008	4	12/1/2009	12
28/5/2007	9	24/3/2008	7	19/1/2009	17
4/6/2007	15	31/3/2008	10	26/1/2009	23
11/6/2007	20	7/4/2008	13	2/2/2009	28
18/6/2007	25	14/4/2008	17	9/2/2009	33
25/6/2007	30	21/4/2008	20	16/2/2009	39
2/7/2007	35	28/4/2008	24	23/2/2009	44
9/7/2007	40	5/5/2008	27	2/3/2009	50
16/7/2007	45	12/5/2008	31	9/3/2009	55
23/7/2007	50	19/5/2008	35	16/3/2009	61
30/7/2007	55	26/5/2008	39	23/3/2009	66
6/8/2007	59	2/6/2008	43	30/3/2009	72
13/8/2007	64	9/6/2008	47	6/4/2009	77
20/8/2007	68	16/6/2008	51	13/4/2009	83
27/8/2007	72	23/6/2008	55	20/4/2009	88
3/9/2007	76	30/6/2008	59	27/4/2009	3
10/9/2007	80	7/7/2008	63	4/5/2009	9
17/9/2007	84	14/7/2008	67	11/5/2009	14
24/9/2007	88	21/7/2008	72	18/5/2009	20
1/10/2007	1	28/7/2008	76	25/5/2009	25
8/10/2007	4	4/8/2008	80	1/6/2009	30
15/10/2007	7	11/8/2008	85	8/6/2009	35
22/10/2007	9	18/8/2008	89	15/6/2009	40
29/10/2007	11	25/8/2008	4	22/6/2009	46
5/11/2007	12	1/9/2008	8	29/6/2009	51
12/11/2007	12	8/9/2008	13	6/7/2009	56
19/11/2007	12	15/9/2008	17	13/7/2009	61
26/11/2007	12	22/9/2008	22	20/7/2009	66
3/12/2007	10	29/9/2008	27	27/7/2009	70
10/12/2007	8	6/10/2008	31	3/8/2009	75

Table 6   *221*

Dates in this table appear day/month/year

Date	Mars	Date	Mars	Date	Mars
10/8/2009	80	7/6/2010	60	4/4/2011	1
17/8/2009	84	14/6/2010	64	11/4/2011	7
24/8/2009	89	21/6/2010	67	18/4/2011	12
31/8/2009	3	28/6/2010	71	25/4/2011	18
7/9/2009	8	5/7/2010	75	2/5/2011	23
14/9/2009	12	12/7/2010	79	9/5/2011	28
21/9/2009	16	19/7/2010	83	16/5/2011	34
28/9/2009	20	26/7/2010	88	23/5/2011	39
5/10/2009	24	2/8/2010	2	30/5/2011	44
12/10/2009	28	9/8/2010	6	6/6/2011	49
19/10/2009	31	16/8/2010	11	13/6/2011	54
26/10/2009	35	23/8/2010	15	20/6/2011	59
2/11/2009	38	30/8/2010	20	27/6/2011	64
9/11/2009	41	6/9/2010	24	4/7/2011	69
16/11/2009	43	13/9/2010	29	11/7/2011	74
23/11/2009	45	20/9/2010	33	18/7/2011	79
30/11/2009	47	27/9/2010	38	25/7/2011	84
7/12/2009	49	4/10/2010	43	1/8/2011	88
14/12/2009	49	11/10/2010	48	8/8/2011	3
21/12/2009	50	18/10/2010	53	15/8/2011	8
28/12/2009	49	25/10/2010	58	22/8/2011	12
4/1/2010	48	1/11/2010	63	29/8/2011	17
11/1/2010	47	8/11/2010	68	5/9/2011	21
18/1/2010	44	15/11/2010	73	12/9/2011	26
25/1/2010	42	22/11/2010	78	19/9/2011	30
1/2/2010	39	29/11/2010	83	26/9/2011	34
8/2/2010	36	6/12/2010	89	3/10/2011	38
15/2/2010	34	13/12/2010	4	10/10/2011	42
22/2/2010	32	20/12/2010	9	17/10/2011	46
1/3/2010	31	27/12/2010	15	24/10/2011	50
8/3/2010	30	3/1/2011	20	31/10/2011	54
15/3/2010	30	10/1/2011	25	7/11/2011	58
22/3/2010	31	17/1/2011	31	14/11/2011	61
29/3/2010	32	24/1/2011	36	21/11/2011	65
5/4/2010	34	31/1/2011	42	28/11/2011	68
12/4/2010	36	7/2/2011	47	5/12/2011	71
19/4/2010	38	14/2/2011	53	12/12/2011	74
26/4/2010	41	21/2/2011	58	19/12/2011	76
3/5/2010	43	28/2/2011	64	26/12/2011	79
10/5/2010	46	7/3/2011	69	2/1/2012	80
17/5/2010	49	14/3/2011	75	9/1/2012	82
24/5/2010	53	21/3/2011	80	16/1/2012	83
31/5/2010	56	28/3/2011	86	23/1/2012	83

Table 6

Dates in this table appear day/month/year

Date	Mars	Date	Mars	Date	Mars
30/1/2012	83	26/11/2012	7	23/9/2013	46
6/2/2012	82	3/12/2012	12	30/9/2013	51
13/2/2012	81	10/12/2012	18	7/10/2013	55
20/2/2012	78	17/12/2012	23	14/10/2013	59
27/2/2012	76	24/12/2012	28	21/10/2013	63
5/3/2012	73	31/12/2012	34	28/10/2013	67
12/3/2012	70	7/1/2013	39	4/11/2013	71
19/3/2012	68	14/1/2013	45	11/11/2013	75
26/3/2012	66	21/1/2013	50	18/11/2013	79
2/4/2012	65	28/1/2013	56	25/11/2013	83
9/4/2012	64	4/2/2013	62	2/12/2013	87
16/4/2012	64	11/2/2013	67	9/12/2013	1
23/4/2012	64	18/2/2013	73	16/12/2013	4
30/4/2012	65	25/2/2013	78	23/12/2013	8
7/5/2012	67	4/3/2013	84	30/12/2013	11
14/5/2012	68	11/3/2013	89	6/1/2014	14
21/5/2012	71	18/3/2013	4	13/1/2014	17
28/5/2012	73	25/3/2013	10	20/1/2014	19
4/6/2012	76	1/4/2013	15	27/1/2014	22
11/6/2012	79	8/4/2013	21	3/2/2014	24
18/6/2012	82	15/4/2013	26	10/2/2014	25
25/6/2012	86	22/4/2013	31	17/2/2014	27
2/7/2012	89	29/4/2013	36	24/2/2014	27
9/7/2012	3	6/5/2013	42	3/3/2014	28
16/7/2012	7	13/5/2013	47	10/3/2014	27
23/7/2012	11	20/5/2013	52	17/3/2014	26
30/7/2012	15	27/5/2013	57	24/3/2014	24
6/8/2012	19	3/6/2013	62	31/3/2014	22
13/8/2012	23	10/6/2013	67	7/4/2014	20
20/8/2012	28	17/6/2013	72	14/4/2014	17
27/8/2012	32	24/6/2013	77	21/4/2014	14
3/9/2012	37	1/7/2013	81	28/4/2014	12
10/9/2012	41	8/7/2013	86	5/5/2014	11
17/9/2012	46	15/7/2013	1	12/5/2014	9
24/9/2012	51	22/7/2013	6	19/5/2014	9
1/10/2012	56	29/7/2013	10	26/5/2014	9
8/10/2012	61	5/8/2013	15	2/6/2014	10
15/10/2012	66	12/8/2013	20	9/6/2014	11
22/10/2012	71	19/8/2013	24	16/6/2014	13
29/10/2012	76	26/8/2013	29	23/6/2014	15
5/11/2012	81	2/9/2013	33	30/6/2014	18
12/11/2012	86	9/9/2013	38	7/7/2014	21
19/11/2012	1	16/9/2013	42	14/7/2014	24

Table 6   223

Dates in this table appear day/month/year

Date	Mars	Date	Mars	Date	Mars
21/7/2014	27	18/5/2015	64	14/3/2016	63
28/7/2014	31	25/5/2015	69	21/3/2016	65
4/8/2014	35	1/6/2015	74	28/3/2016	67
11/8/2014	39	8/6/2015	79	4/4/2016	68
18/8/2014	43	15/6/2015	84	11/4/2016	69
25/8/2014	47	22/6/2015	88	18/4/2016	69
1/9/2014	52	29/6/2015	3	25/4/2016	69
8/9/2014	56	6/7/2015	8	2/5/2016	68
15/9/2014	61	13/7/2015	12	9/5/2016	66
22/9/2014	65	20/7/2015	17	16/5/2016	64
29/9/2014	70	27/7/2015	22	23/5/2016	62
6/10/2014	75	3/8/2015	26	30/5/2016	59
13/10/2014	80	10/8/2015	31	6/6/2016	57
20/10/2014	85	17/8/2015	35	13/6/2016	55
27/10/2014	90	24/8/2015	40	20/6/2016	54
3/11/2014	6	31/8/2015	44	27/6/2016	53
10/11/2014	11	7/9/2015	49	4/7/2016	53
17/11/2014	16	14/9/2015	53	11/7/2016	54
24/11/2014	22	21/9/2015	57	`18/7/2016	55
1/12/2014	27	28/9/2015	62	25/7/2016	57
8/12/2014	32	5/10/2015	66	1/8/2016	59
15/12/2014	38	12/10/2015	71	8/8/2016	62
22/12/2014	43	19/10/2015	75	15/8/2016	65
29/12/2014	49	26/10/2015	79	22/8/2016	69
5/1/2015	54	2/11/2015	83	29/8/2016	72
12/1/2015	60	9/11/2015	88	5/9/2016	76
19/1/2015	65	16/11/2015	2	12/9/2016	80
26/1/2015	71	23/11/2015	6	19/9/2016	85
2/2/2015	76	30/11/2015	10	26/9/2016	89
9/2/2015	82	7/12/2015	14	3/10/2016	4
16/2/2015	87	14/12/2015	18	10/10/2016	9
23/2/2015	2	21/12/2015	22	17/10/2016	13
2/3/2015	8	28/12/2015	26	24/10/2016	18
9/3/2015	13	4/1/2016	30	31/10/2016	23
16/3/2015	18	11/1/2016	34	7/11/2016	28
23/3/2015	24	18/1/2016	38	14/11/2016	34
30/3/2015	29	25/1/2016	41	21/11/2016	39
6/4/2015	34	1/2/2016	45	28/11/2016	44
13/4/2015	39	8/2/2016	48	5/12/2016	49
20/4/2015	44	15/2/2016	52	12/12/2016	54
27/4/2015	49	22/2/2016	55	19/12/2016	60
4/5/2015	54	29/2/2016	58	26/12/2016	65
11/5/2015	59	7/3/2016	60	2/1/2017	70

Dates in this table appear day/month/year

Date	Mars	Date	Mars	Date	Mars
9/1/2017	76	6/11/2017	9	3/9/2018	29
16/1/2017	81	13/11/2017	13	10/9/2018	30
23/1/2017	86	20/11/2017	18	17/9/2018	31
30/1/2017	1	27/11/2017	22	24/9/2018	33
6/2/2017	7	4/12/2017	27	1/10/2018	36
13/2/2017	12	11/12/2017	31	8/10/2018	39
20/2/2017	17	18/12/2017	35	15/10/2018	42
27/2/2017	22	25/12/2017	40	22/10/2018	46
6/3/2017	27	1/1/2018	44	29/10/2018	50
13/3/2017	32	8/1/2018	49	5/11/2018	53
20/3/2017	37	15/1/2018	53	12/11/2018	58
27/3/2017	42	22/1/2018	57	19/11/2018	62
3/4/2017	47	29/1/2018	62	26/11/2018	66
10/4/2017	52	5/2/2018	66	3/12/2018	71
17/4/2017	57	12/2/2018	70	10/12/2018	75
24/4/2017	62	19/2/2018	74	17/12/2018	80
1/5/2017	67	26/2/2018	78	24/12/2018	85
8/5/2017	71	5/3/2018	83	31/12/2018	89
15/5/2017	76	12/3/2018	87	7/1/2019	4
22/5/2017	81	19/3/2018	1	14/1/2019	9
29/5/2017	86	26/3/2018	5	21/1/2019	13
5/6/2017	90	2/4/2018	9	28/1/2019	18
12/6/2017	5	9/4/2018	12	4/2/2019	23
19/6/2017	9	16/4/2018	16	11/2/2019	28
26/6/2017	14	23/4/2018	20	18/2/2019	32
3/7/2017	19	30/4/2018	23	25/2/2019	37
10/7/2017	23	7/5/2018	26	4/3/2019	42
17/7/2017	28	14/5/2018	29	11/3/2019	47
24/7/2017	32	21/5/2018	32	18/3/2019	51
31/7/2017	37	28/5/2018	34	25/3/2019	56
7/8/2017	41	4/6/2018	36	1/4/2019	61
14/8/2017	46	11/6/2018	38	8/4/2019	65
21/8/2017	50	18/6/2018	39	15/4/2019	70
28/8/2017	55	25/6/2018	39	22/4/2019	74
4/9/2017	59	2/7/2018	39	29/4/2019	79
11/9/2017	64	9/7/2018	38	6/5/2019	83
18/9/2017	68	16/7/2018	37	13/5/2019	88
25/9/2017	72	23/7/2018	35	20/5/2019	3
2/10/2017	77	30/7/2018	33	27/5/2019	7
9/10/2017	81	6/8/2018	32	3/6/2019	12
16/10/2017	86	13/8/2018	30	10/6/2019	16
23/10/2017	90	20/8/2018	29	17/6/2019	20
30/10/2017	5	27/8/2018	29	24/6/2019	25

Table 6   *225*

Dates in this table appear day/month/year

Date	Mars
1/7/2019	29
8/7/2019	34
15/7/2019	38
22/7/2019	43
29/7/2019	47
5/8/2019	52
12/8/2019	56
19/8/2019	61
26/8/2019	65
2/9/2019	69
9/9/2019	74
16/9/2019	78
23/9/2019	83
30/9/2019	87
7/10/2019	2
14/10/2019	6
21/10/2019	11
28/10/2019	15
4/11/2019	20
11/11/2019	25
18/11/2019	29
25/11/2019	34
2/12/2019	38
9/12/2019	43
16/12/2019	48
23/12/2019	52
30/12/2019	57
6/1/2020	62
13/1/2020	67
20/1/2020	71
27/1/2020	76
3/2/2020	81
10/2/2020	86
17/2/2020	90
24/2/2020	5
2/3/2020	10
9/3/2020	15
16/3/2020	20
23/3/2020	25

Date	Mars
30/3/2020	29
6/4/2020	34
13/4/2020	39
20/4/2020	44
27/4/2020	49
4/5/2020	54
11/5/2020	59
18/5/2020	63
25/5/2020	68
1/6/2020	73
8/6/2020	77
15/6/2020	82
22/6/2020	86
29/6/2020	1
6/7/2020	5
13/7/2020	9
20/7/2020	12
27/7/2020	16
3/8/2020	19
10/8/2020	22
17/8/2020	24
24/8/2020	26
31/8/2020	27
7/9/2020	28
14/9/2020	28
21/9/2020	27
28/9/2020	26
5/10/2020	24
12/10/2020	22
19/10/2020	20
26/10/2020	18
2/11/2020	16
9/11/2020	15
16/11/2020	15
23/11/2020	16
30/11/2020	17
7/12/2020	18
14/12/2020	21
21/12/2020	23

Table 7: Interpreting Overlapping Cycles

Crossovers of Venus and Mars (Chapter 7)

When this number in the present/future	Is the same as this number at your birth	This is what you can expect
Sun (Table 1: Sun-All)	Venus	Feeling positive about self worth, good relationship experiences; insight into real needs.
Mars (Table 6)	Venus	Feeling impassioned; dramatic surges in self-worth or challenges to it from others; meetings, new relationships; excitability; sexual experiences.
Saturn (Table 2)	Venus	Separations or obstacles arising in relationships; feelings or experiences of limitation; restrictions in financial resources; debt; duties or obligations in relationships; beginning of long-term relationship with some restrictions or relationship with older person. The challenge to reveal a new layer of the self within an existing relationship. The beginning of a long-term development of the heart's desire.
Uranus (Table 2)	Venus	Sudden changes in relationships; sudden endings or beginnings of relationships; brief encounters; sudden windfall or expense; unusual romantic encounters; a great need for independence. The challenge to introduce something new or exciting into an existing relationship. Changes to the heart's desire.
Neptune (Table 2)	Venus	Very romantic experiences or meetings; beginning of relationships under unclear circumstances; romantic illusion; being deceived; infatuation; disillusionment about love; sensitivity; illusions about money; unnecessary expenditure. The challenge to face reality. Confusion about what you want.

Pluto (Table 2)	Venus	Powerful, dramatic or unavoidable transformation of relationships; end of a relationship; being the victim of someone's power or exercising such power yourself; great expenses or outlays; great challenges to self-worth; great attraction or obsessive love; lust; if you're single it can represent the beginning of a relationship with a powerful person or which has a transformative influence; trauma in relationships or financial affairs; cleaning out and starting again. Dramatic changes, endings or beginnings of events related to pursuing true desires.
Sun (Table 1: Sun-All)	Mars	Drives become clear; sexual opportunities; feelings of confidence and self-reliance.
Venus (Table 3)	Mars	Feeling impassioned; strong drive towards relationship or sex but possible confusion between platonic love and romantic love, or between love and lust; you may feel very sexual or not sexual at all and this can cause compatibility issues with a partner.
Mars (Table 6)	Mars (Table 3)	Sexual drive and need strongly emphasized; aggression or frustration (see also Chapter 5).
Saturn (Table 2)	Mars	Frustration, obstacles or limitations in pursuit of sexual drives; feeling very un-sexual; feelings of helplessness, feeling victimized; uncontrollable feelings of despair, sadness, limitation; feeling blocked; lack of sexual expression.
Uranus (Table 2)	Mars	Excitement, sudden opportunities; difficult to control sexual impulses; unexpected developments in relationships; strong but fluctuating sexual drive; difficulty knowing what you want.

Table 7   *229*

| Neptune (Table 2) | Mars | Feeling dreamy and romantic; confusion between romance and sex; low or absent sexual desire. |
| Pluto (Table 2) | Mars | Very strong sexual desire; driven to meet sexual needs; aggression, passion, potential destructiveness through strength of drives; overpowering urges or actions. |

Crossovers of Sun, Saturn, Uranus, Neptune, Pluto

When this number in the present/future	Is the same as this number at your birth	This is what you can expect
Mars	Sun	Drives + Self: a time of great personal energy. Aggression and temper may be high, so are drive and enthusiasm. Possible conflict with others or work-related change. Good for all challenges, pursuit of goals, starting all projects, asserting yourself, getting things done quickly, removing obstacles.
Saturn	Sun	Limitations + Self: a time of greater responsibilities, limitations imposed by self-discipline or external authorities, feelings of melancholy or depression, dealing with the past, getting rid of non-essentials, getting back to basics, having to accept circumstances. Can also represent an increase of status or responsibility, acquiring authority, beginnings of slow, long-term projects.
Uranus	Sun	Change + Self: a time of unexpected or sudden developments, seeing things in a new light, sudden realizations, impulses, intuitions, often requiring adjustments to be made. Crisis, uncomfortable changes, changes in perspective and ideas. A good time for all things requiring individuality, following your intuition. Changes to the self can sometimes be quite dramatic at these times.

Neptune	Sun	Illusion + Self: a time of confusion, vagueness, and when nothing at all seems to be happening. Feelings of powerlessness or dissolution of the self. Being deceived. Strange dreams, over-sensitivity, feelings of isolation or loneliness. May also represent times of vision and idealism.
Pluto	Sun	Transformation + Self: often a time of great personal challenge. Dramatic changes are possible. May be traumatic, circumstances seem out of your control, major changes are demanded. The rug being pulled from under your feet. Power issues, contact with people in power, being victimized by others. Opportunities to make radical changes to yourself. Conflict is possible, as is experience of loss. In this book we have confined our study of the Jupiter cycle to its use to indicate periods of success, as shown in Chapter 4.
Sun	Saturn	Self + Limitation: Limitations are seen clearly and must be accepted. Decisions made and long-term projects can be started, although there may be feelings of depression and reluctance to do things. Meetings with important people, or your own importance may be recognized.
Mars	Saturn	Drive + Limitation: difficulties and obstacles with respect to goals. Urge to overcome limitations impeding progress: a check to progress. Feelings of depression, pointlessness, frustration. Feeling stuck. Can represent dangerous times: do not act until the cycles are out of synch again.
Uranus	Saturn	Limitations + Changes: a time of enforced and difficult changes. It is usually a very unsettling time, challenging us to let go of safe preconceived ideas. Old habits can be changed and limitations overcome if you are willing to trust your intuition.

Table 7   231

Neptune	Saturn	Vision + Limitations: disillusionment, which should not be confused with disappointment. Things that you thought real or important disappear as you come down to Earth. Possible cynicism. At the same time, ideals and visions can take a real form. Barriers can be dissolved and limitations overcome.
Pluto	Saturn	Limitation + Transformation: a time when external power (such as bureaucracy, government, institution) severely limits or imposes on your life. Difficulty achieving results, unwelcome changes enforced. The strategy here is to resist engaging in conflict; it will only make it worse.
Sun	Uranus	Self + Changes: While changes similar to those described in "Uranus à Sun" may occur, this is a less dramatic time. Intuition and "aha!" experiences are possible, or realizations of some changes that must be made. Individuality or need for independence is very strong.
Mars	Uranus	Drive + Changes: sudden changes in progress or direction. Erratic swings of energy, unexpected developments. Possible conflict or even violence. Strong association with accidents, reckless behavior, consequences of foolish actions.
Saturn	Uranus	Limitations + Change: Making changes is difficult at this time, and things may go more slowly than you wish. Freedom or independence is limited. Some restrictions may be imposed.
Neptune	Uranus	Vision + Change: although it may be a confusing time, this is also a time of inspiration, vision, realization, and even spiritual growth.
Pluto	Uranus	Transformation + Change: a time of radical, unpredictable and unwelcome changes. In the long run, these produce great insight and remove much of the clutter in your life.

Sun	Neptune	Self + Vision: This can be a time of great insight, particularly into spiritual or inner things. Secrets may be revealed or there may be important realizations. Some mild confusion is possible. Great for ideas and things requiring imagination.
Mars	Neptune	Drive + Confusion: slow-down of progress, confusion in goals, loss of energy or momentum, suffering the consequences of idealism. Often no consequences are evident; but wait until the cycles are out of synch again.
Saturn	Neptune	Limitations + Vision: disillusionment, which should not be confused with disappointment. Things that you thought real or important disappear as you come down to Earth. Possible cynicism. At the same time, ideals and visions may take a real form.
Uranus	Neptune	Change + Vision: although it may be a confusing time, this is also a time of inspiration, vision, realization, and even of spiritual growth.
Pluto	Neptune	Transformation + Vision: dramatic spiritual growth or changes, sudden enlightenment, idealism, making changes to goals, putting "impossible" things into action, starting very long term projects.
Sun	Pluto	Self + Transformation: opportunities to use or discover your power or effectiveness. Challenges you not to take advantage or manipulate others. There may be opportunities of the mutually beneficial type. There may be traumatic events, though probably not major ones.

Table 7   233

Mars	Pluto	Drives + Transformation: extremely high energy, to the point of unpredictability. Sudden, dramatic developments radically change and often threaten progress towards goals. Possible conflict or even violence. Dealing with external powers affecting goals. Can represent dangerous times: do not act until the cycles are out of synch again.
Saturn	Pluto	Limitation + Transformation: a time when external power (such as bureaucracy, government, institution) severely limits or imposes on your life. Difficulty achieving results, unwelcome changes enforced. The strategy here is to resist engaging in conflict; it will only make it worse.
Uranus	Pluto	Change + Transformation: a time of radical, unpredictable and unwelcome changes. In the long run, these produce great insight and remove much of the clutter in your life.
Neptune	Pluto	Vision + Transformation: spiritual growth, calm enlightenment, idealism, making changes to goals, putting "impossible" things into action, starting very long-term projects.

GLOSSARY

Ascendant: the degree of the zodiac rising over the eastern horizon at birth, representing the persona presented to the world, the "outermost" aspect of the self, and events related to identity and relationship.

Electional astrology: the branch of astrology used to select an auspicious time.

Ephemeris: a book of tables of planetary positions.

Midheaven: in the northern hemisphere, the Southernmost point in the sky; in the Southern hemisphere, the Northernmost point in the sky. Used by astrologers to represent career, potential, status-changing events, and other crucial aspects everyday life.

Natal chart: a symbolic map of the planets' positions at birth which is used to describe the personality as well as make predictions about the future.

Planets (for the purposes of astrology): Sun, Moon, Mercury, Venus, Mars, Jupiter, Saturn, Uranus, Neptune and Pluto.

Retrograde: the apparent occasional backwards movement of a planet, an optical illusion caused by the viewing angle or the earth's own movement.

Transits: the current positions of the planets compared with how they were at birth, used to measure cycles and make predictions.

BIBLIOGRAPHY

Books about cycles, predictions and their meanings

Alexander, Roy, *The Astrology of Choice*, Samuel Weiser 1983

Ebertin, Reinhold, *The Annual Diagram as an Aid in Life*, Ebertin-Verlag 1973

Freeman, Martin, *Forecasting by Astrology*, Aquarian Press 1982

Hathaway, Edith, *Navigating by the Stars*, Llewellyn 1991

Kempton-Smith, *Debbi, Secrets from a Stargazer's Notebook*, Topquark Press 1999

Tyl, Noel, *Prediction in Astrology*, Llewellyn 1991

Related and Connected Areas

Brady, Bernadette, *Predictive Astrology: The Eagle and the Lark*, Samuel Weiser 1999

De Santillana, Giorgio and Hertha von Dechend, *Hamlet's Mill*, David R. Godine 1992 (a study of astrological cycles that is a study in itself.)

Gwynn Press, *Nona, New Insights into Astrology*, ACS Publications 1993

Harding, Michael and Charles Harvey, *Working with Astrology*, Arkana 1990

McEvers, Joan (Ed), *Financial Astrology*, Llewellyn 1991

Szanto, Gregory, *Astrotherapy*, Arkana 1987

West, John A, *The Case for Astrology*, Arkana Books 1992

Books for Complete Beginners

Oken, Alan, *Complete Guide to Astrology*, Bantam 1988

Parker, Derek and Julia, *Parker's Astrology*, Dorling Kindersley 2004

Reference books

de Vore, Nicholas, *Encyclopedia of Astrology*, Littlefield Adams 1977

Ebertin, Reinhold, *The Combination of Stellar Influences*, AFA 1997

Gettings, Fred, *Arkana Dictionary of Astrology*, Arkana 1991

Hall, Manly P, *Astrological Keywords*, Littlefield Adams 1990

Hand, Robert, *Planets in Transit*, Para Research 1976